Closure
in the
Novel

_Marianna Torgovnick_

# Closure
# in the
# Novel

PRINCETON UNIVERSITY PRESS

PRINCETON, NEW JERSEY

C 1

*For Matthew*

## ACKNOWLEDGMENTS

I wish to thank the National Endowment for the Humanities for a summer seminar grant and Williams College for a semester's leave, both of which aided materially in the completion of this book. My thanks also to the editors of *Studies in the Novel* and those of *Twentieth-Century Literature* for permission to reprint portions of chapters six and seven. For careful, judicious typing of the manuscript, Barbara Boltz of Williams College deserves praise.

Many individuals provided encouragement, criticism, or both during the writing of this study: my students at Williams College, my colleagues in the English department, friends like Michael Katz, Carol McGuirk, and Hana Wirth-Nesher. Special thanks are due to Karl Kroeber of Columbia University for readings and advice over a number of years and to Alvin B. Kernan of Princeton University for encouragement offered at crucial times. Seymour Chatman of the University of California at Berkeley, Martin Meisel of Columbia University, and George H. Ford of the University of Rochester also provided some very helpful suggestions for revision. Jerry Sherwood, my editor at Princeton University Press, skillfully and considerately guided the manuscript through the process of publication.

My largest debt and warmest thanks belong to my husband, Stuart, who made completion of the book one of his own priorities, provided constant aid and encouragement, and unobtrusively took over myriad small tasks during my most productive periods of writing.

# CONTENTS

# CONTENTS

Closure
in the
Novel

I

BEGIN to tell the plot of a narrative to an ordinary listener and the result is predictable—a plea at some point not to "give away" the ending. Begin to do the same to a student or critic of literature and although so "sophisticated" a reader might not admit it, he'll probably regret losing the suspense that normally accompanies an unknown text. Go see a movie or read a book knowing that the love scenes are torrid, or that the heroine dies, or that the ending is surprising, and results are similarly predictable: anticipation of the love scenes, waiting for the heroine's death and guessing how it will happen, weighing the probable ending and deducing the nature of the surprise. To see the same movie or read the same book with full knowledge of the ending is to expect and look for signs and anticipations of the way in which things will work out. Try to interrupt someone nearing the end of a novel or sporting event or television program, and, unless the person's interest in his activity is minimal, you'll get a request to wait just a moment until the reading or viewing is completed. All these phenomena testify to the importance most of us, whether devotees of popular or high culture, ordinary readers or literary critics, attribute to the ways in which stories end.

In identifying the attraction fictions exert on the human mind, E. M. Forster reaches a conclusion embarrassingly commonplace yet totally true, which helps to explain our interest in endings: all narratives appeal to the fundamental impulse of curiosity.[1] In any narrative, "what happens next" ceases to be a pertinent question only at the conclusion, and the word "end" in a novel consequently carries with it not just the notion of the turnable last page, but also that of the "goal" of reading, the finish-line toward which our bookmarks aim. In long works of fiction, endings are important for another commonplace but true reason: it is difficult to recall *all* of a work after a completed reading, but climactic moments, dramatic scenes, and beginnings and endings remain in the memory and decisively shape our sense of a novel as a whole.

In more elevated language, Henry James agrees with Forster about what makes a story interesting:

> The prime effect of so sustained a system, so prepared a surface, is to lead on and on; while the fascination of following resides, by the same token, in the presumability *somewhere* of a convenient, of a visibly-appointed stopping-place.[2]

According to James, individuals interrupt the flow of their own lives for immersion in the life of fiction to achieve the satisfaction of an ending. Our sense that fictions will end in part nurtures our desire to read them.

Some critics, especially the Deconstructionists, have lost sight of the individual reader discussed by Forster and James who, like Scheherazade's husband, wants most to know "what happens next." Endings, we are told, both "ravel" and "unravel" the text, with interpretation a constant and constantly self-canceling act.[3] Such ideas have a tantalizing newness and a certain abstract validity. But they violate what common sense and practical experience tell us: novels do have forms and meanings, and endings are crucial in achieving them.

Return for a moment to what James has to say about endings. After discussing the allure of an ending, he goes on to note that "stopping-places" in fictions are never entirely natural or easily found:

> We have, as the case stands, to invent and establish them, to arrive at them by a difficult, dire process of selection and comparison, of surrender and sacrifice.[4]

James moves from the idea of endings as the reader's goal to the idea of endings as fundamentally artistic. A proper ending can be established only by a process of "selection and comparison," by artistic arrangement which makes the novel a unified and organic whole. Forster's thinking about fiction expands in similar fashion. For if human curiosity sustains the reading of novels, a completed novel, he insists, must contain "pattern and rhythm," internal connections which give it meaning and make it art.[5]

Achieving an ending through the selection and comparison that completes a work's pattern and rhythm tests the very artfulness of a writer. As James sees it, skillful endings give readers a sense that the text fully captures life and leaves no relevant aspect of its subject unexplored:

> Really, universally, relations stop nowhere, and the exquisite problem of the artist is eternally but to draw, by a geometry of his own, the circle within which they shall happily *appear* to do so.[6]

Endings enable an informed definition of a work's "geometry" and set into motion the process of retrospective rather than speculative thinking necessary to discern it—the process of "retrospective patterning."[7] Moreover, in completing the "circle" of a novel, endings create the illusion of life halted and poised for analysis. Like completed segments of human lives and as representations of them, completed stories illuminate and invite examination of human experiences. In part, we value endings because the retrospective patterning used to make sense of texts corresponds to one process used to make sense of life: the process of looking back over events and interpreting them in light of "how things turned out." Ordinary readers and literary critics share an interest in endings because appreciating endings is one way of evaluating and organizing personal experience.

II

James's "so sustained a system" and Forster's "pattern and rhythm," restate one of the oldest principles in literary criticism, Aristotle's definition of an artistic whole as "that which has a beginning, a middle, and an end."[8] The formal relationship of ending to beginning and middle is what I call the shape of fictions. Interest in the shape of fictions, in the internal structures of a work, requires the study of novelistic closure, not just of novelistic endings. As I use the term, "closure" designates the process by which a novel reaches an adequate and appropriate conclusion or, at least, what the author hopes or believes is an adequate, appropriate conclusion. My use of the term closure corresponds to what Barbara Herrnstein Smith in *Poetic Closure* calls the "integrity" of a lyric and what David Richter in *Fable's End* calls the "completeness" of an apologue—a sense that nothing necessary has been omitted from a work.[9]

Effective closure cannot be assured solely by the unity or consistency of beginning, middle, and end. Nor need effective closure definitively announce that the work has ended or resolve all the novel's aesthetic and thematic elements. My use of the term thus differs somewhat from Smith's in *Poetic Closure*, in part to include the now familiar tendencies, particularly in Modernist literature, which she calls "anti-closural." My terminology should also be distinguished from Robert Adams' use of the term "closed" to refer to fully resolved meanings.[10] Works that Smith and Adams would call "anti-closural" or "open" can, in my terms, still achieve effective closure. The test is the honesty and the appropriateness of the ending's relationship to beginning and middle, not the degree of finality or resolution achieved by the ending. The word "ending" straightforwardly designates the last definable unit of work—section, scene, chapter, page, paragraph, sentence—whichever seems most appropriate for a given text.

To study closure and the shape of fictions, we begin with the ending, but evaluate its success as part of an artistic whole, as the final element in a particular structure of words and meanings. The discussion of closure includes the discussion of aesthetic shape— verbal, metaphorical, gestural, and other formal patterns. It also includes the study of the themes and ideas embodied in the text and of relevant extratextual contexts that help form those themes and ideas, contexts including the author's life, his times, and his or his culture's beliefs about human experience. To approach fiction by way of closure is not, then, at all narrow. Endings, closures reveal the essences of novels with particular clarity; to study closure is to re-create and re-experience fiction with unusual vividness.

Recognizing the importance of endings, other recent critics have explored the subject. Frank Kermode's fine *The Sense of an Ending* has probably been more responsible than any other single work for initiating renewed critical interest in narrative endings.[11] Kermode's work on endings reflects a general and theoretical interest in the pattern-seeking tendencies of the human mind. He persuasively demonstrates that literary plots and the endings they postulate resemble other fictions men use to make sense of the world (in religion, philosophy, the sciences, etc.), and change as men's ideas about the world do. He nicely documents tension, in all human fictions, between the desire to mime contingency and disorder and the opposing need to create coherence and system.

*The Sense of an Ending* uses Jean-Paul Sartre's novel *La Nausée* as a point of departure. In that novel, the narrator, Roquentin, expresses an idea also known to Herodotus and to the writers of Greek tragedy: the idea that endings confirm the patterns of both lives and texts, but are always unknown for lives in progress.[12] Roquentin insists that "Quand on vit, il n'arrive rien. . . . Mais quand on raconte la vie, tout change" ("Nothing happens while you live. . . . But everything changes when you tell about life").[13] What seem petty details assume significance in narratives because endings confer coherent structure on the flux of experience. An ending transforms:

> tout. . . . Les instants ont cessé de s'empiler au petit bonheur les uns sur les autres, ils sont hâppés par la fin de l'histoire.

> everything. . . . Instants have stopped piling themselves in a lighthearted way one on top of the other, they are snapped up by the ending of the story.[14]

Kermode agrees with Roquentin about how a "piece of information" assumes significance in a novel:

the beginning implies the end. . . . [A]ll that seems fortuitous and contingent in what follows is in fact reserved for a later benefaction of significance in some concordant structure.[15]

Kermode's study is indisputably "major." But it is incomplete in two significant ways. First, its emphasis on theory results in a relative distance from actual texts except, perhaps, from *La Nausée*, hardly a representative novel. Second, as an article by Roy Pascal has shown, Kermode remains fundamentally ambiguous about whether or not reality is purely contingent or contains inherent principles of order.[16] He sometimes loses sight of how endings correspond to very ordinary aspects of experience—to, for example, speculations about our futures in terms of anticipated "endings" (like marriage, graduation, recovery from or descent into illness), to retrospective analyses of history or of our pasts in light of "how things turned out," and to observations of the lives of others and the endings we project for them.

In his seeming acceptance of Sartre's emphasis on the differences between living and reading, Kermode ignores other pertinent analogies between the two. The process of reading without knowing endings is, for example, rather like the process of day-to-day living: we make tentative guesses at direction and meaning by applying our experience of what the data we encounter usually lead to and mean.[17] Since first readings involve the continuous making and revision of guesses, first readings are like the process of living from moment to moment in the present. Second or subsequent readings—when the question of "what happens next" no longer pertains with urgency—differ fundamentally from first readings and resemble the ways in which we experience the past. Upon rereading, pattern and rhythm—connections between beginning, middle, and end—may be more easily discerned and more fully understood by the reader. Appreciating such connections through retrospective patterning provides the primary pleasure of rereadings, just as reliving the facts or perceiving the patterns in our lives forms the basis on which we regard our pasts.

## III

Two other major studies of closure in the novel are marred by too narrow a selection of texts or too polemical a preference for certain kinds of endings. Réné Girard's *Deceit, Desire, and the Novel*, for example, discusses in detail only selected novels by Stendhal, Dostoevsky, and Proust, but proposes to summarize the nature of all novelistic conclusions. According to Girard, novels end with "conversions" in which the hero recognizes the deceitfulness and mediated quality of his desires and thereby comes to share the author's viewpoint and be *"capable of writing the novel."*[18] Any text that does not conform to this paradigm is, for Girard, "romantique" (romance-like), rather than "romanesque" (novelistic). But by converting the word "novelistic" from a description of literary type to an evaluation of literary merit by the standards of nineteenth-century fiction, Girard forces us to omit too many novels (especially non-realistic and Modernist ones) from the ranks of "novelistic" works. More significantly, illuminating though it is for many texts, Girard's thesis obscures the differences that count as much as the similarities in novelistic closure.

Another well-known study of how novels end, Alan Friedman's *The Turn of the Novel*, reverses Girard's standards. For Friedman, the "truer ending" is one that endorses "either an ever-widening disorder or a finally open 'order' which embraces all the opposed directions on whatever ethical compass it has brought along for the trip."[19] Thus, endings in which characters and readers finish with an "open stream of conscience"—with an expanding, unresolved moral consciousness—are, for Friedman, "good" endings. Since such endings are more characteristic of Modernist than of nineteenth-century novels, we must devalue a significant number of nineteenth-century texts if we accept Friedman's vague, polemical criteria. Indeed, the Modernist bias of critics like Friedman has virtually destroyed the usefulness of the terms "open" and "closed" to describe endings, by making "open" a term of approbation, and "closed" a term linked with unadventurous and narrow didacticism. In the conclusion, I will want to return to Friedman's assumption that newer endings are better endings, since my approach to closure will allow us to see continuities, as well as discontinuities, in strategies of closure.

A special issue of *Nineteenth-Century Fiction*, reprinted in book form under the title *Narrative Endings*,[20] indicates a continuing preoccupation with endings; at the same time, it reveals the lack of any consistent framework within which to describe narrative endings, and even the lack of any shared sense of what an ending is. We need for closure in the novel what Barbara Herrnstein Smith has provided for closure in poetry: flexible, non-polemical ways to describe endings and strategies of closure. But Smith's *Poetic Closure* cannot really serve as the model for such a study despite the suppleness of Smith's insights and terminology, to which I am often indebted. In *Poetic Closure*, she rapidly and successfully surveys how closure works in a great many poems. In novels, as in lyrics, the process of closure often begins with the work's first lines. But the greater length of novels renders closure a longer, more intricate process in most novels than in most poems. Following that process requires detailed, sustained analyses of representative works, rather than an attempt at a comprehensive survey.

I have chosen to discuss closure in depth for eleven representative novels: *Middlemarch, Bleak House, War and Peace, The Scarlet Letter, Vanity Fair, L'Education sentimentale, The Portrait of a Lady, The Ambassadors, The Golden Bowl, Light in August,* and *The Waves*. Individual chapters sometimes include brief discussions of a number of other texts. The chapter on *War and Peace*, for example, touches on Tolstoy's other novels; that on James's sense of an ending concentrates on *The Portrait of a Lady* and *The Ambassadors*, but briefly surveys endings in many of James's early works. The novels were chosen for their inherent interest and their importance. They were also chosen to give a roughly historical or chronological sense of developments in the novel since 1848—particularly of developments in reader expectations and in authorial treatment of themes typical of novels (themes like the importance of family life, or the relationship of the individual to society or cosmos).

The endings of these novels follow two common and major formal patterns. Many are epilogues; several are scenes. As defined by the Russian Formalist Boris Eikhenbaum, the epilogue has two formal characteristics: it sets the perspective by a shift in time-scale or orientation; it provides some element of *nachgeschichte* (after-history) for the major characters.[21] Eikhenbaum's definition of the epilogue is more inclusive and less pejorative than the familiar definition of the epilogue, a definition of content based on Henry James's dismissal of the endings to many popular nineteenth-century novels as "a distribution at the last of prizes, pensions, husbands, wives, babies, millions, appended paragraphs, and cheerful remarks."[22] Eikhenbaum's definition allows us to recognize epilogues not just in nineteenth-century novels like Dickens', but also in Modernist works like *Light in August* and *The Waves*. One of its leading practitioners, Henry James, best defines the scenic ending. Modeled after endings in drama, the scenic ending presents a final dialogue between two or more characters, which is intensely focused and usually presented without authorial commentary.

The division of endings into formal kinds like epilogue and scene might satisfy our desire for a description of closural strategies, were it neat enough or informative enough. But as the chapters which follow show, the identification of the form of an ending, while a necessary first step, does not take us far enough in the description of novelistic closure. If we follow Eikhenbaum's definition of the epilogue, for example, all the following major novels end in epilogues: *Pamela, Clarissa, Tom Jones, The Mysteries of Udolpho*, most of Scott's novels, all of Austen's, most of Dickens', *Jane Eyre, Wuthering Heights, Vanity Fair, The Scarlet Letter, The House of the Seven Gables, Madame Bovary, L'Education sentimentale, Middlemarch* and most of Eliot's other novels, *War and Peace, Anna Karenina, The Way of all Flesh, The Waves,*

*Women in Love, Light in August, The Sound and the Fury,* and many, many others. Even cursory thought about the implications of this list reveals that labeling an ending an "epilogue" does not tell us much. The ending of *Tom Jones* differs significantly from that of *Middlemarch,* and both differ significantly from that of *The Waves.* Too simply used, the formal label "epilogue" can, then, distort our sense of each ending's uniqueness. And, of course, we could substitute at will the names of any three novels using the same form of ending in the preceding statement.

Moreover, a number of these epilogues resemble scenes (some being very similar, in fact, to the purely scenic endings of Henry James), or else include scenic elements. I am thinking here of endings like those of *War and Peace, L'Education sentimentale, Women in Love,* and *Light in August*—all epilogues, but all also scenic to one degree or another. It is fairly easy to define forms of endings distinctly; it is much more difficult to find examples from literature that absolutely fit our definitions. We cannot, then, explain how closure works in novels merely by labeling endings with formal terms like epilogue and scene.

We need to supplement our sense of formal kinds of endings with a collection of terms to describe basic strategies for closure in novels, terms applicable to many forms of endings. Such terms should describe the significant relationships that influence closure: the relationship of the ending to the novel's shape, to the author's preoccupations, and to the experience of the reader. Descriptions of closural strategies should apply equally well to epilogues and scenes, and should indicate the differences between these two formal kinds in their purest forms. Ideally, such terms should also be useful for other forms of endings, and for endings in novels rather different from those I discuss—novels less interested in character and plot, in philosophical and moral issues than those I have chosen, novels (for example) like the recent work of authors like Pynchon and Hawkes. Such terms are possible, though they should be used as descriptive and analytic tools rather than substituted for the analysis of individual texts.

## V

We first need a set of terms to describe the relationship of ending to beginning and middle, to the shape of the fiction. We may begin with a geometric metaphor already widely used: the metaphor of *circularity*. When the ending of a novel clearly recalls the beginning in language, in situation, in the grouping of characters, or in several of these ways, circularity may be said to control the ending. One of the most common of closural patterns, circularity may be obvious or subtle, immediately perceived or perceivable only upon retrospective analysis. A familiar and obvious kind of circularity is the "frame" technique common in narratives. When language, situation, or the grouping of characters refers not just to the beginning of the work but to a series of points in the text, we may speak of *parallelism* as the novel's closural pattern. Often less obvious than circularity, parallelism sometimes becomes clear only upon retrospective analysis.

Both circularity and parallelism are geometrical metaphors, and we may use a third geometrical metaphor to describe another closural pattern—*incompletion*. Incomplete closure includes many aspects that suggest circular or parallel closure, but omits one or more crucial elements necessary for full circularity or parallelism. Incomplete closure may result from deliberate authorial choices, or it may result from an inadvertent formal failure, or from some combination of the two. It is quite different from endings that do what students are told never to do at the conclusion of an expository essay—endings that begin a new topic.

When an ending does introduce a new topic, the introduction of that topic (if not incompetent) is usually a deliberate gesture of the kind Smith would call "anti-closural." We can describe this strategy for ending as *tangential*. Because such endings do not lend themselves to detailed analysis, the following chapters include no example of a tangential ending, except for aspects of the ending of *War and Peace*. André Gide's *Les Faux Monnayeurs*, however, provides a well-known example of a tangential ending, one motivated by the author's wish to end his novel with the sense that it could be continued.[23] In *Les Faux Monnayeurs*, the narrator and main character, Edouard, spends the novel pursuing the adventures of a fascinating boy named Bernard. In the novel's last paragraph, Edouard becomes "bien curieux" (very interested) in getting to know Bernard's younger brother, Caloub. Such a new acquaintance could, theoretically, initiate a totally new novel.

One other kind of closural strategy, similar to the tangential ending, also does not lend itself to detailed analysis and will be largely omitted from the following chapters. The strategy is often that of novelists like Balzac and Zola who wrote *romans fleuves*, novels conceived as part of a larger series of works, in which characters reappear in several texts. Novels that form part of such a series sometimes end with the explicit message, "to be continued." Thus, the last chapter of Honoré de Balzac's *Illusions perdues* (in form an epilogue) refers us to future novels for the fate of the main character:

> As for Lucien, his return to Paris belongs to the domain of the *Scenes of Parisian Life*.[24]

Fyodor Dostoevsky ends *Crime and Punishment*, to which he intended to write a sequel, very similarly:

> He did not know that the new life would not be given him for nothing, that he would have to pay dearly for it, that it would cost him great striving, great suffering.
> But that is the beginning of a new story. . . . That might be the subject of a new story, but our present story is ended.[25]

We may call such a closural strategy *linkage*, since an ending like this links the novel not to its own beginning and middle, but to the body of another, often as yet unwritten, novel.

We need a second set of terms to describe the author's and the reader's viewpoint on the novel's characters and major action at the novel's end. Less numerous than the possible relationships of ending to beginning and middle, the two basic possible points of view may be described by the terms *overview* and *close-up*. These terms are analogous to the classic distinction between "telling" and "showing" made by Henry James and Percy Lubbock, though I intend to use them without Lubbock's value judgment in favor of "showing."[26]

In overview endings, authors often explicitly gloss the ending's relationship to the body of the novel for the reader; when no explicit gloss is offered, overview endings still give a clear view of the novel's major action, one that immediately "makes sense" to the reader. In an overview ending, the author's or narrator's understanding (and hence the reader's understanding as well) is often superior to that of the characters. Author, narrator, and reader may know more facts than the characters do, and hence have an overview based on superior knowledge. Or the ending may be told from a point much later in time or more cosmic in knowledge than that available to the novel's characters. In this case too, author, narrator, and reader will have an overview unavailable to characters caught "in the middest."[27] In some instances, characters may share the overview on the novel's major action enjoyed by the author and reader. The protagonist shares the author's overview in novels that conform to Girard's paradigm, for example. Because of the time-shift they involve, epilogues are often overview in technique.

In a close-up ending, no temporal distance separates ending from the body of the novel. Readers, like characters, will—at least initially—lack the overview made possible by temporal distance or by authorial glossing of the action. First-time readers may not even understand why the ending *is* the ending, or may be at a loss for what the ending implies about meaning. They may well have to distance themselves emotionally from characters and action for such understanding to occur. Readers can usually, however, discover both the appropriateness of the ending and its implications for meaning through retrospective analysis and through perception of the pattern that controls the ending (circularity, parallelism, and so on). The implied author or the narrator may pretend to be at sea about the ending, like the characters. But as the "arranger of collocations" in the novel (to use Kermode's phrase), the author only disingenuously pretends to be "in the middest." He usually has very good and very precise reasons for ending at a chosen point. Just as epilogues are often overview endings, scenic endings are often close-up endings.

We need a third set of terms to describe the relationship between author and reader during closure. The slipperiness of the terms "author" and "reader" causes some difficulty in devising and using such terms. Most of my readers are familiar with the idea of the "implied" versus the "real" author. Wayne Booth provides a standard definition of the implied author:

> The "implied author" chooses, consciously or unconsciously, what we read; we infer him [from his novels] as an ideal, created version of the real man; he is the sum of his own choices.[28]

Critics once indicated the difference between "implied" and "real" authors by using quotation marks around the name of the "implied" author: thus we know "Fielding" from his novel *Tom Jones*, but we know Fielding from available biographies, letters, and so on. Today, such devices have largely been dropped. In the following chapters, I deal with discrepancies between "implied" and "real" authors when they are relevant to closure. I do not, however, labor such distinctions, since it is clear when I speak of authors as narrators or as "implied authors," and when I speak of authors as "real" men and women.[29]

The recent spate of reader-response criticism has justly indicated a number of possible readers, readers not always clearly distinguished or distinguishable.[30] These include the ideal reader (who reads the text as it ought to be read), the implied reader (who is explicitly addressed in the text, or whom the author imagines as he writes), and the contemporary reader (who is the typical reader of the author's own times). Depending on how it is used, and on the kind of reader envisioned by a given author, the term "implied reader" can overlap with "ideal reader" or "contemporary reader."

Descriptions of the relationship between author and reader during closure in a novel often differ for "ideal readers," "implied readers," and "contemporary readers." Moreover, "contemporary readers" and "ideal readers" may reach diverse judgments about the success or failure of an ending.

I necessarily deal with all these readers at one point or another. I reconstruct the contemporary reader from historical secondary studies of reading audiences, from contemporary reviews, from tabulations of best-sellers, and from remarks made by authors in notebooks, letters, or texts about the nature of the contemporary audience.[31] I deal with the implied reader as explicitly or implicitly addressed in the text or as identified by authors in extratextual documents. Finally, I try to read the novels as they ought to be read, thus reproducing the viewpoint of the ideal reader. In the chapters to follow it is, I believe, generally clear from context which reader is which; I will, however, use the terms "ideal," "implied," and "contemporary," when they are needed for clarity.

Some novelists, like Jane Austen, assume that they share a variety of ideals and views with their readers. Other novelists, like George Eliot, educate readers to share authorial views by the end of the novel, but are entirely confident that this process of education will take place as a natural result of the reading process, without much resistance by the reader.[32] In both cases, we may describe the relationship between author and reader during closure as *complementary*. In complementary relationships, the reader accepts—more or less uncritically—both the ending itself and whatever meaning (or lack of meaning) the author wishes it to convey.

When the author must more actively coax his reader into accepting an ending, we may describe the relationship between author and reader during closure as *incongruent*. Successful persuasion during closure results in the reader's acceptance of the ending, and converts an incongruent relationship into a *congruent* one. Unsuccessful persuasion results in some continuing degree of incongruence, in some sense for the reader that the ending is flawed. The distinction between a complementary relationship and a congruent one depends upon the degree of resistance the author anticipates from the reader, and the degree to which an author works hard during closure to minimize such resistance.

Finally, some authors exploit incongruent relationships between author and reader. Such authors anticipate that readers will not share the author's own attitude toward his ending. Rather than actively try to create a congruent relationship, they confront their audience with endings that deliberately thwart reader expectations, using the confrontation to achieve desired aesthetic and philosophical ends. We may call such a relationship between author and reader *confrontational*, with the degree and effect of the confrontation varying from book to book. Contemporary readers are usually the target of confrontational endings, especially those that flout popular conventions. They may deem a given ending as unsuccessful, while ideal readers find it successful and experience it as a kind of "in" joke.

We need a fourth set of terms to describe the author's relationship to his own ideas during closure, to indicate the degree of his self-awareness and of his control over the closural process. We may call *self-aware* authors who have mastered their ideas, know what they want to say by way of closure, and successfully go about saying it. Neither ambivalence nor controlled ambiguity need preclude self-awareness.

Most major authors are self-aware during closure. When they are not self-aware, two major possibilities exist. First, they may not have fully thought through their ideas or may have inadequately communicated those ideas in closure. Second, they may display a lack of self-knowledge or a psychological quirkiness during closure. We may call authors of both kinds *self-deceiving*, and distinguish the two varieties of self-deception author by author in the chapters which follow. A discrepancy between the real and implied author often exists when an author is self-deceiving.

In the following chapters and, indeed, even in this introduction, I may seem to violate a major critical precept, that of the intentional fallacy. The formulators of the idea of intentional fallacy rightly point out the limited usefulness of extratextual information, particularly information that is biographical or that concerns the author's intentions. Critics of the intentional fallacy have pointed out, again rightly, the many instances in which biographical information or statements of intention (whether fulfilled or abortive) genuinely advance our understanding of texts. Since an ending is the single place where an author most pressingly desires to make his points—whether those points are aesthetic, moral, social, political, epistemological, or even the determination not to make any point at all—extratextual information and statements of intention are often extremely helpful. I have, therefore, freely used extratextual materials like biography, letters, notebooks, and diaries to illuminate the endings studied. When connections between the text and the extratextual material are deceptive or lack immediacy, I have indicated that in my discussion.

Used in combination, the four sets of terms I propose provide a flexible, non-polemical way to describe endings and closures. They cannot substitute for the close analysis of endings and closures in individual novels. But they can facilitate such analysis and provide a needed vocabulary for the discussion of closure in the novel. The following chapters will provide examples of various patterns, techniques, relationships of author to reader, and relationships of author to self during closure. They will describe strategies of closure in representative novels, using these four interlocking sets of terms.

# ONE

## George Eliot and the "Finale"
## of *Middlemarch*

### I

In nineteenth-century novels, a shift in time scale or perspective at the end of a work is frequently accompanied by what I will call after-history: a brief summary of the "lives" of characters after the conclusion of the novel's major action.[1] The endings of many fictions explicitly testify to the popularity of this form of ending and to the fact that many readers had come to expect it at the ends of novels. At the conclusion of *Old Mortality*, for example, Scott masquerades as a Mr. Pattieson who, as "author" of the novel, "had determined to waive the task of a concluding chapter, leaving to the reader's imagination the arrangements which must necessarily take place after Lord Evandale's death." But admonished by "Miss Buskbody," the reader of her day, that his " 'plan of omitting a formal conclusion will never do,' " he jokingly supplies details of how his characters " 'did live long and happily, and begot sons and daughters.' "[2] Dickens and Trollope also concede to readers' demands for "a few biographical words" about the characters' later "lives" in accordance with "the custom of the thing."[3]

George Eliot wanted to be both a popular novelist and an intellectual one, and her vacillation between these two roles is reflected in the "Finale" of *Middlemarch*. The ostensible purpose of the concluding chapter is that of the after-history in popular fiction: to satisfy readers' curiosity about characters cared for as "people." Yet elements in Eliot's style prevent any simple use of popular conventions: her attitude toward characters is often condescending; she generalizes about characters in a way that works against the reader's emotional involvement; and melodrama and pathos, though present in her works, seem to embarrass rather than to engross her. Eliot's real task in the ending of *Middlemarch* is to convert the basic format of the popular after-history into an appropriate end to her intellectual and philosophical novel. But she accomplishes this task only after some initial hesitations and equivocations.

In the "Finale" of *Middlemarch*, Eliot's high degree of self-consciousness is immediately apparent. She begins by attempting to rationalize and theorize about the kind of after-history many nineteenth-century writers composed spontaneously. She doesn't just write an after-history, she provides multiple justifications for doing so:

> Every limit is a beginning as well as an ending. Who can quit young lives after being long in company with them, and not desire to know what befell them in their after-years? For the fragment of a life, however typical, is not the sample of an even web: promises may not be kept, and an ardent outset may be followed by declension; latent powers may find their long-waited opportunity; a past error may urge a grand retrieval.[4]

At first, the argument here sounds plausible. Eliot maintains that an epilogue is necessary because the "fragments" of lives presented in the novel may be "typical" without being absolute. Ostensibly, Eliot wishes to write after-histories of her characters to record alterations in their personalities or patterns of life that "occurred" after the main actions of the novel. But a reading of the ending reveals that the argument is essentially misleading. The after-histories record no broken promises, unexpected declensions, revived latent powers, or grand retrievals. The sketches of the characters' later lives merely follow through on marriages and decisions made in the body of the novel, and the future of each character is totally consistent with his past as recorded in *Middlemarch*: Fred and Mary remain harmonious, wholesome, and deservedly happy; Lydgate and Rosamund never do resolve their difficulties; Mrs. Vincy still has too much pride in her family's good looks; Baby Arthur remains the center of Celia's world, and so on.

In fact, the after-histories confirm that the portions of the characters' lives covered by the body of the novel were typical of their personalities and lifestyles, and prove that the determining incident in each character's life was the product of the interlinking web which has been the plot of *Middlemarch*. The organization of the epilogue abstracts and condenses the overall construction of the novel and the web metaphor of interconnecting human lives which has been so crucial in the novel.[5] Each of the after-histories ends with the name of the character whose future life will then be discussed, and each after-history conforms to Eliot's stated purpose in writing the novel, "to show the gradual action of ordinary causes rather than exceptional."[6]

## II

The first sentence of the opening paragraph to the "Finale" grapples, however, with an authentic novelistic problem. *Middlemarch* is a multiple plot novel with an omniscient authorial narrator whose presence in the novel contributes a great deal to its unity and structure. As an omniscient narrator, Eliot is always in a position to tell her reader more, and yet compelled to end the novel somewhere. As Eliot sees it, the problem becomes that of finding a satisfying note on which to end, while still preserving the sense of "new beginnings" in the ongoing lives of her characters. In a letter, she expresses her sincere concern over this problem:

> Conclusions are the weak point of most authors, but some of the fault lies in the very nature of a conclusion, which is at best a negation.[7]

The comment was made to her publisher, John Blackwood, whom Eliot used as a test reader and who probably influenced the kinds of endings she wrote. Blackwood liked sentimental endings and highly praised the sentimental after-history that concludes Eliot's first fiction, "Mr. Gilfil's Love Story" in *Scenes from Clerical Life*.[8] She subsequently wrote after-history endings to all her novels, except the last, *Daniel Deronda*. The epilogue of *Middlemarch* is by far Eliot's most sophisticated use of the form. As the above quotation suggests, it reflects her concern that successful characterization and successful story-telling impose a burden on the omniscient author of a multiple-plot novel, and make ending more problematic than it would be in a novel that focuses on a single character and would end, like the biographical form it imitates, on some crucial turning-point in the character's life, or with the character's death. The end of a novel like *Middlemarch*, to avoid being a negation, must round off the novel without closing off the lives of characters.

Two major options for preserving the sense of "new beginnings" at the end of a multiple-plot, omnisciently narrated novel were widely used in the nineteenth-century. One was to write a linking ending, as authors like Balzac and Zola, who conceived of their novels as part of a larger system and had characters from one novel reappear in others, so frequently did. This option clearly did not suit *Middlemarch*. The other was to combine scenic elements into the epilogue form, and to break off in mid-air and simply allow life to go on. The endings of Dickens' *Bleak House* and Tolstoy's *War and Peace* use precisely this technique. The epilogue to *Bleak House* is narrated by Esther Summerson seven years after the completion of the novel's major action and rather gushingly breaks off with a dash, as she waxes enthusiastic over her domestic bliss. The last chapter of *War and Peace* (Book 5, chapter 5) similarly ends with an ellipsis in Natasha's excited speculations with Mary about their future marriages. The first epilogue (the familial epilogue) is dated 1820 (seven years after the climactic events in the novel), and also breaks off with an ellipsis, as Nicholas dreamily plans a future worthy of Andrew, his dead father.

Eliot tries out and rejects the method of breaking off in mid-air to preserve a sense of "new beginnings" in the chapter immediately before the last (Book 8, chapter 86), which deals with the Garth family and gives Mary Garth and Fred Vincy an immediate financial basis on which to marry. The chapter breaks off on a frolicsome and unanswered question, amid a riotous scene of yapping dogs and playing children:

Fred almost in a whisper said—
    "When we were first engaged, with the umbrella-ring, Mary, you used to—"

The spirit of joy began to laugh more decidedly in Mary's eyes, but the fatal Ben came running to the door with Brownie yapping behind him, and, bouncing against them, said—

"Fred and Mary! are you ever coming in?—or may I eat your cake?"   (III, p. 454)

If Eliot authentically wanted a sense of "new beginnings" at the end of *Middlemarch*, she should have ended it here, with Fred and Mary, Will and Dorothea about to marry, and Lydgate and Rosamund entering a new stage in their marriage—"new beginnings" all around in a close-up, scenic ending. But as Eliot probably knew all along, this would absolutely be the wrong ending for the novel. *Middlemarch* demands a long-shot rather than a domestic close-up, a philosophical overview rather than a dramatic scene. Accordingly, the Finale is narrated from thirty-five years after the end of the novel's major action, when many of the characters are dead. Its after-histories are, therefore, inevitably final and inevitably contrary to a sense of "new beginnings."

With one eye firmly fixed on the crowd-pleasing potential of the conventional after-history, Eliot nonetheless never loses sight of the aesthetic and thematic form of her novel. Her equivocations at the beginning of the epilogue do not prevent her from writing the kind of novelistic ending she needs, which is precisely that found in *Middlemarch*—an after-history dominated by the articulate authorial narrator and both firm and final in the viewpoints it offers on the characters.

### III

As we reread the novel, it becomes clear that Eliot worked with closure in mind from the very beginning. The Finale gives unity to the novel's aesthetic and thematic shape by a method she preferred—that of "returning to the key note of the introductory chapter"[9]—or circular form. Indeed, the epilogue re-examines issues raised in the novel's Saint Theresa prologue. Aesthetically, it provides *Middlemarch* with a symmetrical structure and an instant sense that the novel has ended. Thematically, it authentically completes the novel by modifying the narrator's initial evaluation of the relationship between epic life and domestic life, a relationship explored throughout the novel.

In the "Prelude," epic and domestic experiences exist at different levels of life, as contradictory modes of existence. St. Theresa and her brother set forth on their mission against the Moors,

> until domestic reality met them in the shape of uncles, and turned them back from their great resolve.   (I, p. 1)

Yet, as Eliot next indicates, Theresa's "great resolve" ultimately transcended "domestic reality," in a way more useful to society than her childhood mission against the Moors would have been:

> Theresa's passionate, ideal nature demanded an epic life: what were many-volumed romances of chivalry and the social conquests of a brilliant girl to her? Her flame quickly burned up that light fuel; and, fed from within, soared after some illimitable satisfaction, some object which would never justify weariness, which would reconcile self-despair with the rapturous consciousness of life beyond self. She found her epos in the reform of a religious order.   (I, pp. 1-2)

For later-born Theresas, the possibility of transcendent self-expansion through religious activity ceased to be viable, but tension continued to exist between family life ("domestic reality") and higher yearnings (the "epic life"). But "later-born Theresas were helped by no coherent social faith and order which could perform the function of knowledge for the ardently willing soul." Consequently,

> Their ardour alternated between a vague ideal and the common yearning of womanhood; so that the one was disapproved as extravagance, and the other condemned as a lapse.
>
> (I, p. 2)

Dorothea, the primary Saint Theresa figure in the novel, provokes both kinds of disapproval. Celia, Chettam, and Middlemarchers in general condemn her aspirations as "extravagance." And those who knew and admired her in later life view her marriage to Will as a "lapse" from her potential. Typically, in Dorothea's after-history, Eliot contrasts the community's erroneous or narrow judgment with her own sensitivity to the character's predicament. She understands Dorothea's dilemma as few Middlemarchers or Londoners do:

> Many who knew her, thought it a pity that so substantive and rare a creature should have been absorbed into the life of another, and be only known in a certain circle as a wife and mother. But no one stated exactly what else that was in her power she ought rather to have done—not even Sir James Chettam, who went no further than the negative prescription that she ought not to have married Will Ladislaw.
>
> (III, pp. 461-62)

Introduction of the Saint Theresa theme and of Dorothea, a Theresa-like female protagonist, suggests at the beginning of *Middlemarch* that Eliot's theme is the "Woman Question," to be illustrated by the fate of Dorothea. Wary of having her theme thus narrowed, Eliot broadens the issue of epic versus domestic life early in the work by introducing Lydgate into the novel, as a male protagonist subject to the same conflicts that face Dorothea.[10] Her refusal to deal only with a woman's fate in Victorian society accords with sentiments expressed in a letter during the writing of *Middlemarch*:

> There is no subject on which I am more inclined to hold my peace and learn, than on the "Woman Question." . . . I know very little about what is specially good for women—only a few things that I feel sure are good for human nature generally, and about such as these last alone, can I ever hope to write or say anything worth saying.[11]

In fact, the conflict between epic and domestic life is most apparent and striking in the Lydgate, rather than the Dorothea, sections of *Middlemarch*. As Rosamund and family responsibilities undermine Lydgate's lofty scientific ambitions (ambitions already compromised by the celebrated "spots of commonness" the narrator identifies in the doctor), Eliot notes that the course of love often parallels that of high idealism, ending sometimes in "glorious marriage, sometimes frustration and final parting." Moreover,

> not seldom the catastrophe is bound up with the other passion, sung by the Troubadors. For in the multitude of middle-aged men who go about their vocations in a daily course determined for them much in the same way as the tie of their cravats, there is always a good number who once meant to shape their own deeds and alter the world a little.   (I, pp. 218-19)

The explicit purpose of *Middlemarch* is to tell "The story of their coming to be shapen after the average and fit to be packed by the gross," a story "hardly ever told even in their consciousness" (I, p. 219). The themes of *Middlemarch* are thus universal in scope; the lot of Saint Theresa and the women who lived after her serves as a model for the problematic relation of idealism to pragmatism, of lofty aspirations to safe domesticity. In the above quotation, as in the prologue, the narrator regrets the narrowing of epic impulses, but sees the process as fairly inevitable in modern society with the "not seldom" cause being love and marriage.

## IV

The narrator's basic attitude of regret over but resignation to the narrowing of epic impulses is modified and enriched as the novel develops by a different perspective on epic and domestic life, communicated through verbal motifs both major and minor. A minor note, repeatedly sounded, characterizes romantic crises in the lives of Lydgate, Rosamund, and Will as "epochs." This language occasionally belongs to the characters, but more often belongs to the authorial narrator (see, for example, I, p. 177 and III, p. 412). A more major motif, centered in the Dorothea portions, re-examines domestic experience and gradually reveals its potential to fulfill an individual's epic yearnings. As the novel develops, Eliot consistently applies religious vocabulary (associated initially in the novel

with the epic Middle Ages of St. Theresa) to humanitarian experiences. Love and marriage relationships serve as the direct cat-
alysts of the transition and as the most readily available spheres
of humanitarian experience.

During her courtship by Casaubon, for example, Dorothea focuses her Theresa-like yearnings on her husband-to-be. She
swoons like a Bernini Theresa upon reading his proposal of marriage, casting herself "in the lap of a divine consciousness which
sustained her own," and imagining herself "a neophyte about to
enter on a higher grade of initiation" (I, p. 62). Her honeymoon
over, Dorothea changes; in a conversation with Will Ladislaw, she
offers a radically secularized definition of religion as individual
code rather than formal worship. After stating her belief " 'That
by desiring what is perfectly good, even when we don't quite know
what it is and cannot do what we would, we are part of the divine
power against evil—widening the skirts of light and making the
struggle with darkness narrower,' " Dorothea asserts:

> "It [my belief] is my life. I have found it out, and cannot
> part with it. I have always been finding out my religion since
> I was a little girl. . . . I try not to have desires merely for
> myself. . . .
> "What is *your* religion?" said Dorothea. "I mean—not
> what you know about religion, but the belief that helps you
> most?" (II, p. 180)

Thus secularized, religious impulses are next domesticated, as
Dorothea's humanitarian beliefs are tested by her marriage. After
"a litany of pictured sorrows and of silent cries," Dorothea passes
the first test—achieving sympathy and showing tenderness for
Casaubon, now accurately perceived as a narrow-minded pedant,
but one worthy of compassion (II, p. 234). After seeing Will kissing
Rosamund in the Lydgates' parlor, Dorothea undergoes an even
more intense struggle during a sleepless night when she confronts
"lost belief" and experiences one of the "spiritual struggles of
man" (III, p. 388). In the famous "night vigil" chapter, Dorothea
passes her major test by overcoming her jealousy of Rosamund
and deciding to visit her to offer counsel. She successfully expands

the "vivid sympathetic experience" gained through her marriage into an understanding of the Lydgates' marriage and a more broadly humanitarian identification with "the manifold wakings of men to labour and endurance . . . [with] involuntary, palpitating life." (III, p. 392)

The novel's vocabulary thus gradually links domestic experiences with transcendent religious ones. The novel's plot further links the sublimely humanitarian and the mundanely domestic in that Dorothea's decision initiates a chain of actions which improves the family lives of all the major characters: Dorothea visits Rosamund and salvages the Lydgate marriage; Rosamund, "taken hold of by an emotion stronger than her own" (III, p. 405), acts generously for the only time in the novel, informing Dorothea of Will's innocence; Will's final visit to Dorothea assures their marital happiness. The successful resolution of the plot contains terms that bring together religious and epic vocabulary, and applies them to ordinary "everyday life," confirming the overall tendency of the patterns I have traced to bring closer together the epic and domestic levels of life, initially seen as mutually exclusive in the novel:

> But it is given to us sometimes even in our everyday life to witness the saving influence of a noble nature, the divine efficacy of rescue that may lie in a self-subduing act of fellowship. (III, p. 414)

Eliot describes humanitarian "self-subduing fellowship" as not just "noble," but also as possessing "saving influence" and "divine efficacy." Verbally, "domestic reality," everyday life, now provides opportunities for the religious and epic achievements it frustrated earlier in the novel.

In an illuminating letter to Alexander Main, a young man who wished to compile a collection of Eliot's wisest writings, Eliot confided some misgivings about composing the "right" conclusion to *Middlemarch*:

> I need not tell you that my book will not present my own feeling about human life if it produces on readers whose minds are really receptive the impression of blank melancholy and

despair. . . . I am too anxious about its completion—too fearful lest the impression it might make (I mean for the good of those who read) should turn to naught—to look at it in mental sunshine.[12]

Taking upon herself the role of "Victorian sage," Eliot shaped *Middlemarch* to illustrate beliefs which work "for the good of those who read." Her wish to avoid producing "blank melancholy and despair" underlies the verbal patterns I have traced. Throughout *Middlemarch*, she makes verbal allusions to the "Prelude" and reformulates the relationship of domestic and epic life. The process is subtle and fully discernible only upon analysis. But the gradual accretion of epic, religious vocabulary around domestic experience prepares the way for an honest yet consolatory conclusion. In the authorial sections of *Middlemarch*, the narrator eases new ideas about the epic potential of everyday life into the text, presenting them for the consideration of the reader. By the "Finale," Eliot assumes the reader's assent to the narrator's contentions, and her statements therefore become more emphatic. The relationship of author to reader during closure might be seen as initially incongruent, becoming congruent at the end of the novel. Eliot's thorough confidence that the reader will ultimately share her views, however, makes the relationship between author and reader more aptly described by the term complementary.

V

After an uneasy opening in which, as we have seen, Eliot ostensibly aligns her ending with the popular conventional epilogue, the intellectual in Eliot emerges and she moves more decisively toward the joining of the religious-epic and domestic-average levels of life that is the proper resolution of *Middlemarch*'s thematic structure:

Marriage, which has been the bourne of so many narratives, is still a great beginning, as it was to Adam and Eve, who kept their honeymoon in Eden, but had their first little one among the thorns and thistles of the wilderness. It is still the beginning of the home epic—the gradual conquest or irremediable loss of that complete union which makes the advancing years a climax, and age the harvest of sweet memories in common.

Some set out, like Crusaders of old, with a glorious equipment of hope and enthusiasm, and get broken by the way, wanting patience with each other and the world.

(III, p. 455)

The second sentence—with its phrase "home epic"—and the next paragraph, with its references to "Crusaders" and "conquest," refer the reader to the St. Theresa prologue, and its setting in the epic period of the Christian Crusades. The use of the term "home epic" is the culmination of the verbal strands I have traced in the novel, in which epic vocabulary refers to romantic and domestic crises. It elevates marriage and family life as part of the domestic, ordinary level of life, to the epic level. The ending thus fuses the epic/transcendent/religious level of life, which was possible in earlier periods of history, with the domestic/average/humanitarian level of life, which is its closest approximation in Eliot's view of modern times.

The phrase "home epic" gives the reader a crucial framework for reading the after-histories in the "Finale," which detail the success or failure of the major characters in what are, in effect, their home epics. The failure of Lydgate's domestic life conditions his over-all failure: Lydgate, who had "meant to be a unit who would make a certain amount of difference towards that spreading change which would one day tell appreciably upon the averages" (I, p. 221), is rendered worse than average by bitterness and self-reproach and by his problems in domestic life. Conversely, the success of Will and Dorothea, the Garths, and Fred and Mary Vincy, confirms the general rightness of their individual philosophies. The phrase "home-epic" also contains an implied theory of social melioration through good marriages, breeding, and eugenics, a theory further implied at the conclusion of the epilogue.

The last paragraphs of the ending, the only portion of the epilogue usually acknowledged by critics, constitute an explicit defense of Dorothea, and a definition of the way in which her enthusiasm, channeled into her marriage, ultimately touches the larger social world:

> Certainly those determining acts of her life were not ideally beautiful. They were the mixed result of young and noble impulse struggling amidst the conditions of an imperfect social state, in which great feelings will often take the aspect of error, and great faith the aspect of illusion. For there is no creature whose inward being is so strong that it is not greatly determined by what lies outside it. A new Theresa will hardly have the opportunity of reforming a conventual life, any more than a new Antigone will spend her heroic piety in daring all for the sake of a brother's burial: the medium in which their ardent deeds took shape is for ever gone. But we insignificant people with our daily words and acts are preparing the lives of many Dorotheas, some of which may present a far sadder sacrifice than that of the Dorothea whose story we know.
> Her finely-touched spirit had still its fine issues, though they were not widely visible. Her full nature, like that river of which Cyrus broke the strength, spent itself in channels which had no great name on the earth. But the effect of her being on those around her was incalculably diffusive: for the growing good of the world is partly dependent on unhistoric acts; and that things are not so ill with you and me as they might have been, is half owing to the number who lived faithfully a hidden life, and rest in unvisited tombs.
> (III, pp. 464-65)[13]

At the beginning of the novel, Dorothea was disinclined to admit "any error in herself. She was disposed rather to accuse the intolerable narrowness and the purblind conscience of the society around her" (I, p. 52). In the final chapters of the novel and in the epilogue, however, she feels "that there was always something better which she might have done, if she had only been better and known better" (III, p. 461). Eliot's evaluation is somewhere between these two extremes. The sentence, "For there is no creature whose inward being is so strong that it is not greatly determined by what lies outside it," strongly states that society in part determines individual potential. But the point to be made about Dorothea and her society is *not* that society held Dorothea back, but that society in the nineteenth century is reduced in grandeur and inherently less heroic than society in earlier periods of history. Dorothea encounters no heroic opposition; Middlemarch and the Middlemarchers are apt representatives of the anemia of modern society. Great deeds are possible only in a great medium; small deeds are the best that are possible in a reduced medium. In the nineteenth century, the only channels available to an individual's epic impulses are small-scale, mundane, and domestic.

*Middlemarch* focuses squarely on England of the eighteen-thirties in an attempt to illuminate England of the eighteen-seventies. From this point of view, Eliot can envision no hope for the immediate restructuring of society along the lines of her humanistic philosophy. Religion, a force capable of motivating a nation toward noble, self-expanding goals, has ceased to be a force for the communal good in *Middlemarch*. Therefore, Eliot advocates a compromise solution of gradual melioration through the diffusive influence of well-led individual lives. In *Daniel Deronda*, the only one of Eliot's later novels which does not end with an epilogue, the focus on the exotic Jewish community allows Eliot to end with the possibility of a new society structured along religious and humanitarian lines. Deronda will have the religious backing that modern England lacks; his journey to Palestine literally duplicates the route followed by the medieval Crusaders mentioned in the prologue to *Middlemarch*. Perhaps because religious impulse has the potential to build a new society at the end of *Deronda*, there is no need for the consolatory, didactic kind of ending necessary in *Middlemarch*. Deronda's after-history is not supplied for the reader; his fate and Gwendolen Harleth's remain "open."

In the final paragraph of *Middlemarch*, however, Eliot unblinkingly evaluates Dorothea's life in terms of the reduced possibilities she assumes exist for the nineteenth-century man or woman. The language of this final paragraph is avowedly mixed, with words suggesting fullness balanced against words suggesting a partial loss. Positive words (like "finely-touched," "fine issues," "full nature," "incalculably diffusive," and "growing good") and negative or equivocating words (like "not widely visible," "channels which had no great name," "partly dependent," "not so ill," and "half-owing") are strung together in this paragraph. It is difficult to decide which predominates, but within the limited possibilities for positive action axiomatic in Eliot's view of the nineteenth century, Dorothea's life has been a "success," as have those of the other characters who intuitively live by codes the narrator endorses—characters with inner convictions and successful family lives, like the Garths, Will, and Fred and Mary.

## VI

In what I have said thus far, it is clear that though Eliot begins with what looks like conventional after-history, she invests the form with at least some aesthetic value, and with considerable philosophic value. All of the after-history's potentially mindless contents—the summary of characters' later lives, the multiple marriages, the rewarding of virtue and chastisement of vice—are endowed in the "Finale" with considerable, and frankly didactic, philosophical significance by Eliot. She provides a model of the self-aware author during closure. To guarantee the intellectual soundness of her conclusion, she carefully avoids any "sleight of hand" in achieving her didactic consolatory ending. She frankly acknowledges the weaknesses of her conclusions and attempts to meet serious philosophical objections. She admits, for example, that she could have told stories of later-born Theresas "which may present a far sadder sacrifice than that of the Dorothea whose story we know" (III, p. 465). Eliot chose *not to tell* these stories, because such a telling would work against the "mental sunshine" she pursued as her stated goal. But by anticipating the opposition, Eliot blunts charges that she has misrepresented experience.

Eliot's ideas are more seriously vulnerable to charges that not enough positive action emanates from right-minded individuals to the larger social world. In fact, this is a common Marxist criticism of many nineteenth-century thinkers, among them the Positivists, who strongly influenced Eliot. Positivists like Auguste Comte, Ludwig Feuerbach, John Stuart Mill, and George Henry Lewes conceived of their various philosophies as fulfilling for the nineteenth-century the same unifying, purpose-giving functions religion had served for earlier periods. Most believed in progress through the education of the individual away from narrow subjectivity and egoism, toward an objective view of the world, with love and sympathy for others. Like Eliot's philosophy in *Middlemarch*, their beliefs rested upon Comte's view of society as an organism composed of smaller, less complex organic units—the family and the individual.[14] In *Middlemarch*, the narrator's definition of the ardent, enthusiastic self as an instrument for gradual social change is basically consolatory in nature; it emphasizes the immediate goal of making individual lives meaningful, rather than the larger goal of changing society. According to Eliot, the reform of the individual consciousness will serve as an *instrument* in the gradual reform of society. A more radical theory of social change would go directly to society as the entity ultimately in need of reform.

Like the theories of most Positivists, Eliot's philosophy emphasizes continuities in culture, tradition, and order, and hence stops short of revolutionary programs for social change. Eliot is, however, quite frankly meliorist rather than radical, the word *meliorist* having, in fact, been coined by her to describe her social views.[15] She advances a compromise, non-revolutionary theory of social change; compromises can always be accused of conservatism and stand-pattism. But she sees melancholy and general withdrawal as the only alternatives to the meliorist view. And Eliot summarily rejects these alternatives, both as individual tendencies and as the basis for artistic creation:

> Some gentlemen have made an amazing figure in literature by general discontent with the universe as a trap of dullness into which their great souls have fallen by mistake. . . .
>
> (III, p. 174)

There was clearly something better than anger and despond-
ency.   (I, p. 311)

The consolatory nature of the ending, combined with the foray
to meet the opposition, proves an effective narrative strategy. Eliot
establishes a relationship with her reader that is one of teacher to
pupil, and exploits her teacherly persona in concluding the novel.
Most readers willingly enter a complementary relationship with
Eliot during closure and accept her humanitarian view of gradual
melioration through the influence of individual lives and family
lives well led. Even readers who dislike such evolutionary, non-
radical theories of social change will, however, find it difficult to
establish an incongruent relationship with Eliot, since she co-opts
their position. In offering consolation rather than triumphant resolution, the ending accommodates the reader's feeling that her
theories of social change are, to some extent, inadequate.

As a self-aware intellectual and philosophical novelist, Eliot
prepares her reader gradually for the ending, but makes the process
of closure intellectually, novelistically, and artistically valid. Her
novels cover ground slowly, but they do not skip any crucial steps.
In *Middlemarch*, the "Finale," rather than being tacked on and
external to the form of the novel (as the critical neglect it has
encountered would imply), is completely integrated with the aesthetic and, more important, with the thematic shape of the novel.
Once she places her confidence in her strong, Olympian narrative
voice, Eliot is absolutely in control of the overview ending and its
philosophical implications. The conclusions reached through closure in *Middlemarch* cannot be accused of evading issues raised
in the novel, of glossing over objections, or of suggesting a false
"happy ending." Eliot admits her ambivalence, mutes the happiness of the ending, and makes clear the reasons behind her conclusions. As a result, her social philosophy emerges as a coherent,
thoughtful view on man in society.

# TWO

## Closure in Dickens'
## *Bleak House*

### I

WHEN Henry James denounced the endings of nineteenth-century novels as a "distribution at the last of prizes, pensions, husbands, wives, babies, millions, appended paragraphs and cheerful remarks," one suspects that he had in mind the novels of Charles Dickens.[1] Dickens' novels consistently tend toward a happy ending and, though some readers see more happiness than others in the ending to *Bleak House*, the concluding chapter certainly accents the satisfying, successful family life achieved by Esther and Woodcourt rather than any continuing sources of tension or discontent. It is apparent, however, that Dickens' novels offer a more thoughtful consideration of the social world than we find in cheap romantic fiction or in purely conventional novels. To whatever extent it constitutes a happy ending, the marriage of hero and heroine must be invested with thematic significance in *Bleak House*—as it is in *Middlemarch*—or risk seeming an inadequate or false resolution.

Indeed, the ending to *Bleak House* has been frequently criticized. Even some of its earliest reviewers found Esther's marriage a sentimental contrivance rather than a believable fiction and objected to the transfer of Esther from Jarndyce to Woodcourt without the lady's knowledge:

> the final disposal of Esther, after all that had gone before, is something that so far transcends the limits of our credulity, that we are compelled to pronounce it eminently unreal. We do not know whether to marvel most at him who transfers, or her who is transferred from one to another, like a bale of goods.[2]

More recently, critics have seen the ending as an insufficient counterweight to the social criticism in the novel, to its scathing denunciation of Chancery and its revelation of the impotence of organizations for social melioration. As Barbara Hardy puts it:

> The conclusion is only partially responsive to the rest of the novel, squeezes its solace through too narrow an exit. The reconciliation is a part that will not stand for the whole, either intellectually or emotionally.[3]

Hardy espouses the majority view here, and voices objections also raised by several other critics of Dickens.

Still more recently, however, Richard J. Dunn has asserted that the endings to Dickens' middle- and late-period novels are "far, far better things" than they have sometimes been thought and quite different from the glib endings of some of the early novels. Dunn points out submerged elements in Esther's epilogue, elements like the briefly noted, but real enough, woes of Caddy's married life, and like Esther's self-questioning over the extent and meaning of her beauty. Alexander Welsh has also added interest to the ending, with his suggestion that the tapering of Victorian novels to end in marriage is a fictional metaphor for death. Working with Welsh's ideas as well as with some of Edward Said's ideas in *Beginnings*, Garrett Stewart explores the superimposition of marriage, death, and questions of identity at the end of *Bleak House*.[4] But although these views add new richness to our sense of the ending in *Bleak House*, Hardy's analysis still rings true: Esther is more coy than thoughtful in her epilogue; to whatever extent she questions existence and reveals its darker sides, she insists first and foremost on cheerfulness.

To a large extent, the problem of the ending is a problem central to the novel: the role of Esther as narrator, particularly as the narrator who, quite literally, has the last word. Like the ending itself, Esther's role in the novel has been a source of critical controversy. For many years, either wholesale admiration for Esther or a very strong dislike of her coyness were standard features of criticism on *Bleak House*. An important revisionist essay, "Esther Summerson Rehabilitated," by Alex Zwerdling, calls into question these standard views. Zwerdling maintains that Dickens presents

Esther as a clinical case study of "a certain kind of psychic debility," a debility caused by the deprivations and wounds of her childhood, which Esther does not entirely overcome in the novel.[5] In making his case, Zwerdling rather neglects Dickens' sentimental attachment to Esther and the degree to which he—much like the characters in the novel—sees her as fully admirable. He also overlooks the very real possibility that Esther's self-censorship may be typical rather than atypical of the Victorian age, even if it seems patently neurotic to a twentieth-century sensibility. Still, Zwerdling persuasively notes some nuances and oddities in the portrayal of Esther indicating that Dickens knew—and that Esther herself sometimes knows—that she is psychically wounded and that not all the deepest wounds heal.

Although engaged in defending Esther, even Zwerdling balks at the ending of the novel. He finds Jarndyce's breaking of his engagement to Esther—an act Esther utterly refuses to perform for herself—a "sudden, miraculous resolution, in which fantasy elements . . . are totally unconvincing." For all his revisionist intentions, Zwerdling here shakes hands with the Victorian reviewer for *Bentley's Miscellany*. Moreover, Zwerdling sees Dickens' resort to fantasy as typical of his methods and typical of the ending as a whole:

> The same element of fantasy enters into his resolution of the sociopolitical plot of *Bleak House*. . . . The institution of Chancery goes on. . . . All this can hardly be called a retreat from pessimism into fantasy. Yet the book ends not in London but in Eden, where a small group of good and permanently innocent people transform the new Bleak House into a community of love existing outside the blighted world described in the rest of the novel. As Dickens' satire becomes more savage, his need to invent an escape from the world he satirizes becomes more desperate and increasingly forces him to resort to fantasy.[6]

At this point, Zwerdling's views intersect with Barbara Hardy's. Both Hardy and Zwerdling indicate a promising direction for the study of closure in *Bleak House*. Whatever inadequacy we see in the ending of *Bleak House* must involve Esther's role as the narrator of two of the last three chapters in the novel. Unlike Zwerdling, I see no Edenic situation recorded in the last chapter of the novel. But I do see Esther flirting very hard with the idea that the Fall has never occurred and that she and the other characters can regain innocence by pretending hard enough that things are "just as they were." I also see Dickens as allowing Esther's rather dense cheerfulness to stand as the last word in this rather uncheerful novel, thus dissipating its effect slightly. And I see Dickens belying Esther's development through the novel in her final chapters, giving us less than we might expect of Esther at the end.

The weaknesses and strengths of Esther's epilogue as an ending to the novel must ultimately be judged in the context of the novel's development and in the light of Esther's evolution as a character. To assess the ending's weaknesses and strengths, I will first discuss closure and the overall shape of the fiction, and then examine in some detail the last two chapters narrated by Esther: "Beginning the World," and the last chapter, Esther's epilogue.

## II

*Bleak House* begins with three clearly parallel, mutually reflective chapters which introduce London and Chancery, the fashionable world and Chesney Wold, and Esther's world and Bleak House. Since circular patterns are so frequent in narratives, we might expect three concluding chapters. The novel ends, however, with just two concluding chapters: the first an unconventional, poetic after-history devoted to Sir Leicester and Chesney Wold; the second a much more conventional, generalized summary of Esther's life, narrated by Esther herself. Note that no chapter devoted to Chancery's after-history balances the opening chapter; we last see Chancery not in a separate, after-history chapter (like those devoted to Chesney Wold and Bleak House), but at the opening of the "Beginning the World" chapter, which deals primarily with Richard's death. I will return to this aspect of asymmetry in the novel's circular form, but first wish to examine the implications of the basic circularity established by the last two chapters in the novel.

The two concluding after-history chapters underscore generally recognized contrasts present throughout the novel. *Bleak House*'s double narrative method is preserved in the first epilogue's narration by the staccato, journalistic voice adopted by Dickens, the second's by the discursive, emotional Esther Summerson. The novel's basic metaphorical scheme is also carried through, in that freezing snow, fog, repetition, darkness, and impassivity represent the social worlds of Chancery and Chesney Wold, whereas sunshine, summery weather, brightness, and healthy, bustling motion represent the domestic world of Bleak House and Esther Summerson. Ultimately, both in the novel and at its end, Dickens contrasts death and life, with Chesney Wold and Chancery as forces for death, and the benevolence and love of Esther and Jarndyce as forces for life.

Dickens establishes the groundwork for circular closure from the very beginning of his novel. The deservedly famous opening chapter of *Bleak House* immediately enrolls Chancery under the banner of death:

> Smoke lowering down from chimney-pots, making a soft black drizzle, with flakes of soot in it as big as full-grown snow-flakes—gone into mourning, one might imagine, for the death of the sun. Dogs, undistinguishable in mire. Horses, scarcely better; splashed to their very blinkers. Foot passengers, jostling one another's umbrellas, in a general infection of ill-temper, and losing their foot-hold at street-corners, where tens of thousands of other foot passengers have been slipping and sliding since the day broke (if the day ever broke), adding new deposits to the crust upon crust of mud, sticking at those points tenaciously to the pavement, and accumulating at compound interest.[7]

The passage's vocabulary suggests universal annihilation: "black drizzle," "mourning," "the death of the sun"; it ostensibly describes a London street scene, but might easily portray instead an apocalyptic last judgment. Things move in this passage, but with ominous downward movement: smoke "lowering" from chimneys, people jostling one another, and slipping and sliding. There is a marked absence of light, and the living things in the landscape are obscured, buried, and curiously indistinguishable. Four elements in the passage come to symbolize life in the London and Chancery world: the absence of sun, divisive ill-temper, the confused, disorganized medium through which human beings blindly move, and the random accumulation of worthless substance (in this passage, mud). Like the multiplication of Miss Flite's papers and Chancery's self-perpetuating business of "making business for itself," mud's "tenacious" "accumulation at compound interest" is particularly frightening, in that the inorganic monstrously and parasitically imitates organic properties of reproduction.

The second chapter of *Bleak House* introduces the fashionable world in terms that differentiate it from Chancery but also link Chesney Wold and Society to anti-life forces:

> It is not a large world. Relatively even to this world of ours . . . it is a very little speck. There is much good in it; there are many good and true people in it; it has its appointed place. But the evil of it is, that it is a world wrapped up in too much jeweller's cotton and fine wool, and cannot hear the rushing of the larger worlds, and cannot see them as they circle round the sun. It is a deadened world, and its growth is sometimes unhealthy for want of air.   (p. 11)

Chancery and Society both display elemental lifelessness, with the fashionable world explicitly described as "deadened." But although the Chancery world is characterized by wasteful motion and accumulation, the fashionable world's allegiance to death is marked by impassivity, boredom, and constricting insulation. Again, the passage's vocabulary carefully constructs and emphasizes these themes: the fashionable world is "not a large world," it "has its limits . . . its appointed place," "wrapped up in too much jeweller's cotton," it "cannot hear," "cannot see," for "want of air."

In contrast to both spheres, Esther's world represents brightness, benevolence, and purposeful motion. The chapter that introduces Esther as narrator is called "A Progress," a significant chapter title after the claustrophobic preceding chapters, "*In* Chancery," and "*In* Fashion" (my emphasis). Esther's identification with sunshine begins even in the cold atmosphere of her aunt's home, as Esther feels that "When I love a person very tenderly indeed, it seems to brighten," and Mr. Kenge, emissary of Mr. Jarndyce, arrives on a "sunny afternoon" (pp. 17, 20). The identification extends to Bleak House and its inhabitants when, as Richard, Ada, and Esther journey toward their new home, "The day . . . brightened very much, and still brightened as we went westward. We went our way through the sunshine and the fresh air . . . " (p. 57). Jarndyce's face is repeatedly characterized as sunny and bright, and Ada "is like the summer morning" (p. 68). Esther's surname, Summerson, carries through the same image, and Mrs. Woodcourt describes Esther's nature as "like a mountain with the sun upon it" (p. 734). Similarly, although Esther spends a great many pages in the novel rolling along in carriages, she never journeys (like Lady Dedlock), to pass the time or to escape herself, or (like Jo) to follow oppressive, irrational orders. The meaning of these contrasts is fairly clear: the juxtaposition of Bleak House sunshine and healthfulness with the shadowy dullness and malaise of London, Chancery, and the fashionable world embodies the novel's duality of life against death and encourages the reader's identification with Esther's world.

The double ending emphasizes these dualities and, through the stark contrast between its final views of Chesney Wold and Esther's Bleak House, indicates the triumph of life. In the first epilogue, Chesney Wold is a hushed, quiet place, inhabited by ghosts and ghostly stories. Sir Leicester, traces of nobility clinging to him, "holds his shrunken state in the long drawing room." The motifs of constriction and lack of light, introduced in the novel's opening pages, climax here, now explicitly linked with Sir Leicester's death and the narrow darkness of the tomb:

> Closed in by night with broad screens, and illumined only in
> that part, the light of the drawing-room seems gradually con-

tracting and dwindling until it shall be no more. A little more, in truth, and it will be extinguished for Sir Leicester; and the damp door in the mausoleum which shuts so tight, and looks so obdurate, will have opened and received him.  (p. 765)

Making even more explicit the novel's drama of life-affirming versus deadening activities are descriptions of Volumnia and Lady Dedlock's former friends as "like charmers reduced to flirting with grim Death" (p. 764). The only vital elements at Chesney Wold are people foreign to it, and only incidentally present: the stalwart George, the industrious Phil, and the visiting Bagnet family.

Rather poetically, the chapter catalogues the house's abandoned state. With significant irony in relation to the novel's domestic themes, ominous noises in the lifeless structure are described as "an old family." In Dickens' version of the pathetic fallacy, trees lament the house's decay. And in the following passage, verbs of growth and motion are attributed to nature, but not to Chesney Wold:

. . . Lincolnshire life . . . is a vast blank of overgrown house looking out upon trees, sighing, wringing their hands, bowing their heads, and casting their tears upon the window-panes in monotonous depression. A labyrinth of grandeur, less the property of an old family of human beings and their ghostly likenesses, than of an old family of echoings and thunderings which start out of their hundred graves at every sound, and go resounding through the building.  (p. 766)

Dickens' summary paragraph goes on to make clear that Chesney Wold will experience no triumphant rebirth, will never again be a family home. Nature may care for it, but people do not:

Thus Chesney Wold. With so much of itself abandoned to darkness and vacancy; with so little change under the summer shining or the wintry lowering; so sombre and motionless always—no flag flying now by day, no rows of lights sparkling by night; with no family to come and go, no visitors to be the souls of pale cold shapes of rooms, no stir of life about it;—passion and pride, even to the stranger's eye, have died away from the place in Lincolnshire, and yielded it to dull repose. (p. 767)

Like much of Dickens' prose, this paragraph depends for its effect upon repetition and parallel structure (for example, in "With so much . . . with so little"). Its litany of *no*'s reinforces the reader's impression of Chesney Wold's negative existence. And, tellingly for the contrast Dickens plans with his next and final chapter, the paragraph builds to the absence of a family in the house and the house's consequent lack of "soul" and the "stir of life." The phrase "stir of life" reflects the union of purposeful movement and vitality typical of Esther's world. The paragraph then ends with words that reveal the essence of the fashionable world, laid bare in the decay of Chesney Wold—"dull repose."

The first words of Esther's epilogue rouse the reader from the heavy mood of the Chesney Wold chapter. And the last words of the first concluding chapter ("dull repose") contrast sharply and effectively with Esther's opening words: "Full seven happy years I have been the mistress of Bleak House" (p. 767). The effective contrast is furthered by one of Dickens' favorite stylistic mannerisms: the placement of an adjective or adverb at the beginning or end of a sentence, out of its usual syntactical location, for increased emphasis. Esther's account of her life during these seven years follows the conventional marital after-history's tendency to justify good characters and their way of life by recounting their later, gloriously happy condition. When, as in the cases of Caddy and Ada, perfect happiness is impossible, the characters' virtue and cheerfulness are extolled: hence, Caddy is the "best of mothers" in inventing games to cheer her handicapped child.

The epilogue includes an account of characters from the lower to the upper classes—Charlie, Peepy, Turveydrop, Caddy, Woodcourt, Esther, Ada, and Jarndyce. In this epilogue, organic family continuity, domestic good humor, and class harmony are offered as ideals and as alternatives to crippling, inhumane nineteenth-century society. There is bustling motion throughout and a considerable amount of playfulness. The aspect of playfulness is important to Dickens in *Bleak House* (as in other novels, like *Hard Times*), for, as critics have noted, the novel abounds in families which, unlike Esther's, exemplify the perversion of love and imagination. The very name of the Swallweeds suggests, for example, unwholesome proliferation. And one of the salient features of the Smallweeds is the rigorous repression of fancy. When, however, family life promotes fancy and imagination, as it does in Esther's world, Dickens seems satisfied that family life counterbalances the deadening forces of modern society and provides a refuge for individual family members.

## III

Although circularity appears to control closure in *Bleak House*, a significant degree of incompletion exists insofar as the ending includes no after-history chapter for Chancery to match those for Chesney Wold and Bleak House. The absence of an after-history chapter for Chancery seems, at first, minor. As critics rather than mathematicians, we might stretch our sense of what constitutes circular form and accept the substitution of Esther's first-person, past-tense account of the events leading up to Richard's death for a third-person, present-tense after-history for Chancery. But the absence of an after-history chapter for Chancery and certain aspects of the "Beginning the World" chapter which takes its place have significant implications for the novel and blur its social focus in a variety of ways.

At the beginning of the novel, we are told: "Jarndyce and Jarndyce has passed into a joke. That is the only good that has ever come of it" (p. 8). In the third to last chapter, "Beginning the World," the joke reaches a fitting punch-line: the exhaustion of the Jarndyce estate in legal costs. This depletion of the inheritance constitutes a good end to Chancery's story, except that it is not quite so inclusive as Dickens' earlier denunciations of the legal system. Dickens' initial remarks about Chancery are both anti-institutional and filled with a sense that bad institutions hurt individuals:

This is the Court of Chancery; which has its decaying houses and its blighted lands in every shire; which has its worn-out lunatic in every madhouse, and its dead in every churchyard; which has its ruined suitor, with his slipshod heels and threadbare dress, borrowing and begging through the round of every man's acquaintance; which gives to monied might, the means abundantly of wearying out the right; which so exhausts finances, patience, courage, hope; so overthrows the brain and breaks the heart; that there is not an honorable man among its practitioners who would not give—who does not often give—the warning, "Suffer any wrong that can be done you, rather than come here!"   (pp. 6-7)

Dickens' emphasis in passages like this one is broadly social: Chancery influences every shire in Britain; the types it destroys are representative, not singular; Chancery's evil does not just damage random persons—it acts against whole social classes, giving power to the wealthy and disenfranchising the honest poor. So large looms the problem of Chancery that it seems that only wide-ranging solutions can begin to solve it.

By the "Beginning the World" chapter, however, Dickens has thoroughly discredited the possibility of large-scale solutions. Characters like Mrs. Jellyby, Mrs. Pardiggle, and the Chadbands represent organized movements in the novel, and they are a narrow-minded, insensitive lot. At the same time that Dickens shows wide-scale reform to be impossible, he reveals the efficacy of small-scale, one-to-one benevolence, as practiced by Jarndyce. Esther and her guardian aid, in tangible ways, victims of "the system" ignored or abused by charitable agencies—the brickmakers' wives, Jo, Charley and her siblings. Surely, Dickens knew that not all reformers share the vices of Mrs. Jellyby, Mrs. Pardiggle, or the Reverend Chadband. But since he wishes to play down the possibility of organized reform, he tries, from the beginning of the novel, to discredit the reformers.

Founded upon the principle that all contact with social institutions must be shunned, Jarndyce's philosophy gradually emerges as the only true solution to the social ills caused by corrupt institutions. In the "Beginning the World" chapter, Jarndyce's code wins an important convert—the dying Richard. During Richard's death scene, Jarndyce reaches an almost symbolic value: as we are told three times, he is "the picture of a good man." When Richard begs Jarndyce's forgiveness, he acknowledges the rightness of Jarndyce's ways and Jarndyce's philosophy: to be "a good man," one must avoid all contact with the social world, cultivate the private world, and exercise one-to-one benevolence. A significant narrowing of the novel's initially broad social focus thus culminates in the "Beginning the World" chapter. Even the general structure of the chapter serves to mute the call for social reform in the book: the chapter begins with Chancery's ultimate absurdity, the exhaustion of the Jarndyce estate; but it ends with a much longer, much more detailed account of Richard's dying moments, an account which emphasizes the need to separate the private from the social world.

A similarly subtle reduction of the novel's social scope occurs through alterations in the novel's normative patterns of tense near its end. As I have said, the novel introduces Chancery and the fashionable world in the present-tense prose of the third-person narrator. The present-tense narration effectively suggests that these institutions are incapable of change: what Chancery and the fashionable world are, they have always been and always will be. The past-tense farewell to Chancery subliminally suggests a rather different message, one that will not bear a more explicit, examined statement: that individuals engaged with social institutions will be destroyed by that engagement, but that individuals who ignore social institutions will survive to see them recede into the past, with no power to mar a living present. An inversion of tenses in Esther's epilogue supports this covert message. Her chapters are normally in the past-tense; the final epilogue is in the present tense. Chancery, that monster of pre-history, seems (rhetorically, at least) headed for extinction; the private world of Esther's Bleak House seems, in contrast, headed for prosperity and expansion. The subliminal message of these tense shifts is further supported

by a change not in tense but in content from the chapter introducing Chesney Wold to that which bids it farewell. In the introductory chapter, Chesney Wold is the symbol of the fashionable
world; in the concluding chapter, Chesney Wold is simply the
home of the declining Sir Leicester.

Presumably, the fashionable world (being larger than the Dedlock family) continues, like Chancery, to thrive. But we hear
nothing of its continuance or prosperity at the end of the novel.
Like Chancery, the fashionable world is introduced into the novel
with a flourish, but ushered out as quietly as possible. If the ending
does not quite ignore the novel's most problematic social institutions, it certainly tends to minimize their prominence by subtle
devices like these.

The conversion of Esther, Rick, and the reader to Jarndyce's
philosophy and the alteration in tenses near the end of the novel
attempt to make the ending's focus on the private world rather
than the social world more palatable. These are two of the bases
on which Dickens hopes to avoid charges, like Hardy's, that the
domestic ending is only "partially responsive" to the rest of the
novel. Dickens means to demonstrate that though private, small-
scale responses to the social world may produce only local results,
such responses are still more effective than larger, more organized
movements. His demonstration has, however, been only partly
convincing to many readers and critics. Part of Dickens' genius
seems to rest precisely on his ability—in the bodies of his novels
if not at their ends—to reveal how twisted social values impede
and distort private life: think, for example, of the many stunted
families in *Bleak House*, of families like the Gradgrinds in *Hard
Times*, or of the dangerous separation of the private and work
worlds in *Great Expectation*'s Wemmick. When, at the end of
many of Dickens' novels, good characters establish a mental and
often a physical distance between the "little society" of family and
friends and the larger society of hypocrites, exploiters, thieves, and
murderers, many critics justifiably note a conservative accom-
modation with the larger, corrupt society, despite Dickens' efforts
to invest his characters' withdrawal with positive value.[8]

IV

The most disturbing aspect of the "Beginning the World" chapter is, however, the sentimentality with which Esther recounts Richard's death. Dickens intends Richard's death to move the reader, but it is a curiously static moment, largely because of Richard's paleness as a character. George Gissing put the case against him well in an early commentary: "Richard has very little life to lose, and we form only a shadowy conception of his amiably futile personality."[9] Given the "amiably futile personality" of Richard, the sentimentality of his death cloys rather than pleases. In some ways, greater pathos might have been generated by the death of Miss Flite who, curiously, disappears from the novel after Richard's death. As an irremediable victim of Chancery, Miss Flite was perhaps omitted from Esther's epilogue in the effort to downplay Chancery's continuing influence.

After Jarndyce has forgiven Richard, the dying man thinks of Esther's coming marriage to Allan Woodcourt and the consequent birth of a new Bleak House; he fears that he will never live to see her happy home. Amid false reassurances that he will live, Richard turns to Ada in a moment of typical Dickensian melodrama, laden with trite diction startlingly different from the wiry prose characteristic of the novel:

> "I have done you many wrongs, my own. I have fallen like a poor stray shadow on your way. . . . You will forgive me all this, my Ada, before I begin the world?"
>
> A smile irradiated his face, as she bent to kiss him. He slowly laid his face down upon her bosom, drew his arms closer round her neck, and with one parting sob began the world. Not this world, O not this! The world that sets this right.   (p. 763)

Trite, conventional gestures match the dialogue: the parting smile, the kiss, the head laid to bosom, the arms placed round the neck. The chapter then ends with a symbolic—perhaps even an optimistic—gesture: poor Miss Flite releases her captive birds.[10]

Richard's death is the most sentimental in the novel; it edges out even Jo's as winner in this category. Significantly, however, not all the deaths in *Bleak House* are narrated sentimentally. The death of Lady Dedlock—also narrated by Esther—provides an excellent contrast, one I would like to develop, since it accords Esther a new level of growth very near the end of the novel and gives us a standard by which to measure her narration of two of the three last chapters.

The long sequence which leads to the discovery of Lady Dedlock's body certainly contains elements of sentimentality and melodrama: the setting on a cold, snowy night; Lady Dedlock's note, beautifully phrased for a woman about to die of cold and exhaustion; Guster's epileptic fit, which withholds crucial information at a time it is much needed. But the death is more than the total of its sentimental, melodramatic elements. Indeed, many of these melodramatic elements make very good artistic sense in that they contribute to the book's symbolic unity. The snowy setting recalls, for example, the confused medium through which people move in the novel's opening chapter; Esther's horses slip and slide in the snow in a way that circularly repeats the slipping and sliding in the mud with which *Bleak House* begins.

Most important, however, in making the sequence leading to Lady Dedlock's death brilliant rather than sentimental is the new level of narration achieved by Esther. For only the second time in the novel (the first is the very brief section recounting Esther's hallucinations during smallpox), Esther relinquishes all coyness and rejects her usual self-censorship. She receives Bucket's praise for her courage and strength without her customary fencing; she accepts his words gratefully as a much-needed emotional prop. Moreover, she acknowledges and fully expresses the depth of her emotions and of her confused, disorganized impressions. As a result, we get neither conventionalized gestures of grief and concern (like those which surround Richard's bedside), nor Esther's formulaic injunctions to be cheerful, but a franker exploration of a mind disordered by extreme suspense. Again and again, Esther tells us what we feel to be true for somone in her position, fearing every moment to see the body of the mother she loves: "I have the most confused impressions of that walk," "I could repeat this in my mind too, but I had not the least idea what it meant . . . my understanding for all this was gone."

With great honesty, Esther admits that her experiences during the journey forever color her impressions of the Thames:

> I have seen it [the river] many times since then, by sunlight and by moonlight, but never free from the impressions of that journey. In my memory, the lights upon the bridge are always burning dim; the cutting wind is eddying round the homeless woman whom we pass; the monotonous wheels are whirling on; and the light of the carriage-lamps reflected back, looks palely in upon me—a face, rising out of the dreaded water. (p. 678)

With its confusion of the lamps, Lady Dedlock's face, and Esther's own face, the last image marvelously suggests what many motifs in the book have indicated: that Esther's quest for her mother is a quest for her own identity and that until Esther can find and then separate herself from her mother, she will never emerge into full, independent womanhood.

When Esther comes upon Lady Dedlock's body, she believes that she sees before her not her mother's corpse, but Jenny's, whom she identifies as "the mother of the dead child." This description, "the mother of the dead child" is entirely apt. For although the woman is Lady Dedlock, not Jenny, Lady Dedlock for many years thought her child dead and has, in a sense, built her life on this assumption. Metaphorically, Esther has been "the dead child" throughout the novel. At the deepest level of her psyche, she continues to believe what she was told by her aunt: that she really should have died at birth.

When Esther lifts her mother's head, she performs a gesture that parallels that by which she first confronts her own face, changed by smallpox. The similarity of gesture confirms that the confrontation with her dead mother—now openly acknowledged as her mother—is a new break-through to identity. Esther "put the long and dank hair aside and turned the face" and sees her "mother, cold and dead" (p. 714). When Esther finds her mother "cold and dead," the book's themes of problematic identity climax. Esther is now no longer the "dead child"; she is the living child of a dead mother, metaphorically face to face with her own identity, and free to begin her life. She has, moreover, shared deep, intense feelings with the reader and, perhaps, allowed herself to touch those feelings for the first time. She has done both things well. Esther is an engaging, truly sympathetic character in these chapters with no trace of coyness or self-repression. She responds more bravely and honestly to this traumatic experience than she responds to the everyday experiences recorded earlier in the novel.

In this context, Esther's sentimental performance in the last chapters of the novel is disappointing. Coming after Lady Dedlock's death, Richard's death and the material of the epilogue should be narrated with all the force of Esther's experiences during her traumatic journey behind her. We have a right to expect that she will not revert to her earlier weaknesses. But, in the account of Richard's death, Esther does return to sentimentality; and, in her final epilogue, she is both coy and self-censoring.

Richard's loss is very much present in Esther's epilogue, but present in the way that he has himself been present in the novel—palely, and not very convincingly for the reader. His memory exists in the epilogue not as a force in itself (as is Andrew's memory at the end of *War and Peace*), but as a sentimental item: look at his beautiful young widow; look at his poor, orphaned child and namesake. Much of the epilogue consists of the bustling summary of characters' later lives I have already mentioned. When Esther does stop recounting everyone's lot and settles on issues profoundly of concern to her, she does so without the frankness and psychic probing typical of the Lady Dedlock sequence. The discussion of Jarndyce's visits to Esther's new home is typical:

> With the first money we saved at home, we added to our pretty house by throwing out a little Growlery expressly for my guardian; which we inaugurated with great splendour the next time he came down to see us. I try to write all this

lightly, because my heart is full in drawing to an end; but when I write of him, my tears will have their way.

I never look at him, but I hear our poor dear Richard calling him a good man. To Ada and her pretty boy, he is the fondest father; to me, he is what he has ever been, and what name can I give to that? He is my husband's best and dearest friend, he is our children's darling, he is the object of our deepest love and veneration. Yet while I feel towards him as if he were a superior being, I am so familiar with him, and so easy with him, that I almost wonder at myself. I have never lost my old names, nor has he lost his; nor do I ever, when he is with us, sit in any other place than in my old chair at his side. Dame Trot, Dame Durden, Little Woman!—all just the same as ever; and I answer, Yes, dear guardian! just the same.
(pp. 768-69)

Esther "tries to write all this lightly," but she might do better to probe and try to understand her very strong emotions toward Jarndyce—now once again guardian after a stint as lover and fiancé. Defensively, Esther takes up a series of conventional phrases by which to designate Jarndyce: he is her husband's "best and dearest friend," her children's "darling," an "object of our deepest love and veneration," the "fondest father," "a superior being." At the end of the passage, Esther's names—once spontaneous and playful—have become a meaningless and even a regressive ritual. We might, like J. Hillis Miller, see the endurance of these names as one form that fancy and imagination take in Esther's epilogue.[11] But these nicknames are now forced, not playful and natural and, as such, deserve little praise. These nicknames seem especially inappropriate in the light of the novel's themes of identity, discussed earlier: despite her new sense of identity after the discovery and public recognition of her mother, Esther still accepts the second-hand "identity" of Dame Durden and Dame Trot, maintaining—falsely—that all is "just the same as ever."

All is not just the same as ever in Esther's relationship with Jarndyce, else Esther would hardly feel so uneasy about the process of naming him. Nor is all really the same in Esther's world: she herself has risen both in status and in happiness; others in her world have been lost to death or irredeemably marred by the past. But Esther's refusal to admit that things are not just the same and to describe the differences belies her growth and honesty during the psychologically acute sequence in pursuit of Lady Dedlock. Esther is honest here neither with Jarndyce, nor with herself, nor with the reader. And this lack of honesty and depth continues the marked falling-off from the levels Esther achieves during the Lady Dedlock sequence.

The epilogue winds down with a prime example of what must be considered Esther's arch-vice—very vocal amazement that others like and admire her: "The people even praise Me as the doctor's wife. The people even like Me as I go about, and make so much of me that I am quite abashed. I owe it all to him, my love, my pride! They like me for his sake, as I do everything I do in life for his sake" (p. 769). The epilogue then ends with Esther's bemused cogitations about the possibility, suggested by Allan, that she is prettier than she ever was:

> I did not know that; I am not certain that I know it now. But I know that my dearest little pets are very pretty, and that my darling is very beautiful, and that my husband is very handsome, and that my guardian has the brightest and most benevolent face that ever was seen; and that they can very well do without much beauty in me—even supposing—
>
> (p. 770)

Although Richard Dunn calls this a questioning of beauty's value, it yet seems a cute, sugary way to end the novel.

To end with Esther as narrator need not have been a fault in the novel, had Dickens allowed her to speak with the authority gained by her in the text after the death of her mother. Readers could excuse Esther's early sentimentality and coyness as a convention of retrospective first-person narration: such narratives often record things as they seemed to the narrator *at the time*, and reflect the narrator's growth during the novel. But such a narrative perspective demands that Esther tell the end of the novel

with the maturity and depth shown during the Lady Dedlock sequence. To end with Esther need not, in itself, have been problematic; but to end with Esther's sentimental account of Richard's
death and self-censoring epilogue is indeed problematic. It not
only, as Barbara Hardy says, "squeezes . . . the novel's solace
through too narrow an exit," but it also belies what we assume
should be Esther's capacity for honest, probing narration by the
end of the novel. In not allowing Esther to continue her growth
into a narrator capable of effectively summing-up the novel, Dickens settles for an ending that simply does not match the book's
most successful passages.

## V

At issue is not so much the success or failure of the ending in any
absolute terms, as the degree and kind of success it achieves. The
ending of *Bleak House* does succeed in contrasting the forces for
death with the forces for life in the way I have discussed earlier;
in this way, it gives the novel a sense of unity. But the ending
fails to complete the trajectory of Esther's development and it fails
to complete the novel's social themes. An ending more intensely
involved with character and theme might have had even greater
success and would certainly have been more integral to the form
and meaning of the novel. The shortcomings of Dickens' ending
may be illuminated by a brief comparison with Eliot's ending to
*Middlemarch*, the subject of chapter one.

Many objective similarities exist between the situation projected
by Eliot in the "Finale" and the facts of Esther's married life as
she reports them in her epilogue. Like Dorothea and Ladislaw,
Esther and Woodcourt discharge familial and social responsibilities
so as to better the lives of others, promote compassionate relationships, and pass on their beliefs and social values to their children. They thus contribute to the gradual melioration of society
in and through their private lives. One might even say that Woodcourt represents much that Lydgate *might* have become: he lives
a dedicated life as a doctor, well-loved in his community, supported
in his work by his wife and family.

Two important differences in content must, however, be noted. First, though Eliot tells us that Dorothea always felt "that there was always something better which she might have done, if she had only been better and known better," Esther declares herself "the happiest of the happy" (p. 767). Less hyperbolic, the description of Dorothea's evaluation of her life feels closer to the truth. As we have seen, Eliot overtly demonstrates that her ending is a mixed ending, not a happy one, and that its function is consolatory; Dickens' ending at points tries to exceed consolation and to assert the possibility of absolute happiness, despite the scars of earlier experience.[12]

Although Dickens and Eliot both use familial themes to resolve their novels, Dickens attaches a more triumphant value to happy family life than does Eliot. In a sense, this glorification of the family at the end of Dickens' novel is curious, given Dickens' well-known failures in domestic life and the plethora of stunted, even perverse, families included in the novel.[13] In fact, the families chronicled at the end of *Bleak House* are less normal and healthy than those visited at the end of *Middlemarch*. Esther's marriage is curiously sexless, her two daughters appearing as if from beneath the proverbial cabbage leaf. Caddy's family is maimed and handicapped, though contented enough. And the Jarndyce-Ada-young Richard family is at best a substitution for the lost, more natural family of Richard-Ada-young Richard.

The differing effects of the two endings hinges most, however, not on objective differences in content so much as on differences in authorial strategies during closure. Dickens does not, like Eliot, ground his ending in any philosophical context, nor does he present a reasoned, logical argument to convince the reader. Tellingly, Dickens does not even consider that a discrepancy may exist between his own views and those of his reader, a discrepancy that would compel him to flesh out his argument and to make the implicit assertions of Esther's epilogue more concrete and compelling. Here again he contrasts with Eliot who, anticipating her reader's reluctance to accept her meliorist theory and less than happy ending, constructs her argument slowly and in some detail. Dickens too glibly assumes a complementary relationship with his

reader, when even a congruent one requires that the reader over-
look much. Raymond Williams makes a pertinent observation in
a comparison of Dickens' presentation of social ideas with Eliot's:
the process of Dickens' novels involves "conversion [of the reader]
rather than persuasion, acts of transcendence rather than of conclusion."[14]

At the root of this difference in closural strategies may be a
more fundamental difference in the degree to which each author
fully realized the relationship between familial and social themes.
As we have seen, the philosophy articulated by Eliot in *Middlemarch* is fully conscious and based upon wide readings in the
Positivists as well as on Positivist theories about the family's role
in social melioration. Dickens' views on the family's connection
to society are far less philosophical and intellectual. Dickens had
a philosophy of sorts, but that philosophy is not very subtly nu-
anced and is not always clearly reflected in his novels.

Dickens began to write *Bleak House* in 1851, one year after he
initiated his weekly journal *Household Words*. In the first issue
of the periodical, Dickens discussed the purpose of the magazine,
and his comments elucidate the meaning implicitly—though never
clearly and convincingly—given to family life in Esther's concluding chapter. He begins by explaining the motivation behind
the title as the somewhat sentimental aspiration "to live in the
Household affections, and to be numbered among the Household
thoughts, of our readers."[15] He disavows "mere utilitarian spirit"
and the "iron binding of the mind to grim realities," cherishing
instead "that light of Fancy which is inherent in the human breast;
which, according to its nurture, burns with an inspiring flame, or
sinks into a sullen glare, but which (or woe betide that day!) can
never be extinguished." He then resoundingly declares his purpose:

> To show to all, that in all familiar things, even in those which
> are repellent on the surface, there is Romance enough, if we
> will find it out:—to teach the hardest workers at this whirling
> wheel of toil, that their lot is not necessarily a moody, brutal
> fact, excluded from the sympathies and graces of imagination;

to bring the greater and the lesser in degree, together, upon that wide field, and mutually dispose them to a better acquaintance and a kinder understanding—is one main object of our Household Words.

Weighted against the "whirling wheel of toil" and the "moody, brutal" facts of existence are the very qualities exemplified in Esther's epilogue: household affections, the light of fancy, sympathies and graces of the imagination, and a bringing together of the greater and lesser in degree in a harmonious communal relationship. The implicit connections between Dickens' preface to *Household Words*, Esther's epilogue, and the body of the novel may, in fact, be dignified into a coherent social theory or philosophy of life, similar to that in *Middlemarch*, which advocates the elevation of domestic relationships, and of the "sympathies and graces of the imagination" that ideally characterize familial relationships, as a workable model for opposition to a dehumanizing, brutal society. That is, if all human relationships conformed to the familial model, society would be a better, more humane entity. Dickens need not have written a philosophical ending, like Eliot's; the ending which suits *Middlemarch* would not necessarily suit *Bleak House*. But to display full self-awareness during closure, Dickens should have made Esther's epilogue less evasive of crucial issues than I have shown it to be.

One final difference between Eliot's ending and Dickens' should be noted. Some portions of Eliot's "Finale" are rather sentimental and not really essential to the novel; I think here of the cameo, scenic appearances of Fred and Mary Vincy and of Celia and James Chettam. But the opening and closing philosophical paragraphs and the contrast between Dorothea's assessment of her life and Eliot's assessment are entirely crucial to the thematic coherence of the novel. Eliot's argument would, in a very real sense, lack a conclusion were these paragraphs omitted.

In contrast, little of Dickens' concluding chapter is necessary to complete the novel's themes. The last chapter is not quite a collection of (to borrow James's terms) "appended paragraphs." The chapter does serve, as I have described earlier, to give an aesthetically pleasing, circular sense that the novel is ending. It also serves to tip the scales toward life in the novel's symbolic battle of life against death. But part of James's critique of nineteenth-century endings nonetheless holds true for *Bleak House*. Esther's epilogue is more "a course of ices" than a nutritious portion of Dickens' feast. It is pleasant enough, but remains one of the least satisfying aspects of the novel.

# THREE

## "Open" and "Closed" Form
## in *War and Peace*

I

AMONG concordances between the beginning, middle, and end of *War and Peace* used by Tolstoy to communicate meaning, the contrast between life in society and life in the family is one of the most basic. From the first pages of the novel, the world of the clever people—the salons, the diplomatic circles, the tents of generals who believe they control armies—is described in mechanical metaphors. Thus Prince Vasili speaks like "a wound-up clock" and Anna Schérer controls her soirée,

> As the foreman of a spinning mill, when he has set the hands to work, goes round and notices here a spindle that has stopped or there one that creaks or makes more noise than it should, and hastens to check the machine or set it in proper motion.[1]

Pierre is too large and unsuited to the salon because of his "observant and *natural*, expression which distinguished him from everyone else in that drawing room" (p. 9; my emphasis). All other faces in the room automatically, unthinkingly, and mechanically assume the "proper" expressions.

In contrast to the formality and artificiality of the social world, Natasha first enters *War and Peace* amid crashing chairs, irrepressible laughter, and general indecorum; her father, the count, jumps up "and, swaying from side to side," spontaneously embraces her (p. 39). For Nicholas returning from the army, for Pierre during his years of discontent and marriage to Hélène, for Andrew after periods of lassitude, and for the reader, the Rostov household remains a center of vitality and life quite different from the mechanistic social world. As in *Bleak House*, some families corrupt the life force, like those of Prince Vasili and the Old Prince Bolkonski, and those of Hélène and Pierre, Andrew and his wife; but others, like the Rostov family, embody and express it. Glowing scenes of family life—like that of Count Rostov dancing the "Daniel Cooper"—illuminate the novel and punctuate its more weighty social scenes. And even in moments of unhappiness, the Rostov family is described in organic metaphors—as when the novel implicitly compares Natasha's abortive affair with Anatole to the cornering of a fox in a hunt.

Related contrasts and a similar division of metaphors carry over into Tolstoy's later descriptions of the armies as mass as against those of the armies' commanders, who (except Kutuzov) habitually formulate impossible plans. The French army as mass is described as a "wounded beast" (p. 1099). But the reaction of the generals to the mood of that army is described in mechanical terms similar to those used for Anna Schérer's soirée:

> And at once, as a clock begins to strike and chime as soon as the minute hand has completed a full circle, this change was shown by an increased activity, whirring, and chiming in the higher spheres.   (p. 1100)

Ultimately, these consistent metaphorical contrasts reflect another, broader, and more abstract division made by Tolstoy:

> Among the innumerable categories applicable to the phenomena of human life one may discriminate between those in which substance prevails and those in which form prevails.
> (p. 788)

Mechanical metaphors describe the life of form; metaphors drawn from natural animal life (like Tolstoy's repeated comparisons of human life to the bee hive) describe the life of substance. As depicted in the first (familial) epilogue to *War and Peace*—the section of the novel to which this discussion is basically confined—family life follows the rhythms of aging, change, reproduction, and simple day-to-day living characteristic of natural, animal life.[2] For Tolstoy, life within a loving family is thus part of the life of "substance" and an escape from the mechanical life of "form." He attempts to communicate that sense to readers by employing parallelism as a closural strategy.

II

Tolstoy attaches great importance to the assertion that family life can be natural life, and he writes a strongly didactic familial epilogue. The ending is infinitely more sophisticated than the rather Dickensian ending to Tolstoy's first draft of the novel, called *All's Well that Ends Well*, in which Andrew (who, like Petya Rostov, does not die) gives Natasha to Pierre, Sonya gives Nicholas to Mary, and the novel concludes with an account of their joyous double wedding.[3] But the familial ending of *War and Peace* still retains a quality of blithe Dickensian belief that a happy family life solves all significant problems. Tolstoy presents the Rostov and Bezukhov children in a somewhat sentimental, strained, and overly-cheerful manner, perhaps because of his great admiration for Dickens. His portraits of the children stress the organic continuity of family life: Natasha seems reborn in Nicholas' little daughter, Andrew in his son Nicholenka, and so on. Natasha's submersion in motherhood, which many modern readers find disturbing, functions as part of Tolstoy's didactic message. He dogmatically insists that "the purpose of marriage is the family" just as "the purpose of food is nourishment" (p. 1283), and demands that a sympathetic reader view Natasha's transformation as admirable, not limiting. In the novel, Natasha represents the highest level of biological life-consciousness, which all the characters in the first epilogue share to some extent. Life-consciousness means a submersion in the natural processes, a non-rational approach to daily living, and at least some measure of religious faith.

Interpreted in these thematic terms, the content of the familial epilogue clearly relates through parallelism to the philosophical content of the novel and to its more generally didactic form. Most particularly, it is a concrete, detailed, dramatic presentation of life unconsciously lived according to the abstract views Tolstoy expounds in the philosophical second epilogue, which ends the novel. Life in the familial ending embodies his climactic philosophical paradox: the characters are conscious only of spontaneity and freedom in their family lives, but they implicitly recognize "a dependence of which we are not conscious," both in their religious faith and in their ability to flow with the present and not willfully attempt to control the future (p. 1351).

Like all Tolstoy's novels, *War and Peace* moves toward moments of revelation in which major characters experience the meaning of life. In *War and Peace*, as in Tolstoy's own life and in his other novels, the revelation cannot be achieved through rational means; often it is connected with suffering and death, or is transmitted through a "simple" being, like Platon Karataev. Through his captivity and encounter with Platon—an intensely moving section of the novel—Pierre learns to live life instead of questioning it. Like characters' dreams, revelation reveals truth without logical premises and proofs.[4] After Platon's death and his own insight into the meaning of the peasant's life, Pierre

> could not see an aim, for he now had faith—not faith in any kind of rule, or words, or ideas, but faith in an ever-living, ever-manifest God. . . . In his captivity he had learned that in Karataev God was greater, more infinite and unfathomable than in the Architect of the Universe recognized by the Freemasons. He felt like a man who after straining his eyes to see into the far distance finds what he sought at his very feet. All his life he had looked over the heads of the men around him, when he should have merely looked in front of him without straining his eyes.   (p. 1226)

Pierre begins to use this intuitive knowledge when he allows himself to drift into marriage with Natasha and spontaneously live the life of a family man. Similarly, the other married couple featured in the epilogue, Nicholas and Mary, marry only after their natural feelings overcome elaborate "reasonable" arguments that "forbid" their union. As Tolstoy depicts his characters' lives in the familial epilogue, those lives are made possible by and illustrate a non-rational understanding of the blessedness of life, learned by the adult characters during the war years and innate in the children; this intuitive knowledge illuminates each moment of daily living in their after-histories.

Unlike their wives, Pierre and Nicholas have occupations outside the family, but—as the epilogue takes care to point out—domestic life nurtures the spiritual self. Nicholas' charitableness and justness as a landowner stem in part from Mary's influence on his violent temper; his marriage enriches and controls his outside activities. Similarly, though Pierre has just returned from important political and social negotiations in Moscow, "in spite of much that was interesting and had to be discussed, the baby with the little cap on its unsteady head evidently absorbed all his attention" (p. 1288). Tolstoy further assures us that the "general opinion . . . that Pierre was under his wife's thumb . . . was really true" (p. 1284), and that Pierre's outside activities are only a temporary furlough and distraction from Natasha's central principle, which is "that every moment of his life belonged to her and to the family" (p. 1284). Moreover, "After seven years of marriage Pierre had the joyous and firm consciousness that he was not a bad man, and he felt this because he saw himself reflected in his wife." Significantly, "this was not the result of logical reasoning but was a direct and mysterious reflection," precisely the same kind of "direct and mysterious reflection" that for Tolstoy constitutes the essence of revelation (p. 1285).

Most tellingly, when Natasha, attributing "great importance" to her husband's social responsibilities, asks Pierre how Platon Karataev would regard his work in Moscow, her husband thinks a moment and then makes a significant answer. He decides that Platon would see his political life as trivial and as divisive of men in the same way that Pierre's earlier experiences with the Masons had been trivial and divisive. As Pierre understands the meaning of his meeting with Platon Karataev and subsequent enlightenment, life informed by daily revelation is not life in the social world, but life which promotes spiritual peace and harmony—for him, life in the family. The highest endorsement possible in this novel is placed on family life when Pierre says to Natasha that Platon Karataev would have approved of their family life, finding "seemliness, happiness, and peace in everything" (p. 1307). *War and Peace* accordingly shows its characters, seven years after the end of the novel's major action, safely and contentedly nestled into family life and living out, in ordinary events, earlier, spiritual revelations.

## III

If we use the terms "open" and "closed" to describe the familial epilogue to *War and Peace*, the segment as discussed thus far appears to be fully "closed." The ending's parallelism and its over-view perspective contribute greatly to our sense that the ending is "closed." Strongly didactic in its advocacy of family life, the epilogue vividly embodies the characters' after-histories from 1813 to 1820 as representative of the total span of their later lives and as a triumphant respite from the searching of earlier years. Parts of the familial epilogue give, however, hints of "openness" and indications that family life can offer only temporary and precarious happiness. At the beginning of the first epilogue and again at the beginning of the second, for example, Tolstoy abstractly invokes continual change as a basic principle of history and of nature:

> Seven years had passed. The storm-tossed sea of European history had subsided within its shores and seemed to have become calm. But the mysterious forces that move humanity (mysterious because the laws of their motion are unknown to us) continued to operate. . . . The coming formation and dissolution of kingdoms and displacement of peoples was in course of preparation.   (p. 1253)

Since individual human lives are influenced by the forces of nature and history throughout the novel, some readers may see the fa-milial epilogue in part as a prelude to future events every bit as momentous as those of 1812, which will once again reshuffle the characters' lots.

Similarly, though less explicitly, the characters' after-histories contain subtle hints of coming disruptions. Indeed, many scenic elements in the epilogue suggest a slightly tangential pattern that directs us *beyond* the boundaries of the novel, rather than back into the text, as its primary pattern of parallelism does. Nicholas' concern over Mary's abstracted, other-worldly expression suggests, for example, that Mary may indeed die young and that Nicholas' materialistic conservatism may no longer be modified by her spiritual instincts. Pierre's continued pursuit of activities outside the family also opens possibilities for disruption. The political quarrel between Nicholas and Pierre indicates possible repercussions from Pierre's commitment to radical causes, particularly in the upcoming Decembrist revolution. Tolstoy's original plan was that Pierre be involved in the Decembrist revolt and that *War and Peace* be about the Decembrists, not about the Napoleonic era. Since the finished novel differs so radically from that originally planned by Tolstoy, this information cannot be used to definitively confirm the direction of Pierre's later "life." But like many narrative sections towards the end of the novel, the familial epilogue ends with a dash, as the young Nicholas Bolkonski dreams of the coming revolution, thus giving suggestions of future turmoil and change a privileged place in the novel.

A general pattern of strong resolution, followed by a hint of irresolution, exists throughout the familial epilogue and especially at its end. Consider the rhythm of the last episodes. Chapter three of the first epilogue in the Maude translation presents harmonious family scenes that feature laughing children and the parents' contentment with this "delightful music" (p. 1295). The end of chapter fourteen introduces, however, dissent between Nicholas and Pierre over politics, with Nicholas' vow to resist Pierre's radical movement even if, in an actual revolution, it means killing his beloved brother-in-law. Combined with Nicholas Bolkonski's eager questions and everyone's depression and concern over the quarrel, the incident allows elements of discord and premonitions of future instability to enter the epilogue.

Discord and instability are partly allayed at the beginning of chapter four, as Mary assures Nicholas that Pierre will not become involved in armed revolution, noting that " 'though we might expose ourselves to risks we must not risk our children' " (p. 1303). The chapter passes on to intimate and harmonious family talk, but disconcertingly ends its first section with Nicholas' un-resolved and foreboding sense that Mary will die while still young. The second section of the chapter once again restores stability and harmony through conjugal conversation, this time between Na-tasha and Pierre, as the two exchange ideas magically, by only partial utterance. It is in this conversation that Pierre reveals the superiority of family life to political causes, perhaps indicating that Mary is right in predicting Pierre's eventual rejection of political life. The chapter and the familial epilogue end, however, with Nicholas Bolkonski's open-ended promise to lead a coming revo-lution. With just a few changes in emphasis to magnify the ending's unstable elements, the familial epilogue can be made to seem considerably open, although it continues to be essentially "closed."

Let us examine in more detail the important scene between Natasha and Pierre, which precedes Nicholas Bolkonski's final rev-erie and tapers off without the kind of explicit authorial gloss Tolstoy usually makes on his action. As I have noted, Tolstoy introduces the conversation as one of intuitive communication, not dependent on ordinary logic and, therefore, as an action similar to Tolstoy's conception of harmonious, spiritual living:

> Natasha and Pierre, left alone, also began to talk as only a husband and wife can talk, that is, with extraordinary clear-ness and rapidity, understanding and expressing each other's thoughts in ways contrary to all rules of logic, without prem-ises, deductions, or conclusions, and in a quite peculiar way.   (p. 1305)

Reading the entire scene with Tolstoy's initial comment in mind, we might justifiably stress Pierre's satisfaction with domestic life and the ability of family life to enrich the spirit. By allowing the text to speak for itself and bypassing Tolstoy's guidance, however, it becomes possible to see a *potential*, though not an actual, impasse between husband and wife indicated in the scene.

Despite his evident enjoyment of family life, for example, Pierre states that, besides ideas, " 'for me nothing else is serious' " (p.

1306). Like Andrew and other male characters in Tolstoy's works who seek perpetually for meaning, Pierre in his later life continues his political activities rather than, like Tolstoy's typical female characters, finding complete fulfillment and an absolute boundary for activity in the family.[5] Moreover, although Natasha shows no resentment toward her husband's ideas and is, in fact, proud of them, she displays neither the ability nor the inclination to understand this part of Pierre's existence. *If* Tolstoy had pressed the scene just a bit further, their final exchange might be read as a *failure* of communication rather than as a unique form of contact. For the scene ends with Pierre engrossed in political ideas which (much like his younger self) he believes can save the world, and verbalizing those ideas for Natasha. Natasha smilingly but obliviously responds with news of their nursing baby. Had Tolstoy mentioned Pierre's slight disappointment that Natasha does not truly share his enthusiasms, or his decision to keep henceforth his ideas to himself, or indicated Natasha's uneasiness about the future effect of Pierre's activities on the family, the scene would clearly point to trouble between husband and wife and a progressive growing apart in the marriage as, we shall see, a parallel scene in *Anna Karenina* does. Nothing in the scene as it stands entirely justifies such a reading. But different critics may wish to emphasize or to play down this and similar "open" elements in the familial epilogue, to believe that domestic life is, as Tolstoy insists, conducive to spiritual life or, as Tolstoy barely hints between the lines, to believe that domestic life promotes mental and spiritual vegetation.

The dual temporal orientation of the narrative ending—its relationship both to the "past" events of the narrative (through parallel closure), and to the "future" events hinted at in the epilogue (through tangential closure)—helps to explain some of the critical controversy which surrounds the text, most of whose critics are sure they know exactly what the epilogue means, yet some of whom disagree radically. A critic like George Steiner in *Tolstoy or Dostoevsky*, interested in the ending's elements of openness, naturally tends to read the epilogue differently from one like Isaiah Berlin who, in *The Hedgehog and the Fox*, relates the epilogue to the "past" (the body of the novel).[6] The former sees stagnation and decay in the characters' after-histories (somewhat perversely ignoring Tolstoy's clear didactic endorsement of family life), and welcomes the ending's indications of coming change; the latter sees in the epilogue the successful end of the characters' struggles, reading it as a stable and triumphant ending to the novel's narrative sections.

The two conflicting interpretations of the familial epilogue published by Georg Lukács similarly reflect this dual temporal orientation and double pattern of closure. In *The Theory of the Novel* (published during World War I), the Hegelian Lukács, like Steiner, sees "only the subdued colours of Flaubertian hopelessness, the frustration of the purposeless searchings and impulses of youth, their silting-up in the grey prose of bourgeois family life" in the epilogue.[7] Later, the Marxist Lukács revises these views and emphasizes the epilogue's tangential "open" elements and hints of future events:

> the real great philosophical and psychological content of the epilogue to *War and Peace* is the process which after the Napoleonic wars led the most advanced minority of the Russian aristocratic *intelligentsia*—a very small minority, of course—to the Decembrist rising, that tragically heroic prelude to the secular struggle of the Russian people for its liberation.[8]

Once again like Steiner, Lukács ignores the epilogue's clear indications that the characters' domestic lives should be viewed positively and that the "process" which leads them to revolution—as disruptive of natural, family ties—may be undesirable, even if inevitable.

Clearly, the epilogue to *War and Peace* is both "open" and "closed"; in fact, it reveals the inadequacy of these terms when applied didactically or absolutely to complex literary works that evoke deeply personal responses from readers and, like the best "classic" texts, can evoke different responses on different readings. For me, however, irresolution is subtexture and counterpoint in the epilogue rather than dominant. The immediacy of the characters' contented lives supersedes the epilogue's often oblique hints of irresolution. While not fully "closed," the epilogue creates the illusion of being so, largely because, at this point in his life, Tolstoy is unwilling or reluctant to give fuller play to irresolution or uncertainty in connection with familial themes.

## IV

In his autobiography, *My Confession*, Tolstoy describes the period during which he composed *War and Peace* as one in which family life—with its numerous petty joys and concerns—covered over troubling questions in life to which his mind would in the future inevitably return. He speculates that his euphoria as a newly married man staved off "that state of absolute despair" he reached "fifteen years later," in part from his lost belief in the curative powers of family life:

> The new circumstances of a happy family life by which I was surrounded [in the 1860's] completely led my mind away from the search after the meaning of life as a whole. My life was concentrated in my family, my wife, and children, and consequently in the care for increasing the means of supporting them. The effort to effect my individual perfection, already replaced by the striving after general progress, was again changed into an effort to secure the particular happiness of my family.[9]

The older Tolstoy diagnoses in his younger self a tendency to idealize family life as a defense mechanism and as a justification for neglecting matters thought truly important.[10] Tolstoy includes in the familial epilogue hints of instability and irresolution that anticipate his later disillusionment with family life. But he underplays these hints, perhaps to persuade himself that family life may after all prove a manageable ideal and to stave off his later breakdown.

In his later novels, Tolstoy progressively abandons the attempt to endow family life with transcendent value and allows his endings to be less fully resolved. The later novels increasingly expose the irrelevance of family life to spiritual enlightenment—to the "search after the meaning of life" and the striving after "individual perfection" that come to count for Tolstoy as finally more significant than even "the striving after general [social] progress." Like his great epic novel, *Anna Karenina* and *Resurrection* are structured to give maximum effect to the philosophical ideas dearest to Tolstoy at the time of their composition. Each builds toward a profound and life-altering revelation granted to a major character near the end of the work. The terms of the revelation differ slightly in each novel, and become progressively more religious. Yet there is a fundamental difference between the endings of *Resurrection* and *Anna Karenina* and that of *War and Peace*. In the later novels, rather than jumping ahead years in an attempt to fix and demonstrate the interrelationship of insight and later life, Tolstoy deliberately eschews making any firm predictions about the characters' future.

Although written shortly after *War and Peace*, *Anna Karenina* (1876) signals a changed emphasis in Tolstoy's engagement with familial themes even in its opening sentence. If "All happy families resemble each other, but each unhappy family is unhappy in its own way,"[11] then *unhappy* rather than happy families constitute the more interesting subject for fiction. The beginning of the novel prepares us to see each family —including Levin and Kitty's—as uniquely unhappy. How different this is from *War and Peace*, in which unhappy families are merely foils to the happy families which engage Tolstoy's greatest and most detailed attention—the families of Count Rostov and, later, those of his children, Natasha and Nicholas.

Like *War and Peace*, *Anna Karenina* ends with an epilogue, but one dissimilar to the earlier novel's. Set only two months after Anna's death—just enough of a time lapse to demonstrate the continuity of life, and to complete the Levin plot in the novel— it has no air of finality. Vronsky, glimpsed in transit to the Crimean

War, journeys into an unknown future. Levin's history is in the process of resolving itself in terms that must be read with *My Confession* in mind, since Levin is in part an autobiographical projection of Tolstoy just after his discontent with the family had begun to come to the surface. As in *War and Peace*, toward the end of the novel a simple being, here Fyodor, casually gives the answer to the doubts tormenting the main character. For Levin as for Pierre, in clearly parallel passages, a revelation follows that is non-rational and involves the emotional understanding of basic truths:

> "I looked for an answer to my question. But reason could not give me an answer—reason is incommensurable with the question. Life itself has given me the answer, in my knowledge of what is good and what is bad. And that knowledge I did not acquire in any way; it was given to me as to everybody, *given* because I could not take it from anywhere."
>
> (p. 722)

For Levin, this insight stimulates the gradual growth of religious faith (p. 724). In the next chapters, however, family life proves, if not a hindrance to Levin's spiritual development, at least something apart from it. He repeatedly quarrels with his wife, Kitty. Resubmerged in the details of family life, Levin feels "disillusionment with the change that should have taken place in him" (p. 736).

After a series of petty quarrels, Kitty and Levin patch up their discord. But the chapter immediately following their reconciliation—the last chapter in the novel—gently but sadly shows that lack of communication has become a way of life for Kitty and her husband. The potential impasse between Natasha and Pierre at the end of *War and Peace*, discussed earlier in this chapter, has become a reality for this couple in *Anna Karenina*. "When on leaving the nursery Levin was alone, he at once remembered the thought that had not seemed quite clear" (p. 738): implicity, Kitty's presence inhibits thought for Levin, as Natasha's presence does not hinder

Pierre. Once alone, Levin begins to ponder the movement of the earth and its relationship to God's will, *until* Kitty rejoins him and begins the following conversation:

> "Nothing has upset you, has it?" she inquired, peering attentively into his face by the starlight.
>
> But she would not have been able to discern its expression had not a flash of lightning that effaced the stars lit it up. By the light of that flash she saw the whole of his face and, noticing that he was calm and happy, she smiled at him.
>
> "She understands," thought he, "she knows what I am thinking about. Shall I tell her or not? Yes, I will. . . ." But just as he was going to speak, she began:
>
> "Oh, Kostya! Be good and go to the corner room and see how I have arranged things for Sergius Ivanich! I can't very well do it myself. Have they put in the new washstand?"
>
> (p. 740)

Quite literally, Kitty deflects Levin from the sublime to the ridiculous, from pondering the mysteries of the universe to pondering the proprieties of the toilet. All the implications that domestic life is limiting, left undeveloped and latent in the scene when Pierre expounds his philosophy to a motherly Natasha, are developed and active here: Kitty understands and lives in the details of family life; more reluctantly and with less enjoyment than Pierre, Levin shares this familial world but cannot be satisfied by it. Moreover, in reaction to Kitty's remark, Levin consciously and explicitly decides to keep parts of himself secret from his wife, to suppress in the future his thoughts in her presence. His decision marks both the difference between Pierre's marriage and Levin's, and the difference between Tolstoy's ideas about marriage as developing the individual's fullest potential in *War and Peace* and in *Anna Karenina*.

At the end of the novel (in the paragraph immediately following the above scene), Levin accepts a future informed by meaning through religious faith, but continuing to unroll at a mundane, not illumined, level:

"I shall still get angry with Ivan the coachman in the same way, shall dispute in the same way, shall inopportunely express my thoughts; there will still be a wall between my soul's holy of holies and other people; even my wife I shall still blame for my own fears and shall repent of it. My reason will still not understand why I pray, but I shall still pray, and my life, my whole life, independently of anything that may happen to me, is every moment of it no longer meaningless as it was before, but has an unquestionable meaning of the goodness with which I have the power to invest it." (p. 740)

The meaning of life has changed for Levin, but life—especially domestic life—continues to unroll with all its banality and tedium. The almost magical conjugal communication in the familial epilogue of *War and Peace* has, in *Anna Karenina*, given way to more commonplace silences and misunderstandings. At the end of *War and Peace*, family life is viewed as a direct expression of the harmony of things, as a perpetual enactment of praise to the creator. But at the end of *Anna Karenina*, family life exists separately from, and even in conflict with, the characters' path of spiritual development. Significantly, in the later novel, Tolstoy includes no weighty endorsement of family life like that imputed to Platon Karataev. Although he is not yet ready to abandon positive familial ideals, Tolstoy has begun to distance himself from them and to question their value. In *Anna Karenina*, he appropriately modifies the kind of familial epilogue he wrote for *War and Peace*, making it less conventional and sentimental. The ending to *Anna Karenina* is also more "open," and closer in time to the novel's main action and to the unresolved dynamism of the body of the novel than is the familial epilogue of *War and Peace*.

## V

*Resurrection* does not end with after-history, and its ending focuses on the immediate experience of revelation, which Tolstoy no longer considers related to family life. Indeed, familial themes are only minimally present in the novel. Motivated by a misguided wish to atone for the seduction of Maslova years before, Nekhludov breaks off his engagement to a young society woman and seeks Maslova's hand in marriage. Neither the broken engagement nor the projected one, however, has an authentic role in Nekhludov's life, and he must dismiss the simple notion of atonement by marriage to Maslova to experience the spiritual resurrection of the title. The family's only other notable appearance in the novel almost parodies Natasha's motherliness in *War and Peace*. The wife of a provincial official, in whose house Nekhludov is a visitor, insists that he view her sleeping children and earnestly seeks his praise for their beauty. Nekhludov responds mechanically with the required praise, but the incident conveys absolutely no sense that marriage or family life are worthy ideals or even worthy matters of concern.

Near the end of *Resurrection*, the novel considers matters that are, for Tolstoy at this point in his life, truly weighty, although distinctly non-epic. Dismissed by Maslova after being exposed to the terrible wrongs of prison life, Nekhludov undergoes a process that closely parallels that recorded by Tolstoy in his spiritual autobiography.[12] First, there is the realization that faith comforts man, as yet unaccompanied by actual belief. The feeling that goodness and wisdom may be found in the Gospels follows. After a period without rationalizing or comprehension,

> it happened to Nekhludov as it often happens to men who live a spiritual life. The thought that at first had appeared so strange, so paradoxical, even laughable, had been more and more frequently confirmed by life, and now rose before him as an indisputable truth.[13]

The character then applies his new consciousness to the course of his own life and to the basic questions of human existence—particularly to questions of evil and free will. After pondering the parable of the vineyard, Nekhludov's revelation is complete:

> "We do the same," thought Nekhludov. "We live in the belief that we are the masters of our own lives, and that they were

given us for enjoyment. That is frankly absurd. If we have
been sent into this world, it is obviously by someone's will
and for some purpose. . . . If men but follow the will of the
Master as expressed in these [God's ten] commandments, the
Kingdom of God will be established on earth. . . . Here, then,
is my life's work. One task is completed and another is ready
to my hand." (p. 430)

The process undergone by Nekhludov at the end of the novel
resembles those experienced in Tolstoy's earlier novels by Pierre
and Levin and, like those earlier processes, it leads to a simple
revelation that rejects reason for faith and for life in accordance
with natural, divine law. At the end of *War and Peace*, as we have
seen, Pierre lives his revelation through his family life. At the end
of *Anna Karenina*, Levin seeks fulfillment as a married man, but
ultimately realizes that he will find it only apart from his family
life, in his private inner being. Nekhludov is not shown in later
life, after the moment of revelation, but insofar as he remolds his
life, he will clearly do so alone, as a single man. The endings to
*Anna Karenina* and *Resurrection* thus suggest that as Tolstoy's
desire and need to idealize the family and to see family life as a
spiritual force diminished, new and more abstract sets of values
replaced the family at the ends of his fictions to resolve the works'
philosophical questions. After *War and Peace*, Tolstoy increasingly
rejected both happy endings and the idealization of family life,
which (as in Dickens' novels and in other popular nineteenth-
century fiction) so often are closely linked.

The ending to *Resurrection* dramatically indicates one further
significant change in Tolstoy's attitude toward the relationship of
revelation and daily life. The novel ends with the following authorial comments:

That night a new life began for Nekhludov, not because the
conditions of his life were altered, but because everything that
happened to him from that time held an entirely new and
different meaning for him.

Only the future will show how this new chapter of his life
will end. (p. 430)

Tolstoy the narrator approves Nekhludov's insights, but explicitly declines to predict the quality of his future life and thereby "fix" the interrelationship of insight and daily existence as he had in *War and Peace*. The ending was to be a linking ending, but since Tolstoy never wrote a projected sequel to *Resurrection*, a sequel that would have made the ending less dramatically unresolved, it is best classified as tangential. Written late in Tolstoy's life, long after experience had proven to him that neither domesticity, nor philosophical insight, nor faith necessarily yields permanent serenity, the ending's inconclusiveness seems particularly apt, especially in view of the well-known and extreme alteration Tolstoy made in his life shortly before his death.[14] The prophet-author-pilgrim who never found finality and rest very properly declines to predict the future of the major character in his last novel, who, like all of Tolstoy's major characters, is a projection of some part of Tolstoy himself, this time at a late stage in his protean existence.

It thus becomes clear in the context of Tolstoy's later novels precisely how the ending to the narrative sections of *War and Peace* functions. Each of the novels is frankly didactic. Only at the end of *War and Peace*, however, does he attempt to justify his characters through a variation on the tactic used at the end of many nineteenth-century *Bildungsromane* (like *Jane Eyre* and *David Copperfield*)—the presentation of after-lives that, through their success and naturalness, confirm the efficacy of the characters' growth and insight during the novel. In *Anna Karenina* and *Resurrection*, conflict, even after revelation, remains fundamental to meaning. Only in *War and Peace* is conflict merely hinted at and all but postponed until some vague future time. Only in *War and Peace* is there a partial attempt at a stable, resolved ending through the presentation of family life as life *in* nature and, therefore, as a perpetual spiritual hymn of peace and praise. Viewed in the context of Tolstoy's life and canon, the familial epilogue to *War and Peace* may be seen as an attempt to smother Tolstoy's own doubts about the spiritual value of family life and to convince the reader—and the author himself during the 1860's—that a permanent rather than an interim solution to the problems of existence had been found.

Tolstoy's ending to *War and Peace* is both more honest and more satisfying than Dickens' ending to *Bleak House*; it is a highly effective piece of literature. Yet ultimately both these endings claim too much for the power of family life as a refuge from the disruptive and harmful influences of society, and reveal their authors as self-deceiving. Dickens never does face up to the problems in his family-centered ideology. Tolstoy does face these problems—indirectly and tentatively at the end of *War and Peace*, explicitly and firmly in his later works. It is tempting to speculate that, in *Middlemarch*, Eliot resists idealizing the family and avoids making it the center of her philosophy rather than an illustration of it, precisely because, unlike Tolstoy and Dickens, she had no personal traumas, insecurities, or compulsions to satisfy by means of the glorification of family life. In contrast to Tolstoy and Dickens in *War and Peace* and *Bleak House*, she therefore avoids writing an ending that tries too hard for stable and triumphant resolution through familial themes, although she certainly uses familial themes in resolving the novel.

The familial epilogue of *War and Peace* illustrates a danger inherent in the self-deceptive use of a novel's closure to support an author's beliefs. In the familial epilogue to *War and Peace*, Tolstoy advances in complete good faith a more permanent, easily achieved solution to the problems of existence than he was able to find in life. This is perhaps the ultimate example (to use Isaiah Berlin's terminology) of Tolstoy, a natural fox (pluralist), masquerading with confidence as a hedgehog (a monist). The titles of Tolstoy's late aesthetic and social tracts are often questions; in *War and Peace*, the young Tolstoy prematurely announces an answer. The writer and reader of a carefully wrought, internally consistent ending written by a self-deceiving author must always beware of the possibility that the ending's beliefs are wrong or inadequate, or oversimplified—or will become so in time.

# FOUR

## Communal Themes and the Outer Frame of *The Scarlet Letter*

### I

THE strong formal unity of *The Scarlet Letter* has been frequently noted by critics and variously described. Malcolm Cowley calls it a novel conceived in architectural terms,[1] and Harry Levin describes its structure as "a tense alternation of public tableaux and private interviews."[2] The symmetry of the novel is effected by its construction in five balancing parts:

| Introduction | Beginning | Body of the Novel | Climax | "Conclusion" |
|---|---|---|---|---|
| \| | \| | | \| | \| |
| "The Custom-House" | | | | Epilogue |
| | Scene before the prison and first scaffold scene | | Election Day sermon and third scaffold scene | |

The "private interviews" of which Levin speaks constitute what I have called the body of the novel. This major section presents a series of meetings between pairs of characters, as many chapter titles indicate: "The Elf-Child and the Minister," "The Leech and his Patient," "Hester and Pearl," "The Pastor and his Parishioner." Surrounding these middle chapters, this series of one-to-one confrontations, are the chapters which open and close the novel's major action and contain the first and third scaffold scenes—the "public tableaux" noted by Levin. These chapters may be considered the novel's inner frame; they portray the larger community, with the four major characters occupying the foreground, but not filling the entire stage. The inner frame endows *The Scarlet Letter* with a double pattern of circularity and parallelism. The ending is parallel when we consider the second scaffold scene (Dimmesdale's midnight vigil); it is primarily circular when we examine the stronger concordances between the first and last scaffold scenes.

"The Custom-House" and the "Conclusion" form an additional,

markedly authorial outer frame for the novel, which intensifies
our basic sense of the novel's circularity. This outer frame has
been almost totally ignored by critics, many of whom discuss the
novel as though it ends with Dimmesdale's death. The fairly mechanical way in which the "Conclusion" balances "The Custom-
House" and contributes to the aesthetic unity of the novel might
seem to justify the absence of critical commentary. But the thematic role of the outer frame is highly significant. In "The Custom-
House" Hawthorne reflects on his own communal ties—his ancestral links to Puritanism and to Salem, his disillusionment with
Brook Farm, his years as a civil servant in the Custom-House.[3]
In the final chapter, he considers his characters' ties to the Puritan
community, and he makes a final evaluation of this relationship.
The outer frame of *The Scarlet Letter* is thus crucial to an interpretation of a major theme in novels: the proper relationship of
the individual to his society. Hawthorne's personal remarks in the
introduction suggest, moreover, that this theme was of profound
emotional importance to the author. It is not too strong to say that
without its last chapter *The Scarlet Letter* would be a rather different novel, one only partly responsive to Hawthorne's intentions.

II

Hawthorne's statements in "The Custom-House" introduce attitudes important in the thematic structure of the novel. The plural,
"attitudes," is significant here, as his statements pull in several
directions. The essay focuses on the Custom-House as the symbol
of society, just as the novel's opening pages focus on the cemetery
and the prison, "the black flower of society." Through his choice
of images, Hawthorne implicitly criticizes social institutions. And
quite explicitly in the prologue, he declares that social establish-
ments hinder spiritual development:

> I was led to conclusions in reference to the effect of public
> office on the character, not very favorable to the mode of life
> in question.[4]

And again, more pithily:

> Neither the front nor the back entrance of the Custom-House
> opens on the road to Paradise.   (p. 13)

In the prologue, Hawthorne's suspicions about society and public
life in general are fairly clear; his attitude toward Salem, his personal social milieu, is considerably more mixed. On the one hand,
the native son must instinctively feel attached to his native soil:

> It is no matter that the place is joyless for him; that he is
> weary of the old wooden houses, the mud and dust, the dead
> level of site and sentiment, the chill east wind, and the chillest
> of social atmospheres;—all these, and whatever faults besides
> he may see or imagine, are nothing to the purpose. The spell
> survives, and just as powerfully as if the natal spot were an
> earthly paradise.   (p.11)

Thus "though [I am] invariably happiest elsewhere, there is within
me a feeling for old Salem, which, in lack of a better phrase, I must
be content to call affection" (p. 8). On the other hand, connections
to one's ancestral home are harmful and should be avoided because
"Human nature will not flourish, any more than a potato, if it be
planted and replanted, for too long a series of generations, in the
same worn-out soil" (pp. 11-12). Hawthorne goes further and
declares: "My children have had other birthplaces, and, so far as
their fortunes may be within my control, shall strike their roots
into unaccustomed earth" (p. 12). Moreover, he approves of pre-
Civil War America's increasing tendency to relocate with each
generation: "Few of my countrymen can know what it [attachment
to native soil] is; nor, as frequent transplantation is perhaps better
for the stock, need they consider it desirable to know" (p. 9). Yet
Hawthorne's attachment to his native place reasserts itself; he ends
his prefatory essay with the wistful hope that although he is leaving
Salem to become "a citizen of somewhere else," his writings will
become a part of his town's traditions and help to conserve a sense
of the community's past (pp. 44-45).

A similarly divided attitude controls Hawthorne's introduction of the Puritan community that forms the setting for *The Scarlet Letter*. At the beginning of the novel, the Puritans in their "sad-colored garments," come to witness Hester's humiliation, seem to embody society at its worst. But the narrator emphasizes that the reality of the community represents a falling away from the idealism with which it was founded:

> The founders of a new colony, whatever Utopia of human virtue and happiness they might originally project, have invariably recognized it among their earliest practical necessities to allot a portion of the virgin soil as a cemetery, and another portion as the site of a prison.  (p. 47)

The tension between Utopian idealism and social necessity—between what men "originally project" and "their earliest practical necessities"—was familiar to Hawthorne from his personal experience with Brook Farm, an episode that Hawthorne mentions in "The Custom-House," and that should be considered in evaluating the resolution of his attitudes toward society in *The Scarlet Letter*.

## III

The facts will be familiar to many of my readers. In 1841, Hawthorne invested one thousand dollars, his savings from his first years at the Custom-House, in Brook Farm, a Utopian community founded by his friend, George Ripley, who was an ardent Transcendentalist. Hawthorne was never fully in sympathy with Transcendentalism, and from the very beginning feared that the community would not be able to establish a brotherhood of man in rapport with the rest of society. But the mere fact that he committed himself and his savings to Brook Farm seems compelling evidence of his interest—if not faith—in the perfecting of human communities and social relationships. Hawthorne's letters during the first few weeks at Brook Farm provide further evidence: he calls his companions at Brook Farm "Brethren," speaks of "the fopperies and flummeries which have their origin in a false state

of society," and pronounces the way of life at Brook Farm "right-
eous and heaven-blessed."[5]

From the beginning of his involvement with Brook Farm, however, Hawthorne's practical considerations balanced his idealistic
impulses. Hawthorne had two eminently practical reasons for
going to Brook Farm: first, he hoped to earn his living by a half-
day's work (versus the full day at the Custom-House), and to
devote the other half to writing; second, he hoped that communal
life on Brook Farm would provide the financial basis on which to
marry Sophia Peabody, to whom he had been engaged for two
years.[6] Sophia's reactions to Brook Farm typify the moderate and
middle-class attitudes of the couple. After inspecting Brook Farm,
Sophia enthusiastically wrote to her sister:

> It's a splendid place, and I like these men and women who
> say why not have our daily life organized as Christ's own
> idea. And they are evidently going to preserve the idea of
> private property—merely exclude competition. It is a life that
> aims beyond the stars, as Mr. Ripley puts it, but it does remain
> on earth.[7]

It is hard to know where Sophia's emphasis falls—on the pious
emulation of "Christ's idea," or on the very pragmatic retention
of "private property."

The bantering tone of Hawthorne's letters and notebooks during
the Brook Farm period belies any deep emotional turmoil. A dung
heap becomes "the Gold Mine," and much is jokingly made of
learning to milk a cow.[8] Yet Hawthorne several times writes very
earnestly to Sophia about the question of whether Providence
"calls" them to Brook Farm;[9] his letters reflect an increasing sense
that the call was not to come. Shortly after his arrival in April,
the "Brethren" become "these people." At the end of a month,
Hawthorne muses on the isolation of Brook Farm from the rest
of society: "I read no newspapers, and hardly remember who is
President, and feel as if I had no more concern with what other
people trouble themselves about than if I dwelt in another
planet."[10] He next designates himself a "slave" and finally an-

nounces to Sophia: "I am becoming more and more convinced that we must not lean upon this community. Whatever is to be done must be done by my own undivided strength."[11] By September, and his first return visit to Salem, the emotional break with Brook Farm was complete:

> But really I should judge it to be twenty years since I left Brook Farm; and I take this to be one proof that my life there was an unnatural and unsuitable, and therefore an unreal, one. It already looks like a dream behind me. The real Me was never an associate of the community; there has been a spectral Appearance there. . . .[12]

After a year of life at Brook Farm, Hawthorne withdrew, eliciting a promise from Ripley to repay the one thousand dollars he had invested. Part was in fact repaid. But in 1845, under financial pressure, Hawthorne sued George Ripley for the remainder of his investment, at a time when the community was stricken by small-pox and struggling against bankruptcy.[13] By 1849 and the prologue of *The Scarlet Letter*, Brook Farm was far behind him; he calls his Utopian experiment "my fellowship of toil and impracticable schemes, with the dreamy brethren of Brook Farm" (p. 25).

## IV

Hawthorne's involvement with Brook Farm clearly indicates a man capable of idealism but ruled by practicality, one able to conceive of individual and social perfection but resigned to the imperfections observed and compromises demanded in day-to-day living. By 1850 and the completion of *The Scarlet Letter*, he clearly no longer believed in the possibility of a Utopia. And yet he could not quite reject the ideal of a humane community. Hawthorne's treatment of the "Voice of Society," which, as in some of Dickens' late novels, has its say in *The Scarlet Letter*, is illustrative. The novelist sat-irizes the particular Puritan community and its public dicta, but he consistently measures the Boston community against a general, abstract ideal of community he admires. In fact, what evolves in

*The Scarlet Letter* is a dual sense of the term "community" that complicates the divisions I have already noted in Hawthorne's attitudes toward society. He distinguishes between the social mind as an essentially humane and natural phenomenon and the social mind as an institutionalized, collective phenomenon, which has become mechanized and has lost contact with the emotions.[14] Though he is invariably critical of the latter, he never loses faith in the former.

I will take as an example a passage in which Hawthorne recounts, with characteristic deviousness, an instance of Approved Puritan Public Opinion:

> the Reverend Arthur Dimmesdale's best discerning friends, as we have intimated, very reasonably imagined that the hand of Providence had done all this [brought Chillingworth to live with Dimmesdale] for the purpose—besought in so many public, and domestic, and secret prayers—of restoring the young minister to health. But—it must now be said—another portion of the community had latterly begun to take its own view of the relation betwixt Mr. Dimmesdale and the mysterious old physician. . . . The people, in the case of which we speak, could justify its prejudice against Roger Chillingworth by no fact or argument worthy of serious refutation. . . . [They merely sensed] there was something ugly and evil in his face. . . .
>
> To sum up the matter, it grew to be a widely diffused opinion, that the Reverend Arthur Dimmesdale, like many other personages of especial sanctity, in all ages of the Christian world, was haunted either by Satan himself, or Satan's emissary, in the guise of old Roger Chillingworth.
>
> (pp. 126-28)

Many phrases which ostensibly indicate approval in this passage really are meant to be read ironically: "the Reverend Arthur Dimmesdale's best discerning friends" (Dimmesdale has no friends and no one around him discerns the truth), and "very reasonably imagined," for example. Truth in the passage rests upon foun-

dations that look, at first, unsound. The feeling against Chillingworth rests on a "prejudice" not "worthy of serious refutation"
and yet ultimately correct. This feeling against Chillingworth
grows from an intuitive reading of facial expression and the dis-
cernment of "something ugly and evil in his face" (a vague, yet
just, observation). Those prejudiced against Chillingworth include
"persons of such sober sense and practical observation, that their
opinions would have been valuable in other matters" as well as
those—less practical and sober—inclined to see devils everywhere.

The truth is more complex than either Chillingworth's sup-
porters or his detractors imagine. Chillingworth *does* help heal
Dimmesdale and may thereby serve as an agent of Providence. But
he "heals" Dimmesdale only unintentionally and only spiritually,
whereas the community expects a deliberate, and physical, cure.
Similarly, Chillingworth's motives are malicious and demonic,
though we have little real reason to imagine him as a direct emissary of Satan. Amid all the complexities and ambiguities of this
passage, however, there appears an important, fairly straightforward gloss by Hawthorne, a gloss relevant to the idea of the two
kinds of community I have been discussing:

> When an uninstructed multitude attempts to see with its eyes,
> it is exceedingly apt to be deceived. When, however, it forms
> its judgment, as it usually does, on the intuitions of its great
> and warm heart, the conclusions thus attained are often so
> profound and so unerring, as to possess the character of truths
> supernaturally revealed.   (p. 127)

Dimmesdale's "friends"—the community's elite—judge things
solely by appearances and are, therefore, deceived. Though they
differ in motivation and in the accuracy of their impressions, Chillingworth's detractors form their judgments on the instincts of the
heart as well as on the observations of the eye and, therefore, come
closer to the truth.[15]

The most important concordance in *The Scarlet Letter*—that
between the first and third scaffold scenes—must be read in the
context of this distinction between judgments made empirically

and judgments made intuitively. The two scenes have the same settings, the Market Place, Meeting House, and scaffold; both occur on a significant public occasion, amidst a gathering of the entire Boston community; Dimmesdale is the featured speaker in each; the Scarlet A is revealed first on Hester's breast and then on Dimmesdale's; Chillingworth lurks in the crowd in each scene, present to Hester's mind as a threatening figure. In addition, characters forgotten or marginal since the opening scene reappear in the final scene: Governor Bellingham, the Reverend Wilson, the jailor, and the group of women who formed the initial chorus of public opinion in the novel.

The many similarities between these two scenes strikingly set off the essential difference beween them: in the first scene institutionalized ritual is uninterrupted; in the second, ritual breaks down, and a more immediate kind of experience is offered the Puritans. As the novel opens, the Puritan officials, like the crowd, are serene and confident. Hawthorne describes them (in terms deliberately similar to those later used for Chillingworth) as incapable of judging questions concerning human emotions, yet unhesitatingly making such judgments on Hester. Governor Bellingham, for example, is, at the beginning of the novel,

> not ill fitted to be the head and representative of a community, which owed its origin and progress, and its present state of development, not to the impulses of youth, but to the stern and tempered energies of manhood, and the sombre sagacity of age; accomplishing so much, precisely because it imagined and hoped so little.   (p. 64)

At the end, however, Bellingham's imaginative faculties expand: "although a man not readily obeying the vague intimations that pass from one spirit to another," he refrains from stopping Dimmesdale's ascent onto the scaffold (p. 252). Similarly, the crowd, tranquil during the first scene, is later

> in a tumult. The men of rank and dignity, who stood more immediately around the clergyman, were so taken by surprise,

and so perplexed as to the purport of what they saw,—unable to receive the explanation which most readily presented itself, or to imagine any other,—that they remained silent and inactive spectators of the judgment which Providence seemed about to work.   (p. 253)

Dimmesdale's ascent and the revelation of the Scarlet A on his chest appear to educate the Puritans in the true nature of the human heart. The crowd seems, in fact, to have a "privileged moment" of enlarged sympathies and quickened moral perceptions, like moments in the works of Eliot and James:

> Partly supported by Hester Prynne, and holding one hand of little Pearl's, the Reverend Mr. Dimmesdale turned to the dignified and venerable rulers; to the holy ministers, who were his brethren; to the people, whose great heart was thoroughly appalled, yet overflowing with tearful sympathy, as knowing that some deep life-matter—which, if full of sin, was full of anguish and repentance likewise—was now to be laid open to them.   (p. 254)

Having become a "great heart," the community seems about to respond humanely and sympathetically. "Some deep life-matter was now about to be laid open to them," to which they will presumably be able to attend with an expanded consciousness. At Dimmesdale's death, the crowd "murmurs" "in a strange, deep voice of awe and wonder," which appears to avoid logical speculation and rational speech in deference to the mystery at the heart of things (p. 257).

If this were the only frame to the story and the novel ended here, the community would, in Hawthorne's terminology, have progressed from being deceived by its eyes to being enlightened in "so profound and unerring truths" by "the intuitions of its great and warm heart." It would have ceased to be an unfeeling social unit and have become a genuinely humane and feeling sympathetic community. The climax of the action would, therefore, dispose not only of the characters' fates, but also of Hawthorne's ambivalent attitudes toward society and community. But great novels rarely resolve their thematic conflicts so simply or triumphantly. One major function of the ending is to deny this apparent movement to triumphant resolution and to reaffirm Hawthorne's sense of the social order as faulty.

## V

The community's moment of insight is characterized by intuition rather than knowing and silence rather than speech.[16] In *The Scarlet Letter*, true knowledge means the appreciation of the essential mystery in human emotions and human life and the greatest sin is Roger Chillingworth's—violating the "sanctity of the human heart." The Puritan community, however, always seeks to articulate opinions and hence to deny the validity of emotional, intuitive experience. The opening section of the "Conclusion" emphasizes that what has been the climactic scene for the protagonists has *not* also been a climactic transformation of the Puritan community:

> After many days, when time sufficed for the people to arrange their thoughts in reference to the foregoing scene, there was more than one account of what had been witnessed on the scaffold. (p. 258)

Only temporarily silenced, the community almost immediately reverts to cold-hearted rationalism, missing the lessons of the third scaffold scene:

> Most of the spectators testified to having seen, on the breast of the unhappy minister, a SCARLET LETTER—the very semblance of that worn by Hester Prynne—imprinted in the flesh. As regarded its origin, there were various explanations, all of which must necessarily have been conjectural. Some affirmed that the Reverend Mr. Dimmesdale, on the very day when Hester Prynne first wore her ignominious badge, had begun a course of penance,—which he afterwards, in so many futile methods, followed out,—by inflicting a hideous torture

on himself. Others contended that the stigma had not been produced until a long time subsequent, when old Roger Chillingworth, being a potent necromancer, had caused it to appear, through the agency of magic and poisonous drugs. Others, again,—and those best able to appreciate the minister's peculiar sensibility, and the wonderful operation of his spirit upon the body,—whispered their belief, that the awful symbol was the effect of the ever active tooth of remorse, gnawing from the inmost heart outwardly, and at last manifesting Heaven's dreadful judgment by the visible presence of the letter. The reader may choose among these theories. . . .

It is singular, nevertheless, that certain persons, who were spectators of the whole scene, and professed never once to have removed their eyes from the Reverend Mr. Dimmesdale, denied that there was any mark whatever on his breast. . . . According to these highly respectable witnesses, the minister, conscious that he was dying,—conscious, also, that the reverence of the multitude placed him already among saints and angels,—had desired, by yielding up his breath in the arms of that fallen woman, to express to the world how utterly nugatory is the choicest of man's own righteousness. . . . Without disputing a truth so momentous, we must be allowed to consider this version of Mr. Dimmesdale's story as only an instance of that stubborn fidelity with which a man's friends—and especially a clergyman's—will sometimes uphold his character. . . .   (pp. 258-59)

Hawthorne handles these explanations with customary dexterity: generally, they reveal themselves as deliberate falsification, as oversimplification, or as some mixture of the two. As in the passage quoted earlier concerning Chillingworth's coming to live with Dimmesdale, the least tenable position is that of Dimmesdale's "friends." Against all evidence—seen, heard, and especially felt—"these highly respectable witnesses" deny Dimmesdale's involvement with Hester in anything other than a religious parable. At the end of the passage above, Hawthorne violates his usual neutrality to dismiss the explanation of Dimmesdale's friends as thoroughly inadequate and self-serving.

The first three explanations given are harder to dismiss, though all "must necessarily have been conjectural." The first sees Dimmesdale's masochism as a sole and sufficient cause. Having earlier told us of a "bloody scourge" with which Dimmesdale "tormented" himself, Hawthorne anticipates this explanation and lends it color. But ultimately, this explanation oversimplifies: if Dimmesdale is masochistic, what social and psychological factors motivate his perversity? What role, moreover, did Chillingworth play in driving Dimmesdale to this method of penance?

The second explanation again oversimplifies, this time by attributing too much power to Chillingworth and to the agency of "magic and poisonous drugs." Surely, those who hold this opinion correctly judge that Chillingworth had tormented Dimmesdale and delved "into the poor clergyman's heart . . . like a sexton into a grave." But his influence alone would not have produced the stigma, and the recourse to drugs and magic lacks the subtlety of Hawthorne's sense of the psychological interplay between the doctor and his prey. Chillingworth alone will not serve as the final cause for Dimmesdale's stigma.

Hawthorne accords the third explanation a special status by observing that it constitutes the opinion of "those best qualified to appreciate the minister's peculiar sensibility, and the wonderful operation of his spirit upon the body," that is, those, like Hawthorne himself, attuned to the interdependence of spirit and substance and to the complexities of a personality like Dimmesdale's. The interaction of body and soul is the vaguest of all the explanations offered; it therefore comes closest to acknowledging the mystery at the heart of things and to the sense of wordless pity and awe that grips the community during the final scaffold scene. It is, moreover, an explanation "whispered," not "affirmed" or "contended." This last explanation, vague though it may be, emerges as the most inclusive opinion offered by the community: it does not, for example, rule out either of the two prior explanations, though it deems each inadequate, nor does it ignore those aspects of the minister's behavior that are indeed "peculiar."

Only this third explanation seems at all adequate to what we know of Dimmesdale. Yet it is the minority opinion and—like all the other explanations—is a verbalization and a rationalization of matters ultimately inaccessible to words and to reason. By showing the community in the process of denying its intuitive knowledge of the third scaffold scene and seeking instead the delusory comfort of rational explanations, the opening of the "Conclusion" caps Hawthorne's portrait of the community as spiritually inadequate. The ending's calculated anticlimax emphasizes the community's failure to assimilate the lessons of the third scaffold scene. In this way, the epilogue completes Hawthorne's negative evaluation of community, which is begun in "The Custom-House" and in the opening chapters of *The Scarlet Letter*. It confirms that the nature of the community as institution is to repress the heart and suppress the spirit.

But the "Conclusion" carries through an opposing thematic movement that ends the novel with the same kind of ambivalence expressed in "The Custom-House." The epilogue begins by stressing the faulty nature of the social order, but ends by emphasizing the importance of the individual's integration with and submission to the community. This final emphasis completes one of the major themes in *The Scarlet Letter*: social integration takes priority over the expression of individuality and assumes a sacramental quality. Once again, Hawthorne emphasizes this theme through circularity and parallelism.

The beginning of the novel establishes each of the major characters as an isolated individual, removed from the Boston community (see pp. 54, 66, 93-94). The climax and epilogue reverse the action of the opening chapters, reintegrating each character into the community. By the end of the novel, confession to the community and acceptance of its justice become equivalent to spiritual salvation. Thus, in the final scaffold scene, after Chillingworth fails to dissuade Dimmesdale from mounting the scaffold, he imputes this meaning to the minister's action:

"Hadst thou sought the whole earth over," said he, looking darkly at the clergyman, "there was no one place so secret,—

no high place nor lowly place, where thou couldst have escaped me,—save on this very scaffold!"

"Thanks be to Him who hath led me hither!" answered the minister.  (p. 253)

Salvation means publicly returning to the communal fold, and Dimmesdale is the first of the characters to abandon his isolation from the larger community. Upon kissing her dying father, Pearl similarly reintegrates herself:

A spell was broken. The great scene of grief, in which the wild infant bore a part, had developed all her sympathies; and as her tears fell upon her father's cheek, they were the pledge that she would grow up amid human joy and sorrow, nor for ever do battle with the world, but be a woman in it. (p. 256)

The two remaining protagonists, Hester and Chillingworth, are, at the end of the climactic scene, still outside of the community. Another function thus served by the ending is to explain how these characters later found their places. Chillingworth's potential to throw off his demonic character and join society is clearly less than that of the other characters. That he leaves his wealth to Pearl indicates, nonetheless, the triumph of human sympathy over revenge and the possibility (as Hawthorne speculates) that Dimmesdale and Chillingworth have been "mutual victims," and that the ties of love and hate exist as the same bond in the spiritual world. Only the reintegration of Hester remains; her pride must be converted into genuine penitence to complete the thematic scheme of the novel. This is accomplished only in the epilogue, with the narrator's account of how a chastened Hester returns to Boston and undertakes penitential good works.

## VI

The ending to *The Scarlet Letter* is thus consistent with the aesthetic shape of the novel, with its themes, and with Hawthorne's beliefs and intentions. But there is a sense in which it is not congruent with some of the best things in the novel and with the reader's emotions.[17] Signs exist that Hawthorne thought that his criticism of the social order might lead the reader to identify too strongly with the magnificent Hester, and to side with her rebellious attitudes toward the community. He feared that the relationship between author and reader during closure would be incongruent as the novel moved toward its "darkening end."

In fact, the emotional center of the novel is the scene between Hester and Dimmesdale in the forest, when they decide to leave New England and to assume new identities in the Old World. Hawthorne exercised some care in introducing this scene, placing Hester's suggestion of flight in a moral context appropriate to the novel's handling of communal themes. His marvelous opening description of Hester balances admiration for her strength and courage against a sense that they have "taught her much amiss" (p. 200):

> Hester Prynne, with a mind of native courage and activity, and for so long a period not merely estranged, but outlawed, from society, had habituated herself to such latitude of speculation as was altogether foreign to the clergyman. She had wandered, without rule or guidance, in a moral wilderness; as vast, as intricate and shadowy, as the untamed forest. . . . (p. 199)

Hester's individuality and unlimited freedom are associated with the wilderness (the forest), which belongs to Satan, and with vast, confused space. The imagery of an "intricate and shadowy . . . untamed forest" recalls that earlier in the novel, when Hawthorne describes Hester's mind as a "dark labyrinth" (p. 166). And the forest's wide and free geography is, for Hawthorne, a "moral wilderness."

In the same passage, Hawthorne goes on to contrast Dimmesdale with Hester:

> The minister, on the other hand, had never gone through an experience calculated to lead him beyond the scope of generally received laws; although, in a single instance, he had so fearfully transgressed one of the most sacred of them. But

this had been a sin of passion, not of principle, nor even
purpose. . . . At the head of the social system, as the clergymen
of that day stood, he was only the more trammelled by its
regulations, its principles, and even its prejudices. As a priest,
the framework of his order inevitably hemmed him in. (p.
200)

At this point in the novel, society "hems" men in and "trammels"
them—both negative images. But Hawthorne nonetheless considers Hester's solution the product of social isolation and consequent
moral individualism and, as such, dangerous. Hester's presence is
strong, but demonic; like Chillingworth, she violates the "sanctity
of the human heart" by "instinctively exercising a magnetic power
over a spirit [Dimmesdale's] so shattered and subdued, that it could
hardly hold itself erect" (p. 197). At first associated with constriction and arbitrary limits, obedience to rules later assumes positive
value as prefiguring the appropriate relationship of mortal man to
infinite spiritual order.

In the forest scene, Hester re-enacts the original seduction scene.
The most moralistic and simplistic of Hawthorne's readers would
incline to overstate Hester's evil resemblance to Satan and Eve in
this scene and to ignore the moral complexity of her responses to
sin and ostracism. Yet most of Hawthorne's contemporary readers
and most modern readers as well both perceive the biblical and
Miltonic parallels and move beyond those parallels to feel basic
human sympathy with Hester and Dimmesdale. Hawthorne is not
unaware that many readers will sympathize with Hester in this
scene, and that her proposal of flight produces the same sense of
affirmation and hope in the reader as it does in nature, which
responds to Hester's suggestion of flight with a "flood of sunshine":

Such was the sympathy of Nature—that wild, heathen Nature
of the forest, never subjugated by human law, nor illuminated
by higher truth—with the bliss of these two spirits! (p. 203)

But by describing nature as heathen in this sentence, and by making
"subjugated by human law" and "illumined by higher truth"

parallel conditions, Hawthorne tentatively states the connection between human law and higher truth that controls the climax and end of the novel, and he moves to consolidate a congruent relationship with the reader. For Hawthorne to avoid an incongruent ending, the reader, like Hester, must be led to reject the illusory hope that "natural" impulses rather than "social laws" most fully approximate "higher truth." And the process must be gradual, since Hawthorne knows that his thematic statements run counter to ordinary human emotions and advocate the sacrifice of the individual's happiness to social and spiritual laws.

The rest of the novel is in some sense a weaning of characters and readers from what seems "natural"—the search for individual happiness. Pearl's insistence on her mother's re-assumption of the Scarlet Letter is the first step in this direction; Dimmesdale's spiritual turmoil in the chapter entitled "The Minister in a Maze" is another. But until Hester can reject her absolute individuality and idiosyncratic morality, the process cannot be complete. Hester's chastisement begins in the marketplace, during the Founder's Day Procession, when Hester thinks of "the dim forest, with its little dell of solitude, and love, and anguish," and resents Dimmesdale's "being able so completely to withdraw himself from their mutual world" (pp. 239-40). As the social world embodied in the procession overshadows her private "bond" to the clergyman, Hester begins to appreciate the necessity of her disappointment. But acceptance comes only in the final chapter and it is there that Hawthorne must complete the process of re-channeling Hester's and the reader's emotions.

Hester's after-history in the final chapter begins with the following authorial assertion:

> But there was a more *real life* for Hester Prynne, here, in New England, than in that unknown region where Pearl had found a home. Here had been her sin; here, her sorrow; and *here was yet to be her penitence.* (pp. 262-63, my emphasis)

Hester's acknowledgment of the necessity for penance and her voluntary resumption of the Scarlet Letter run counter to what readers desire, but they are necessary for the thematic resolution Hawthorne projects. In a sense, he insists that Hester share his view of her earlier experience. Hawthorne's account of Hester's new life as nurse and counselor asserts the rightness of Hester's rejection of prideful individualism:

> Hester comforted and counselled them, as best she might. She assured them, too, of her firm belief, that . . . in Heaven's own time, a new truth would be revealed, in order to establish the whole relation between man and woman on a surer ground of mutual happiness. Earlier in life, Hester had vainly imagined that she herself might be the destined prophetess, but had long since recognized the impossibility that any mission of divine and mysterious truth should be confided to a woman stained with sin, bowed down with shame, or even burdened with a life-long sorrow. The angel and apostle of the coming revelation must be a woman, indeed, but lofty, pure, and beautiful; and wise, moreover, not through dusky grief, but the ethereal medium of joy; and showing how sacred love should make us happy, by the truest test of a life successful to such an end!   (p. 263)

Hester thus sadly abandons her rebellious role, which she once thought could effect broad social changes. As in *Middlemarch*, the main character must reject her hopes for immediate and wide-scale social reform and her potential for effecting that reform; like Dorothea, Hester must content herself with a life of minor good works, and relegate the improvement of the world to a vague, indefinite future. Since Hawthorne believed in no meliorist philosophy, Hester is denied even the gradual power to influence the world granted Dorothea in the "Finale" of *Middlemarch*. And, certainly, the ending of *The Scarlet Letter* is more depressing and grim than those of *Bleak House*, *War and Peace*, and *Middlemarch*, in part because of its absence of familial ideals and the consolatory middle ground they provide between the individual and the larger society. Neither charitable ardor, nor a humane circle of family and friends, nor passing on one's noble views through children has any broader, cumulative social value in *The Scarlet Letter*. As Hawthorne warns in the first chapter, the novel moves to a "darkening close of a tale of human frailty and sorrow," relieved only by "some sweet moral blossom" (p. 48). The "Conclusion," with the temporal distance often found in overview endings, ends with an examination of Hester's tombstone, which is gray, somber, gloomy, and "relieved only by one ever-glowing point of light" (p. 264).

The prevailing imagery of darkness at the end of the novel indicates that Hawthorne's judgment on Dimmesdale and Hester and his thematic resolution of *The Scarlet Letter* were reluctant rather than eager, heart-rending rather than heartily endorsed. They sadden the author and must necessarily sadden the reader. Hawthorne's letters provide interesting extratextual confirmation of his intentions at the end of *The Scarlet Letter*. Hawthorne finds his wife's reaction to the end of the novel "a triumphant success": "It broke her heart and sent her to bed with a grievous headache." And, marveling at Thackeray's reported stoniness at the end of his novels, Hawthorne contrasts his own reaction to completing *The Scarlet Letter*:

> I cannot but wonder at his [Thackeray's] coolness and compare it to my own emotions, when I read the last scene of *The Scarlet Letter* to my wife, just after writing it—tried to read it rather, for my voice swelled and heaved, as if I were tossed up and down on an ocean as it subsides after a storm.[18]

The metaphor is instructive: the body of the novel creates a storm of conflicting views on the individual's obligations to a flawed society; the ending, like an ocean subsiding after a storm, gradually calms and diffuses powerful forces.

In *The Scarlet Letter*, rebellious or isolated individualism and covert one-to-one relationships are dominant modes of experience only while characters are abnormally estranged, through sin and secrecy, from the larger community. The climactic scaffold scene and the post-climactic "Conclusion" clearly establish the importance of the characters' reintegration into the existing society, while still confirming the unreformed and unreformable flaws in the social order. The paradigm introduced early in the novel of "practical necessities" overpowering what individuals "originally project" holds true: Hawthorne remains suspicious and critical of social institutions, but he is finally even more suspicious and fearful of unbridled individuality and the undermining of the established social order. For Hawthorne, a society's flaws—however serious—do not cancel the necessary ties between the individual and the larger community. The spiritual perils of self-government are finally more serious than the spiritual failures of social organization.

At the end of his novel, Hawthorne needs both to present a censorious judgment on the Puritan community and to assert that the individual must still be a part of his society. Because he sees the validity of both the individual's desires and the prerogatives of the larger community, he repeatedly needs to examine the problematic relationship between the two. The inner and outer frames of *The Scarlet Letter* give Hawthorne the form he needs to construct his position by the alternation of conflicting perspectives, and gradually to rechannel the novel's and the reader's emotional energy. The "Conclusion" allows a self-aware Hawthorne to make a final juxtaposition of criticism and endorsement of the established social order. His compromise resolution is essentially the tough-minded statement that both viewpoints do and must coexist.

# FIVE

# Discomforting the Reader:
## the Confrontational Endings of
### *Vanity Fair* and *L'Education sentimentale*

I

WHEN we first meet Becky Sharp at Miss Pinkerton's school, she has already set her basic pattern for action throughout the novel. She sees through the conventions and forms of her culture and parodies them in her actions, but she does not break with culture in the creation of new roles. Instead, she exploits the feminine roles her society has mapped out for her, always trying to parlay her good looks and charm into possibilities for social advancement. Her conduct repeatedly indicates problems with contemporary notions of feminine conduct without exploring alternatives to them. Becky thus remains a part of Vanity Fair, whose values she holds in contempt, yet imitates. When she leaves Miss Pinkerton's, Becky expresses her contempt for her benefactor and for decorous social norms by an emblematic action—flinging Johnson's "Dixonary" out the window. She succeeds in shocking Miss Pinkerton and wounding the sensibility of the timid but kindhearted Jemima.

The two novelists discussed in this chapter have things in common with Becky. They both shrewdly perceived the conventional social values expressed by happy endings in which hero marries heroine and everyone who deserves to lives happily ever after—the things valued including marriage, the family, the ability of men to learn from experience, and the possibility of living contentedly and happily in the world. But they were unwilling or unable to share those values. Cool and, like Becky, "lively on the wire,"[1] they enjoyed shocking the hypocritical and dismaying the sentimental. For both Thackeray and Flaubert, negative sensibility, brought to bear upon both their societies, and the narrative conventions for ending approved by those societies, was an important impetus to novelistic creation and a major motivation of closure. The endings of *Vanity Fair* and *L'Education sentimentale* are confrontational. They "throw the book" at the nature of the times in which their authors lived and at reader expectations for a happy or idealistic ending.

## II

Many of Thackeray's works—particularly *The Yellowplush Papers, Barry Lyndon,* and *Rebecca and Rowena*—marked him even in his own day as a parodic writer. Before *Vanity Fair,* he wrote outright burlesques of contemporary novels that appeared in *Punch* as "Punch's Prize Novelists" as the early numbers of *Vanity Fair* were published.[2] The subtitle to *Vanity Fair,* "A Novel without a Hero," both indicates Thackeray's dislike for popular conventions and announces his peculiar attitude toward his characters. Each character—the generally fine as well as the generally nasty— emerges as a rogue, a fool, or a bit of each. There is no character whom the author fully admires, and no one with whom the reader may comfortably identify. Thackeray's mixed evaluations of his characters—each finally colored by satiric scorn—define the way characters in *Vanity Fair* must be viewed: from beginning to end, author and reader are distanced from Thackeray's "puppets" and denied both emotional involvement and emotional identification with them.

Consider Thackeray's attitude toward the best of his characters— the admittedly silly William Dobbin. Like Fielding's Parson Adams, Sterne's Uncle Toby, and Dickens' Mr. Pickwick, Dobbin is a perfectly good man who lacks common sense and worldliness. But whereas Fielding, Sterne, and Dickens feel free to satirize these characters while simultaneously offering them to readers as objects of affection and as models of disinterested conduct,[3] Thackeray takes care to make Dobbin at least as foolish as he is admirable. The Major's stupidity in forcing the marriage of George and Amelia, which causes fifteen lost years in Amelia's life and his own, minimizes the nobility of his conduct toward the young couple. Similarly, his capacity for love, although deep and genuine, always approaches idolatry as, in the course of the novel, he worships in turn George, Amelia, and his daughter Janey. In case readers fail to feel contempt for Dobbin, Thackeray explicitly tells them toward the end of the novel that "This history has been written to very little purpose if the reader has not perceived that the Major was a spooney" (p. 641). And in the final pages of *Vanity Fair*, Dobbin and his paternal affection are rendered slightly ridiculous by Thackeray's repeated references to the Major's beloved but presumably pedantic "History of the Punjaub," the thing the Major loves most, after his child.

With high irony, Thackeray expresses his awareness that the climax and final pages in fiction conventionally recount the marriage of young lovers in the novel. He unites his lovers with distinct bitterness and open scorn, in what I shall call the novel's first ending:

> The bird has come in at last. There it is with its head on his shoulder, billing and cooing close up to his heart, with soft outstretched fluttering wings. This is what he has asked for every day and hour for eighteen years. This is what he pined after. Here it is—the summit, the end—the last page of the last volume. Good-bye, Colonel—God bless you, honest William!—Farewell, dear Amelia—Grow green again, tender little parasite, round the rugged old oak to which you cling!
> (pp.660-61)

The stale imagery, the breathless dashes, the ironic exclamations, and the cutting oxymoron, "tender parasite," effectively demolish any sentimental pleasure the reader might derive from the accomplishment of the long-awaited union of Amelia and Dobbin. Rhetorically, Thackeray underlines his point with the parallel structure of "There it is" (which reduces Amelia to the neuter "it"), "This is what," "Here it is." He further conveys his sense that the conventional climax is both thoroughly expected and intolerably silly in the ironic, dash-enclosed "the summit, the end—the last page of the last volume," for in the case of *Vanity Fair*, the betrothal of the lovers is *not* the real end of the work.

The final pages of *Vanity Fair* constitute the novel's real ending and provide after-history: they hint that Becky slays Jos, record an encounter between Becky and the Dobbin family, and inform us that Amelia wistfully recognizes Dobbin's greater love for their daughter than for her. But the primary purpose of the after-history is not genially to provide information about characters the reader cares for as people. Throughout his novel, notably in the years after Waterloo, Thackeray elides long periods in the characters' lives, without feeling obliged to fill in details that a novelist who conceives of his characters as inhabiting an invented, but dense, social world might. Moreover, Thackeray's anti-conventional image of characters as puppets, reiterated in the novel's last line and final sketch, destroys the sense implied by most after-histories— maintained even in Scott's humorous ending to *Old Mortality*— that characters have "lives" that expand beyond the borders of the narrative and need to be summarized in after-history. The novel, you will recall, ends with the following words and then with a sketch of children shutting lifeless puppets away in a box:

> Ah! *Vanitas Vanitatum*! Which of us is happy in this world?
> Which of us has his desire? or, having it, is satisfied?—Come
> children, let us shut up the box and the puppets, for our play
> is played out.   (p. 666)

The author conventionally gives after-histories at the end of his novel, but satirically mocks the premises that make them possible; he satisfies his readers' expectations, but implicitly ridicules their naiveté.

In a letter, Thackeray explains the true motivation behind his anti-conventional double ending:

> I want to leave everybody dissatisfied and unhappy at the end
> of the story—we ought all to be with our own and all other
> stories.[4]

The ending indicates pretty clearly why the characters should be dissatisfied. Dobbin wins Amelia only after he has realized her unworthiness, and he is dutiful, not joyous, in the climactic scene. His realization is, however, not so much a transcendence of folly as a patient daily bearing of its consequences. And Amelia, though she bills and coos like the exalted heroine of any romance when she wins Dobbin, later sighs with the recognition that she no longer represents an ideal in his life (p. 666). As for Becky, the final chapter portrays her as Jos's murderess (whether believably or not), and thereby counterbalances whatever favorable opinion the reader may have formed of her actions in bringing Dobbin and Amelia together. In addition, the after-history's presentation of the pious "Lady Crawley" is singularly appropriate: Becky's "success," founded on collecting the money from Jos's sudden death, condemns her to living a hypocritical and dull existence that, we may note, is in accord with surface patterns of Victorian morality.

The final chapter dissatisfied its contemporary readers by denying them the expected treatment of characters as "people" (not puppets), and by withholding the generalized marital after-history and rewarding of vice and virtue usually found at the end of novels. It dramatizes something Barbara Hardy notes about Thackeray's methods of characterization, his "refusal to differentiate sharply between the lives of the good and the bad,"[5] in that neither Dobbin nor Amelia nor Becky is entirely happy in later life. Moreover, his ending undercuts what the conventional happy ending implies about the nature of novels and their ability to provide an "escape" from real life. As Kathleen Tillotson notes, Thackeray's final address to the reader is "a recall to life and individual responsibility as the preacher lays his cap and bells aside."[6] The recall rouses and unsettles the reader, since it denies both the conception of fiction as an escape from life and the efficacy of a novel's happy ending to prove that life at or after the altar holds anything beyond the muted, circumscribed, and slightly contemptible happiness Thackeray allows to Dobbin and Amelia in the epilogue to *Vanity Fair*.

But if Thackeray succeeds in leaving his characters and his contemporary readers dissatisfied at the end of his novel, the ending nonetheless reflects more subtle dissatisfactions felt by Thackeray himself. For by ridiculing the muted happiness of Dobbin and Amelia, Thackeray denies himself, as well as the reader, a comforting (if bland), domestic solution to the problems of human existence in the world of Vanity Fair. He rejects for himself as well as the reader the domestic ideals endorsed at various points in *Vanity Fair* (as so often in his other works) as a solid basis for existence. The Sedleys, for example, especially before their bankruptcy, provide a model of marital contentment and enjoy a number of cozy, conjugal conversations. And Thackeray moralizes over Lady Rose Crawley's rejection of young Peter Butt in marrying Sir Pitt by invoking the once possible image of Lady Rose as "a cheery lass; Peter Butt and Rose a happy man and wife, in a snug farm, with a hearty family, and an honest portion of pleasures, cares, hopes, and struggles" (p. 83). At another point in the novel, when Amelia and Dobbin are placidly traveling in Europe, Thackeray alters his usual attitude toward his characters. In his description of their muted, rather domestic happiness, his satire abates and he becomes uncommonly affectionate:

> I like to dwell upon this period of her life, and to think that she was cheerful and happy. . . .
> Perhaps it was the happiest time of both their lives indeed, if they did but know it—and who does? . . . It was on this very tour that I, the present writer of a history of which every word is true, had the pleasure to see them first, and to make their acquaintance.   (pp. 601-02)

The author who dismisses his characters as puppets is thus capable of a sentimental fiction: he can pretend that he met and liked several characters in the novel. Even Thackeray's drawings soften at this point. The illustration called "A Fine Summer Evening" presents a more attractive image of the characters than most; Dobbin's looks have improved considerably, and Amelia wears a more tranquil expression (p. 599).

The second ending to *Vanity Fair* denies, however, the ideals implied at these points in the novel. It not only deflates the contemporary reader's expectation of a happy ending, but also checks Thackeray's own yearnings toward a moderate but happy mode of existence, his own impulse to view the first ending, which joins Dobbin and Amelia, as a happy one. To some extent, the conventional reader's pleasure in the union of Dobbin and Amelia has already been lessened by its long postponement and by the fact that the united couple is no longer young. And, as I have noted, Dobbin has fully perceived the hollowness of his victory. The real function of the overstated first ending may thus be to discredit the importance of domestic happiness in Thackeray's own mind. Biographical speculations are natural here and, as Praz's and Ray's analyses of Thackeray's life and works have shown, the facts of Thackeray's life strongly influenced his development as a man and writer.[7] Amelia was modeled on Thackeray's own wife. And the tragedies in Thackeray's life—in particular his wife's insanity—may well motivate the presentation in the ending of domestic life as sweet, but somewhat contemptible and ridiculous. Excluded by an accident of nature from the course he had chosen for his own happiness, Thackeray defensively undercuts the worth of marital contentment for Dobbin and Amelia. At whatever level of consciousness, Thackeray's ending in part seeks to compensate for his personal disappointment; it is, in this ending, very difficult to decide whether he is fully self-aware, or at least partly self-deceiving.

Because the book wobbles between the sentimental idealization of, and the ridicule of, family life, many of Thackeray's readers—more attuned to the idealization than the ridicule—misread the ending. As I see it, the ending is clearly confrontational and, as the quotation from Thackeray's letter indicates, was intended as such. Many of his contemporaries, however, missed the harsher, more ironic tones in the narrator's voice, hearing instead only its kinder, paternal tones and emphasizing those moments when Thackeray idealizes the family or moralizes in the genial manner of a Fielding. As it stands, the text somewhat accommodates such misreadings. But it would be a mistake to see Thackeray as a kindly moralist, and to miss the ending's confrontational nature.

Thackeray relishes the moralist's pose but, unlike the true moralist, distressed at the discrepancy between ideal and real, he enjoys the absurdity of the action he chronicles. He neither considers the role of social reformer, nor would he have found life in a perfected world very interesting. His personal views and sensibility entirely lent themselves to literary impulses anti-conventional and parodic; his confrontational style is prompt with criticism for what did exist, but slower with suggestions for what might profitably have existed instead. At the end of *Vanity Fair*, Thackeray can only ridicule the conventional happy ending, distancing himself and his readers from ideals of human happiness and social betterment, rather than write an entirely different kind of ending. Like the novel itself, closure in *Vanity Fair* is clever and amusing, but disengaged from human affairs despite its surface moralizing.

## III

Like *Vanity Fair*, *L'Education sentimentale* has more than one ending, each of greater textual complexity than those in Thackeray's novel. The end of the novel's main action takes place in December, 1851, as a series of cataclysmic events overtake both Frédéric's personal life and the political life of France, completing the novel's extensive parallels between the lives of characters and events in public life. The two after-history chapters focus on Frédéric's personal connections, moving the novel's historical parallels from center stage. Chapter VI, the first concluding chapter, begins with an after-history of Frédéric and Flaubert's famous, remarkably succinct summary of ten years: "Il voyagea," "He traveled."[8] Most of the chapter recounts, however, the final meeting of Madame Arnoux and Frédéric when she visits him in March of 1867. Chapter VII, the final chapter in the novel, takes place in the winter of 1867 (or, perhaps, 1868-69), and consists of a conversation between Deslauriers and Frédéric, who have been reconciled "par la fatalité de leur nature."

The two closing chapters induce a sense of closure by slowing down the tempo of the novel, which has become increasingly rapid

through its second and third parts and has built to a frenzied pace
as Frédéric's world collapses against the background of Louis-Na-
poleon's coup d'état. They present scenes that, unlike most in the
novel, are allowed to unroll without interruption, to proceed without the abrupt substitution of characters and sudden changes in
direction typical of action in the novel. But although the pacing
in the final chapters is more tranquil than elsewhere in *L'Education
sentimentale*, they produce anything but a sense of peaceful resolution.

As I read them, the endings to *L'Education sentimentale* are
among the most discomforting passages in all of literature: they
initially invite the reader to be moved, and then abruptly withdraw
the invitation. As in *Vanity Fair*, the reader can adopt no conventional attitudes toward the characters. He clearly looks down
on Frédéric, "homme de toutes les faiblesses," but the action in
the endings inspires neither full contempt, nor true laughter, nor
pure empathy. The concluding chapters deal with the most permanent of Frédéric's relationships—those with Marie Arnoux and
Charles Deslauriers—but the duration of this love and this friendship do not prove them genuine. To borrow one of Flaubert's own
words, the conclusions "exhume" the ideals of love and friendship,
which have been discredited in the body of the novel, thus implicitly seeming to inflate them. But by exposing the hollow foun-
dations upon which these relationships rest, the endings ultimately
deflate love and friendship, making empty forms of lofty ideals.
Shorter than most chapters in the novel, the concluding chapters
have the same kind of deflationary effect that so many of Flaubert's
one-sentence paragraphs have after a long paragraph of inflated
imaginings.

The first concluding chapter discredits the one ideal Frédéric has
maintained, his love for Madame Arnoux, and is an important
addition to the treatment of love in the novel. Without it, Frédéric
might indeed emerge as a genuine lover, since his last actions
before the ending (and especially his break with Madame Dambreuse) stem from his loyalty to Madame Arnoux. His actions
in their final meeting reveal, however, that Frédéric's love is based

on pretense, vanity, and imagination rather than on a genuine attachment to a real woman.[9]

The chapter uses with considerable effectiveness the deflationary technique characteristic of Flaubert's style in *L'Education sentimentale*. Each time the scene becomes emotionally moving, a detail or incident is inserted that reminds the reader that the characters' relationship is highly artificial.[10] When the couple sentimentally goes for a stroll, for example, the luminous description that follows is undercut by the final simile:

> La lueur des boutiques éclairait, par intervalles, son profil pâle; puis l'ombre l'enveloppait de nouveau; et, au milieu des voitures, de la foule et du bruit, ils allaient sans se distraire d'eux-mêmes, sans rien entendre, comme ceux qui marchent ensemble dans la campagne, sur un lit de feuilles mortes.
>
> (p. 602)

> The lights of the shops illuminated intermittently her pale profile; then the darkness closed in on it again; and they moved among the carriages, the crowds, and the noise, oblivious of everything but themselves, hearing nothing, as if they had been walking together in the country, on a bed of dead leaves.   (p. 413)

Again, when Marie indicates that Frédéric's reserve convinced her that she was truly loved, he is momentarily dignified: "Il ne regretta rien. Ses souffrances d'autrefois étaient payées" (p. 604). But the revelation of Marie's white hair and Frédéric's ignoble reaction immediately follow.

Flaubert's account of his characters' thoughts when Marie removes her hat is totally incongruous in a "tender love scene" and illustrates Flaubert's success in discomforting the reader. Madame Arnoux is vain, foolish, and downright vulgar in her lack of perception that Frédéric automatically utters compliments merely to hide his confusion, and in her subsequent questions about his other women and his plans for marriage. Frédéric's words of adoration, which have previously been quite sincere when addressed to Madame Arnoux, here assume the mechanical, unfeeling quality his vows to Rosanette and Madame Dambreuse have had throughout the novel. Given the large amount of indirect discourse in *L'Education sentimentale*, Frédéric's speech *could* have been omitted and the summary, "il . . . se mit à lui dire des tendresses," might have stood without further detail. But Flaubert includes the speech because its overly-romantic imagery and empty meaning embarrass the reader and definitively reveal the true nature of Frédéric's love:

> —Votre personne, vos moindres mouvements me semblaient avoir dans le monde une importance extra-humaine. Mon coeur, comme de la poussière, se soulevait derrière vos pas. Vous me faisiez l'effet d'un clair de lune par une nuit d'été . . . [et] je me répétais [votre nom], en tâchant de le baiser sur mes lèvres.   (p. 604, from a much longer passage)

> "Your person, your slightest movements seemed to me to possess a superhuman importance in the world. My heart used to rise like the dust in your footsteps. The effect you had on me was that of a moonlit night in summer. . . . I repeated it [your name] again and again, trying to kiss it with my lips."   (p. 414)

As Frédéric reaches for clichés to mask his disappointment that Madame Arnoux has aged, the passage reveals his passion as mere romantic illusion sustained by pasted-together phrases; it suggests that his great love originates in weakness of mind rather than in transcendent emotions. For the love Frédéric has nurtured for over two decades, to which he has sacrificed his life, cannot withstand the "revelation" that Madame Arnoux is no longer a young, dark-haired Andalusian beauty. Toward the end of this speech, he directly lies for the second time in the scene to Madame Arnoux, and his falseness further belies whatever idealization we might be tempted to see in the meeting.

The chapter becomes even more discomforting when Frédéric perceives Madame Arnoux's conduct as seductive. The reader reacts in as confused a manner as he does, but the passage is distasteful and reveals him as vacillating, weak minded, and ultimately more pragmatic than loving:

> Frédéric soupçonna Mme Arnoux d'être venue pour s'offrir; et il était repris par une convoitise plus forte que jamais, furieuse, enragée. Cependant, il sentait quelque chose d'inexprimable, une répulsion, et comme l'effroi d'un inceste. Une autre crainte l'arrêta, celle d'en avoir dégoût plus tard. D'ailleurs, quel embarras ce serait! et tout à la fois par prudence et pour ne pas dégrader son idéal, il tourna sur ses talons et se mit à faire une cigarette.  (pp. 605-06)

> Frédéric suspected that Madame Arnoux had come to offer herself to him; and once again he was filled with desire, a frenzied, rabid lust such as he had never known before. Yet he also had another, indefinable feeling, a repugnance akin to a dread of committing incest. Another fear restrained him— the fear of being disgusted later. Besides, what a nuisance it would be! And partly out of prudence and partly to avoid degrading his ideal, he turned on his heel and started rolling a cigarette.  (p. 415)

A basis for the revelation that supreme love of the kind Frédéric has imagined is unattainable in an earthly context is here, in the feeling akin to incest and religious taboo which quells Frédéric's lust. But Frédéric's mind has no revelations; it moves on from the religious and psychological contradictions in his conception of love to the mundane concerns of the middle-aged gentleman—"what a nuisance it would be!" At the end of this passage, Madame Arnoux misinterprets Frédéric's actions in a way which underscores the irony in the scene and further de-idealizes the characters:

> Elle le contemplait, tout émerveillée.
> —Comme vous êtes délicat! Il n'y a que vous! Il n'y a que vous!  (p. 606)

> She gazed at him admiringly.
> "How considerate you are! There's nobody like you! There's nobody like you!"  (p. 415)

There follows one of the most embarrassed silences in all literature—uncomfortable and distancing. The reader, like the characters, watches Frédéric's cigarette burn down and hears the ticking of the clock, waiting for the stroke of a quarter past eleven when Madame Arnoux must go. As she leaves, she performs a gesture which is both ridiculously sentimental and genuinely touching: she cuts off a lock of the white hair that has so dismayed Frédéric. We are not told what use he makes of this love-token, but from his cool attitude toward Madame Arnoux in the second concluding chapter, we presume it was not a cherished momento.

At the very end of the first concluding chapter, as Frédéric watches from the window and Marie Arnoux leaves his life forever, the scene once again becomes touching. But the coldness of the narrative's final line, like the chill produced by all the exposition in this chapter, distances the emotion and leaves the reader uncomfortable rather than moved: "Et ce fut tout," "And that was all" (p. 606; p. 416). Indeed, in Frédéric's talk with Deslauriers, Madame Arnoux takes her place with the other characters, and is no longer a privileged object in Frédéric's consciousness.

Thus far, Flaubert's targets are similar to Thackeray's. The meeting between Madame Arnoux and Frédéric clearly parodies the union of lovers that often ends conventional romantic fiction, and parodies it more extremely and disturbingly than the first ending of *Vanity Fair*. Flaubert may also have had in mind the ending to Balzac's recent success, *La Lis de la vallée*, which also deals with the love of a younger man for an older woman. Balzac's novel ends unhappily (with the separation of the lovers and the woman's death), but preserves the ideal quality of the love as Flaubert's ending stubbornly refuses to do.[11]

The cold lamplight, Marie's white hair, and the ticking clock are the only concrete, genuine things in the scene; even the metaphorical "dead leaves" have more substance than the action and dialogue, which are reduced to pretense, second-hand romantic language, illusion, and nonproductive memory. In this chapter, as more emphatically in the next, the characters choose to hover in an idealized version of their past rather than to invest the present with meaning. Much of the love that should be vital and realized in this scene is diverted into a recreation of the past: the first time Frédéric saw Marie, her singing, Arnoux's habits, and so on. The negative power of memory—its impoverishment rather than enrichment of the present—underlies this chapter and emerges as a major theme in the second concluding chapter, which broadens the implications of the ending.

Just as we are tempted to see ideal love in the meeting of Frédéric and Madame Arnoux, we may also be tempted to see an archetypal masculine friendship in the reunion of Frédéric and Deslauriers. But the second concluding chapter, like the first, reveals that hypocrisy rules this potentially "ideal" relationship. When Deslauriers confesses that he slept with Rosanette, we are told:

> Cet aveu était une compensation au silence qu'il gardait touchant sa tentative près de Mme Arnoux. Frédéric l'eût pardonnée, puisqu'elle n'avait pas réussi.
>
> Bien que vexé un peu de la découverte, il fit semblant d'en rire. . . .    (pp. 608-09)

> This confession made up for his silence concerning the attempt he had made to seduce Madame Arnoux. Frédéric would have forgiven him for this, since it had not succeeded.
>
> Although slightly annoyed by his friend's revelation, he pretended to laugh at it. . . .    (p. 417)

Rather than qualifying the novel's alignment of friendship and betrayal, these evasions further debase the characters: the two men continue to cling to the destroyed ideal of friendship, and they both ignore their failures and betrayals as friends.

The concluding chapters—in which the reader looks down on the characters—recall by inversion the endings one finds in first-person *Bildungsromane* contemporary with *Vanity Fair*—like *Jane Eyre* and *David Copperfield*—that confirm the wisdom characteristic of or achieved by the protagonist-narrator in the body of the novel by showing, in the after-history ending the novel, how successful and happy his later life has been. The final chapters of *L'Education sentimentale* demonstrate quite the opposite: the characters have achieved no wisdom, and rather than learning from the past, compulsively relive it in memory. In their coldness and one-sentence brevity, the after-histories of minor characters in the second concluding chapter are similarly parodic of the sentimentality often found in after-histories (see p. 608 in the French edition, pp. 416-17 in the English). The effect is to dismiss each character and to reveal, through the two men's tone, the ties of envy which exist among their "friends." The clipped brevity of these after-histories is much like the dismissal of characters as puppets at the end of *Vanity Fair,* and this effect is highly appropriate; for despite the multiplicity of characters in the novel, few except the major characters emerge with any real distinctness. Their after-histories may thus be quickly listed at the end.

The final "incident" in the novel—the characters' journey in memory to Nogent—intensifies the ending's bitter irony by an unusual kind of circularity. The friends recall an abortive visit to a whorehouse that had taken place in 1837, years before the beginning of the novel. Any shift in time-scale at the end of a novel ordinarily involves a movement forward in time; Flaubert parodically inverts this traditional element by having the novel end with an "incident" that had occurred before the beginning of the novel's action. The inversion has thematic value, for it indicates that our heroes' journey through life is regressive rather than progressive. The mental journey to Nogent caps the pseudo-picaresque elements in the novel. Characters in *L'Education senti-mentale* move about constantly, but almost all their movement is fruitless: it consumes time rather than covers ground.[12] The final memory aptly summarizes the novel's inversion of the picaresque mode: the action began with Frédéric's actual journey home to Nogent and ends with a circular sentimental journey back in memory.. This portion of the second concluding chapter also reinforces the reader's perception that neither Frédéric nor Deslauriers has developed through the action of the novel. Indeed, in their first conversation, they allude to the very same incident at the whorehouse.[13] Once again, the ending reminds the reader that *L'Education sentimentale* is a parodic *Bildungsroman*: it focuses on the life of one character, Frédéric, but denies him any moral growth or insight, and subjects him to experiences from which he learns nothing.

The incident recalled at the end of the novel may be said to encapsulate the novel as a whole.[14] The interrupted action, mental vacillation, and changed purposes that typify action in the novel characterize Frédéric's conduct at the whorehouse. And, as has been noted by critics, all the novel's personal, social, and political relationships involve figurative forms of prostitution. As in his wish that Frédéric supply the funds for a newspaper, Deslauriers looked to Frédéric to provide money for their youthful venture, but Frédéric simply didn't come through. The final memory is thus of an event failed of completion, of a desire unfulfilled, and every level of mental and physical action in the novel is similarly incomplete and unfulfilled.

In some sense, the final conversation between Frédéric and Deslauriers also inverts the typical form and ending of the *récit*. In the *récit*, a first-person narrator explains to an auditor within the text how he has reached his present condition through immaturity, love, or some damaging flaw of character. At the end of his tale, both the first-person narrator and the reader have achieved at least some genuine understanding of the protagonist's life through the process of the narrative. In the final chapter of *L'Education sentimentale*, Frédéric and Deslauriers get their chance, like the first-person narrators of *récits*, to tell their stories to each other and thereby understand the emptiness of their lives. In this context, the incident at the whorehouse would emerge as an emblematic event, symbolically repeated in different terms throughout the novel.[15] Frédéric and Deslauriers are, however, incapable of self-analysis or psychological purgation. They do not intensely try, like the hero of the *récit*, to understand how and why things went wrong in their lives; instead, after some desultory attempts at explanation, they begin to relive and to enjoy the attitudes that have made them what they are.

Flaubert, who transformed his sense of disillusionment and disgust into a motivating source of his art, might have extrapolated from the final action to make a profound philosophical statement, perhaps in an explicit, overview ending. But the shape of his fiction—its efforts to avoid overt authorial commentary and to tell the novel through the limited consciousness of the characters—precludes his doing so. The novel accordingly ends with a banal exchange between Frédéric and Deslauriers about their adolescent misadventure with the prostitutes:

> — C'est là ce que nous avons eu de meilleur! dit Frédéric.
> — Oui, peut-être bien? c'est là ce que nous avons eu de meilleur! dit Deslauriers.   (p. 612)

> "That was the happiest time we ever had," said Frédéric.
> "Yes, perhaps you're right. That was the happiest time we ever had," said Deslauriers.   (p. 419)

The ending is scenic in form and close-up in technique, despite the seven years elapsed since the end of the novel's major action. It is intensely close-up in its ability to disorient and confuse the reader. Flaubert no doubt had an overview on the ending and could have allowed the reader to share that point of view immediately. An additional sentence or two, glossing the final statement, would have done the trick. Two factors prevented him from doing so. First, though superior to his characters, he recognized the sense in which their experiences correspond to his—hence, his famous utterance, "Madame Bovary c'est moi." The close-up ending preserves this identification, simultaneously objectifying the foolish romanticism that caused Flaubert to resemble his characters. Second, overview endings normally seek either a complementary, or at least a congruent, relationship with the reader during closure; author and reader often cosily share insight that the characters do not. Flaubert's reader may ultimately share Flaubert's insight: but he will have to *work* for it *through* the close-up, confrontational ending, since Flaubert will give him little.

The ending recalls that to *Madame Bovary*, in which Charles' last words are also a cliché. Surveying the ruin of his life in the company of Emma's lover, Rodolphe, Charles ironically arrives at a phrase Rodolphe has previously used first to seduce Emma, and then to abandon her—"C'est la faute de la fatalité!" "Fate is to blame." The phrase discomforts the reader as it is both banal and wise, corrupted by its association with Rodolphe and yet sincere in its use by Charles. The ending to *L'Education sentimentale* similarly seeks to discomfort the reader. Stubbornly reflecting Flaubert's dislike of the nineteenth century, the ending refuses to offer either climax, or moral, or insight, or comfort, or even a stable vantage point from which to regard the novel.[16] Less good-natured than Thackeray's ending to *Vanity Fair* and, as befits its later date, more self-consciously critical of a wider variety of novelistic forms, the ending to *L'Education sentimentale* is one of the most bitter and satiric in all of fiction.

## VI

At the ends of *Vanity Fair* and *L'Education sentimentale*, Thackeray and Flaubert have comparable motivations: an aloofness from modest aspirations for happiness, a dislike for contemporary society, a debunking of all possible ideals, an awareness of what sentimental authors and readers want at the ends of novels, and a refusal to satisfy those wants. These endings are the product of bitter men, who suppress the kind of warmth and fellow feeling that Eliot, Dickens, Tolstoy, and even Hawthorne display toward their characters in the endings I have examined.[17] Like Becky Sharp's, the motivations of Thackeray and Flaubert are essentially negative and anti-conventional, rather than authentically unconventional; like her, they protest the *bêtises* of nineteenth-century society, without articulating any positive ideas for change. Characteristically, Thackeray accompanies his ending with a gently condescending smile, Flaubert with a bitter grimace. Neither writes an ineffective ending, though Flaubert's is more crucial to the effectiveness of his novel because it crystallizes and completes the novel's themes, whereas Thackeray's ending basically reiterates them.

Without denying the greatness of Thackeray and Flaubert, it is nonetheless important to realize an oddity in the artistic development of each. Although it is not at all unusual for novelists to write parodic novels with markedly parodic endings, such novels usually occur at the *beginning* of a career, as a way of defining an author's difference from the received tradition and of clearing the path for original, essentially non-parodic creation. Thackeray's sojourn in the parodic mode was, however, unusually protracted. Half his literary career (from about 1834 to 1850), is largely dedicated to literary parody, with his major novel, *Vanity Fair*, as the culmination of his parodic art. His later novels, though not always seen by critics as parodies, "repeatedly make their statement in terms of their rejection of a romantic pattern of action which they cannot seem to do wholly without,"[18] a process analogous to the use of anti-convention as I have described it. Flaubert's three major novels—*Madame Bovary* (1850), *L'Education sentimentale*, and *Bouvard et Pécuchet* (1880)—become increasingly parodic, perhaps because (unlike some of his non-novelistic works of the 1870's, which end in revelation), they insistently deal with French life in the nineteenth century. Indeed, the burlesque "Dictionnaire des idées reçues," which ends *Bouvard et Pécuchet*, emerges as the most striking evidence of Flaubert's utter disgust with contemporary values.

As illustrated by the cases of Thackeray and Flaubert, the writing of confrontational endings based on literary anti-convention or parody sometimes leads authors into what we might call the Becky Sharp syndrome. For anti-convention and parody often involve a dependence upon, rather than a break with, the forms ridiculed. They complexly mirror dissociations of sensibility in an age or an author and help prepare the ground for new literary conventions and techniques. But the realization and exploitation of new forms depend not upon the ridicule and scorning of old ideas and the conventions which express them, but upon the internalization of new ideas—whether philosophical, aesthetic, or both—and upon the creation of new literary forms and techniques expressive of those ideas. For Thackeray and Flaubert, confrontational endings became almost a goal in themselves. They can, however, more positively be used as a means to a greater end. In the next chapter, which surveys the development of James's sense of an ending, we shall see a classic case of an author who began with quasi-parodic forms of endings and wrote some confrontational endings based upon popular conventions, but whose convictions about fiction, once fully realized, led to the evolution of new forms of ending that leave parody behind.

# SIX

## James's Sense of an Ending: The Role Played in its Development by James's Ideas about Nineteenth-Century Endings

### I

IT IS not at all difficult to demonstrate James's disdain for nineteenth-century endings. In his famous essay of 1884, "The Art of Fiction," James resoundingly contrasts the expectations of the Victorian reading public and its judgment of what constitutes a "good" ending with the artistic "search for form" that interests him:

> Literature should be either instructive or amusing, and there is in many minds an impression that these artistic preoccupations, the search for form, contribute to neither end, interfere indeed with both. They are too frivolous to be edifying, and too serious to be diverting; and they are moreover priggish and paradoxical and superfluous. That, I think, represents the manner in which the latent thought of many people who read novels as an exercise in skipping would explain itself if it were to become articulate. They would argue, of course, that a novel ought to be "good," but they would interpret this term in a fashion of their own. . . . One would say that being good means representing virtuous and aspiring characters, placed in prominent positions; another would say that it depends on a "happy ending," on a distribution at the last of prizes, pensions, husbands, wives, babies, millions, appended paragraphs, and cheerful remarks. . . . The "ending" of a novel is, for many persons, like that of a good dinner, a course of dessert and ices, and the artist in fiction is regarded as a sort of meddlesome doctor who forbids agreeable aftertastes.[1]

Later in his career, in elevating the dramatic form of his own novels, James complains that "Exhibition may mean in a 'story' twenty different ways, fifty excursions, alternatives, excrescences, and the novel, as largely practised in English, is the perfect paradise of the loose end."[2] He goes on to note that in a drama a scenic ending must be "mathematically right, and with the loose end as gross an impertinence on its surface, and as grave a dishonour, as the dangle of a snippet of silk or wool on the right side of a tapestry."

James's delightfully pejorative comments on the endings of nineteenth-century novels are, of course, polemical and largely inaccurate. Nineteenth-century novels did not uniformly end with the comedic, happy-ending epilogue James describes in "The Art of Fiction," in which hero marries heroine after the obstacles to their union have been removed, and the virtuous are rewarded while the villainous are punished as a new community forms around the bride and groom.[3] Indeed, major novels, like those discussed in the preceding chapters, endowed the conventions common to epilogues—a change in time scale at the end of the novel and a summation "setting the perspective or informing readers of the *Nachgeschichte* [after-history] of the characters"[4]—with considerable variety and complexity of both form and effect. Moreover, authors like Eliot, Dickens, Tolstoy, and Hawthorne used precisely the same kinds of concordances to communicate meaning that James himself did, though they were less insistent that readers perceive and appreciate such concordances, and often evolved the aesthetic shape of a novel primarily to support its thematic content. As the analyses of nineteenth-century closure contained in this study show, in major novels, endings were emphatically *not* "appended paragraphs." My concern in this chapter is, however, to examine the role James's *notions* of the epilogue played in the development of his own fictional endings, rather than to criticize or correct his perceptions.

Comments like those above from the prefaces and "The Art of Fiction" show James aware and even resentful of the popular epilogue and consciously charting his own course as a writer toward "the search for form" and away from received conventions, which he considered unaesthetic impediments to formal perfection. Instead of readers who "read novels as an exercise in skipping" and look for "happy endings," James wanted readers capable of discerning and understanding the author's process of "selection and comparison" in ending his novel, the method by which the author solves the artist's "exquisite problem"—that of limiting in fact limitless "relations" and giving art the perfect form life lacks.[5] His ideals for endings are, then, congruent with his well-known artistic goals: to make aesthetic form and the reader's active engagement in its perception the guiding principle of the ending, and to change the gratification felt at novel's end from being sloppily emotional to being rigorously aesthetic and intellectual. The use of confrontational endings helped James to achieve these goals.

In their recurrent attention to the endings of individual texts, critics have sufficiently noted the complexity of James's endings and their importance in interpretation. Less noted, however, is the gradual process of artistic self-discovery that allowed James to realize fully his own characteristic form of ending—the scenic ending, bare of authorial commentary, focused intently on the final conversation of two protagonists, and rich in formal connections to the body of the novel—a process that included playing with and working through the popular nineteenth-century forms of ending he despised. This chapter traces some steps in the development of James's sense of an ending, as he moved from a playful manipulation of nineteenth-century conventions for ending to a full-scale alternative in the scenic ending. I have selected texts on the basis of their relationship (direct or inverse) to the epilogue form as James conceived of it, and examined most texts briefly to allow for a fuller examination of the ending of *The Portrait of a Lady*—in which he definitively and strikingly recognized his ideals for fictional endings—and that of *The Ambassadors*, which richly embodies those ideals.

II

James never wrote a fully conventional epilogue of the popular type. As a novice writer, however, he began by exploiting the epilogue as a familiar form of ending, readily accessible as a model. The result is what might be called a quasi-epilogue: a short (sometimes a single-sentence) after-history, which, rather than resolving the themes of the fiction and neatly disposing of the characters' fates, unsettles the reader or compels him to re-examine the story.

James's use of the quasi-epilogue can be playful, sometimes complicating even what his prefaces call the simplest question that may be asked of any narrative: "of whom necessarily is it told?" (p. 181). In an early short story, "De Grey: A Romance," he concocts an elaborately gothic tale about the curse dooming the first love of male heirs in the De Grey family. The tale ostensibly focuses on Paul De Grey and Margaret, the young woman he loves, and their abortive attempt to avoid the curse. Peripheral to the story are De Grey's mother and Father Herbert, the mentor-priest who resides with the family; their major function seems to be that of providing background information about Paul's father and the pathetic death of the young Italian woman he had loved. But the tale has a quasi-epilogue that re-focuses the story. In it the reader learns that Father Herbert is the unhappy "survivor" of the tragic death of Paul's father's first love: rather than being a passive spectator of the earlier events (as the reader has believed throughout the narrative), he was an active participant in them, since he loved the girl before and after her contamination by the elder De Grey. This information casts new light on the actions of Father Herbert in the tale, and makes the more interesting story in "De Grey: A Romance" the one that precedes the main action. The quasi-epilogue makes the story "about" Father Herbert and his lost love, rather than simply "about" Paul and Margaret.

An analogous kind of displacement occurs in James's first notable novel, *Roderick Hudson*. At the beginning of the novel, James introduces Rowland Mallett, who has come to visit his cousin Cecilia at Northampton, before he introduces the title character. The plot apparently centers, however, on the young sculptor, Roderick. But the reader never loses a sense of Roderick's essential vacuity, nor does James: Rowland is a more fully realized character than Roderick and a much more interesting one. In his prefaces,

James acknowledges this flaw in the novel; as a young novelist he miscalculated by focusing on Roderick's collapse, but indirectly achieved some success in the novel by unwittingly making Rowland the real center of interest:

> My subject, all blissfully, in face of difficulties, had defined itself—and this in spite of the title of the book—as not directly, in the least, my young sculptor's adventure. This it had been but indirectly, being all the while in essence and in final effect another man's, his friend's and patron's, view and experience of him. One's luck was to have felt one's subject right— whether instinct or calculation, in those dim days, most served. . . .   (p. 15)

The end of the book, like its beginning, is true to the real spirit and subject of the work: Roderick's death does not end the novel; there is a circular return to Northampton, to Rowland's relationship with his cousin, and to his equivocating passion for Mary Garland. This truncated epilogue shows the young James moving toward his later subject matter, for Rowland is the prototype of the too sensitive gentlemen (like Hyacinth Robinson, and Marcher), who figure prominently in James's later and better-known works.

A more confusing effect is produced by the quasi-epilogue to another of James's early stories, "Osborne's Revenge." Phillip Osborne, a systematic and vain New York lawyer, learns of his best friend's suicide. An acquaintance, Mrs. Dodd, informs Osborne that she knows what caused Graham's suicide: he had been jilted by a Miss Henrietta Congreve. Osborne decides to avenge his friend's death by beguiling Miss Congreve and then jilting her. Predictably, Osborne is instead enchanted by her. He decides, as a romantic ploy, to arouse her jealousy by announcing that a portrait he has purchased at random is the image of his beloved, whom he identifies as a "Miss Thomson" of Philadelphia. The ploy fails when Henrietta, with supreme composure, seems to recognize the portrait as that of a "Miss Dora Thomson" of Philadelphia; Osborne lamely christens the portrait "Angelica." At this point, Mr. Holland, the man for whom Miss Congreve had reportedly "jilted" Graham, appears on the scene, and Osborne decides to return to New York. He is accompanied by the gossiping Mrs. Dodd and her military brother-in-law. Confused and despairing, Osborne considers drowning himself and becoming Henrietta's second victim. But he is interrupted by Major Dodd, who had also witnessed Graham's "jilting" but interprets the events differently. He asserts that Henrietta Congreve was innocent of all flirtatiousness in the matter, and affirms that her conduct was that of a proper and engaged young woman, confronted by an infatuated and slightly mad suitor. Osborne finds this explanation to his liking, and the story ends with a playfully cryptic quasi-epilogue:

> *Aux grands mauxs les grands remèdes.*
> Phillip is now a married man; and curious to relate, his wife bears a striking resemblance to the young lady whose portrait he purchased for the price of six dozen of his own. And yet her name is not Angelica Thomson—nor even Dora.[6]

James's ironic French motto ("Great woes demand great remedies") mocks the importance given to marriage by the popular conventional epilogue. Moreover, the short after-history forces the reader to re-evaluate the story. First of all, it beclouds the clarity of Henrietta Congreve's "innocence": she was aware of Osborne's love for her but never informed him of her engagement and, in the portrait-naming incident, was capable of the coquettish fiction of "Dora Thomson." More important, however, is the view of character implied in this ironic after-history. Osborne's future marriage is determined by a willed consistency with his past. Having declared the purchased portrait to be that of his beloved, Osborne marries to prove the "truth" of this lie. The story is not major, nor is it one of James's best known, but in it the absolute conception of character which James espouses in "The Art of Fiction" is already discernible.

In his essay, James notes: "When one says picture one says of character, when one says novel one says of incident, and the terms may be transposed at will. What is character but the determination

of incident? What is incident but the illustration of character?"
(p. 839). In "Osborne's Revenge" James has just begun to realize
the implications his view had for fictional endings and the conventional after-history: if character so strongly determines incident, then what follows the main action, the protagonist's after-
history, is completely controlled by character as established in the
body of the fiction. Later in his career, James fully exploits his
assumptions at the ends of his novels. But, as he notes in his
prefaces, James found ending his fictions something of a problem
at this point in his development as a writer (see pp. 5, 15, 30, 31),
and he continued to experiment.

Many of James's early works end in noncommittal, sardonic
ways. His early fictions sometimes seem to end reluctantly and
even arbitrarily. Fairly typical is the ending of James's second
major novel, *The American*, significant in this context as an early
experiment with the scenic ending. After Newman has been rejected by Claire de Cintré and uncovered her family's secret, the
novel unrolls in a leisurely and somewhat disjointed manner, with
Newman making and unmaking decisions about whether to avenge
himself on the Bellegarde family by revealing its secret. It ends
with Newman's decision to burn his incriminating evidence in the
presence of his friend, Mrs. Tristram. The final passage contains
her evaluation of Newman's relationship with the Bellegardes, and
a final change of Newman's mind that *might* re-open the novel
were it not already ended:

> "It is most provoking," said Mrs. Tristram, "to hear you
> talk of the 'charge' when the charge is burnt up. Is it quite
> consumed?" she asked, glancing at the fire.
> Newman assured her that there was nothing left of it.
> "Well then," she said, "I suppose there is no harm in saying
> that you probably did not make them so very uncomfortable.
> My impression would be that since, as you say, they defied
> you, it was because they believed that, after all, you would
> never really come to the point. Their confidence, after counsel
> taken of each other, was not in their innocence, nor in their

talent for bluffing things off; it was in your remarkable good nature! You see they were right."

Newman instinctively turned to see if the little paper was in fact consumed; but there was nothing left of it.

(pp. 324-25)

In this last sentence, James coyly alludes to the novel's winding down. Newman's action suggests the possibility of continuing, but the final sentence gives a definite sense that the novel is ending: these are the last words on the last page of the novel, and just as there is nothing left of the note, there is nothing left of the novel.

For his next novel, *The Europeans*, James wrote an epilogue *fairly* like the conventional, popular sort. The novel's action ends with the European Felix winning the hand of the American Gertrude Wentworth, while Felix's sister—the consummately European Eugenia—fails to ensnare an upright American named Robert Acton and returns to Europe. The epilogue records in straight-faced fashion the marriage of Felix to Gertrude, tossing in the marriages of Charlotte Wentworth to Mr. Brand (Gertrude's former suitor), Clifford Wentworth to Lizzie Acton, and Robert Acton to a presumably bland and deliberately anonymous "nice young girl." In its celebration of multiple marriages, and particularly in its union of the European Felix with the descendant of Puritans, the epilogue seems to conform to the usual formula, even to the extent of promising a "new society" of sorts from the marriage of Felix and Gertrude. The epilogue adds, however, some complicating facts.

Felix and Gertrude are pronounced "imperturbably happy," but the adverb—less reassuring than the conventional "perfectly happy" or "blissfully happy"—implies disharmony, probably between the married couple and Boston society, for the epilogue also tells us that "they went far away" and that in Boston the echo of their gaiety was distant. None of this is very promising for the new society that should conventionally form around the bride and groom. Even less promising for the general enlivening of American stock is Acton's marriage to that "nice young girl" instead of to the lively and accomplished, though amoral, Eugenia.

The epilogue, despite its conventional surface, really serves to underscore questions raised in the body of the novel, questions Richard Poirier describes as concerning "what is lost and what is gained by the fact that this American society cannot finally include within itself a woman whose style resembles James's, even while James himself is often critical of the uses to which she puts it."[7] The ending contains some nice touches that nudge speculation along and make American readers less complacent than they might otherwise be, but it does not finally seem the inevitable end to this particular novel. All important issues have already been raised in the body of the novel and are, in fact, contained in the deliberate ambiguity of Eugenia's parting words to Felix immediately before the epilogue. Felix has just assured Eugenia that they will meet again in Europe and Eugenia replies: "I don't know. . . . Europe seems to me much larger than America." In the case of Eugenia's destination, a tiny principality, Europe is surely not physically larger; but how trustworthy is Eugenia's assessment of qualities for which "larger" stands—like tolerance, social ease, individuality? The later James—as we shall see—might well have ended the novel here before the epilogue, on an ambiguous statement for the reader to evaluate, rather than writing a clever but coy version of a nineteenth-century ending.

III

Around the time of *Washington Square*, James gained a firmer sense of his endings, as he began to perceive the wider implications of his views on fictional characterization. The one sentence conclusion to this brief but major novel performs all the functions of the nineteenth-century after-history, with none of the epilogue's formal features. As he leaves the Sloper house after being rejected by Catherine, Morris Townsend encounters Aunt Penniman, who, filled with sentimental expectations, assures him that Catherine will relent and accept him as a husband. As Morris dismisses Aunt Penniman as a foolish old woman, "Catherine, meanwhile, in the parlor, picking up her morsel of fancy-work, had seated herself with it again—for life, as it were." Catherine's action, rendered metaphoric by the "for life, as it were,"[8] makes after-history in the usual sense superfluous: by this point in his career, James has sufficient confidence in his delineation of character that, having brought Catherine thus far in her history, he is sure that everything (or, in Catherine's case, what little remains) may be inferred by the reader. He has, in effect, now begun to confidently redefine the "stable point" that ends the novel to mean not marriage, not death, but the character's full realization of his or her personal morality and determination to follow through the dictates of that morality. It is important to note that the character's morality may be questioned or even condemned by the reader, and that the characters' choices will often prove at odds with popular, conventional notions of a "happy ending" (like Aunt Penniman's hope for a belated marriage between Catherine and Morris). The dubious quality of the characters' crucial choices is especially marked in James's next major novel, *The Portrait of a Lady*, and, as the critical literature on James attests, in his three late novels.

The ending to *The Portrait of a Lady* combines the scenic ending (with which James experimented in *The American*), with the view of character implicit in the endings of "Osborne's Revenge" and *Washington Square*, and articulated in "The Art of Fiction," published, not surprisingly, three years after *Portrait*. The novel ends with a scene between Henrietta Stackpole and Caspar Goodwood after Caspar has failed to convince Isabel to leave Osmond and his victim-daughter Pansy and has instead shown her "a very straight path" back to Rome. Not insignificantly, the scene recalls that between Aunt Penniman and Morris: as he confidently recognizes his own characteristic form of ending, James now looks to his own earlier works for models of endings rather than to the works of earlier novelists.

Although forced to inform Goodwood that Isabel has returned to Rome, Henrietta still offers hope:

> Henrietta had come out, closing the door behind her, and now she put out her hand and grasped his arm.

"Look here, Mr. Goodwood," she said; "just you wait!"
On which he looked up at her.

This is a wonderful example of a close-up ending. To understand the novel, the reader must assess Henrietta's final words, perceive that Isabel will not return to Caspar however long he waits, and characterize Goodwood's look as chagrined or disbelieving. Only a very naive reader would fail to do so and finish the novel thinking that Isabel has returned to Rome to pack her things and elope with Caspar, though, as we shall see, many contemporary readers made this mistake. James gambles by ending his novel with a false indicator that must be rejected by the reader, but he is not gambling too wildly. For despite the tangle of issues raised by the ending, every careful reader of *The Portrait of a Lady* knows that Henrietta's words do not mean that Isabel will elope with Caspar, and knows this on the basis of Isabel's character as delineated in the novel.

Isabel's initial fascination for James, for the reader, and for Ralph Touchett, is her freedom and her potential. As James notes in *The Art of the Novel*, Isabel is a "vivid individual—vivid, so strangely, in spite of being still at large, not confined by the conditions, not engaged in the tangle, to which we look for much of the impress that constitutes an identity" (p. 47). Isabel becomes entangled through her actions in the novel and, by choosing her entanglements, creates her identity. Consistency and Isabel's native moral seriousness largely determine her final choice. As James advises his reader earlier in the novel:

> She was a person of great good faith, and if there was a great deal of folly in her wisdom, those who judge her severely may have the satisfaction of finding that, later, she became consistently wise only at the cost of an amount of folly which will constitute almost a direct appeal to charity.    (pp. 95-96)

The reader sensitive to his responsive role in the novel—as James wished his reader to be—cannot miss the network of expectations and judgmental roles James establishes in passages like this one.

To the ideal reader, Isabel's final rejection of Caspar shows her as consistently wise with a vengeance and accepting the consequences of the "folly" of entangling herself with Osmond which, by limiting her freedom, has established her identity.

James wants his reader to recognize a tangle of motivations in Isabel, some admirable, some foolish. Played against the hollow "freedom" claimed by Mrs. Touchett, Isabel's decision shows, first of all, a responsible moral nature: she accepts rather than shuns her duties, even unpleasant ones like returning to Osmond and keeping her promise to her stepdaughter, Pansy. Her refusal of Caspar similarly shows that she has learned, in the course of the novel, the limits of human freedom. When Caspar offers her unlimited freedom in a "very large" world, Isabel instinctively fears him, for all her claims to be "very independent" have led her into the small, restrictive world of her marriage. Moreover, Caspar urges upon Isabel a childish dependence uncongenial to her. " 'You don't know where to turn; turn to me!' " exclaims Goodwood (p. 543). But Isabel is not ready to exchange one cage for another. In a marriage with Osmond she of necessity works out her destiny, however unhappily, alone; the Isabel who pities rather than despises Madame Merle is too deep and too complex a woman simply to "cling" to Goodwood.

Though primarily inviting us to see Isabel's final decision as morally commendable, however, James also suggests that it is weak, foolish, and even rather perverse. Early in the novel, the pragmatic Henrietta Stackpole and Mrs. Touchett both predict Isabel's fate in terms which underscore its wastefulness. Henrietta maintains that Isabel will marry some "horrid" European and make "some great mistake" (p. 153), an apt description of her marriage to Osmond, despite his American birth. And Mrs. Touchett, when she hears that Osmond has a daughter, jokingly but prophetically observes, "we shall have Isabel arriving at the conviction that her mission in life is to prove that a stepmother may sacrifice herself" (p. 255). Although their straightforward common sense renders Mrs. Touchett and Henrietta less morally complex and interesting than Isabel, it similarly, and quite sensibly, dictates against her return to Osmond. But for Isabel, to pursue the pragmatic course they advise would too strongly deviate from the "heroic line" she characteristically pursues.

Although well within the bounds of a decent pursuit of happiness, a decision to leave Osmond would jar with Isabel's lofty views of herself and of fair moral conduct. Significantly, her decision to preserve her marriage conforms to the latest of her many theories about moral conduct, one engendered in her last conversation with Osmond before leaving Rome: to return to Rome, to resume her married state, will affirm "something sacred and precious—the observance of a magnificent form," and this stirs "her passion for justice" (p. 496). The line between Isabel's honest desire to "accept one's deeds" (p. 450), and Osmond's trickily "sincere" "wish to preserve appearances" (p. 496), blurs uncomfortably at the end of the novel; Isabel acts nobly but almost cynically and hypocritically in accepting her marriage as a "determining act."

James prepares for this negative reading of Isabel's decision early in the novel, though the preparations may only be discernible retrospectively or upon rereading. In one of her first conversations with Ralph, Isabel naively declares her willingness to suffer as a means to knowledge (p. 45); James's narration confirms Isabel's romantic notions of suffering several times, as in the following comment:

> Sometimes she went so far as to wish that she should find herself some day in a difficult position, so that she might have the pleasure of being as heroic as the occasion demanded.
>
> (p. 48)

Similarly, when Isabel refuses Lord Warburton, she tells him that she cannot marry him because she cannot escape her "fate": " 'I can't escape unhappiness. . . . In marrying you, I shall be trying to' " (p. 122). Her return to Osmond perversely, but certainly, seals this self-chosen "fate." Indeed, aspects of Isabel's character anticipate later and more negative Jamesian protagonists, like Marcher in "The Beast in the Jungle." And, like Osborne in "Osborne's Revenge," Isabel works hard to predict her "fate" and then to *will* her future development into accordance with it.

Finally, as has been generally recognized despite James's reticence, the novel suggests that Isabel rejects Caspar and returns to Osmond from a fear of physical, sexual closeness. The burly Warburton inspires a "certain fear" in Isabel, undefined but probably sexual (p. 76). The "stiff," "firm" Caspar Goodwood noticeably affects Isabel at all their interviews (he is the only character to make her cry), and finally, through over-aggressiveness, precipitates her flight back to Osmond, who presumably does not offer "lightning" kisses. The language of the final scene intensifies the novel's latent sense of Isabel's sexual anxieties: she "scents" Caspar's idea and resents his "pressing her close" by his suggestion of flight (p. 542); then, when "it was as if he were pressing something that hurt her," and kisses her, "She never looked about her; she only darted away from the spot" (pp. 543, 544).

At the end of *The Portrait of a Lady*, then, James suggests a number of contexts in which to judge Isabel's return to Osmond. He simultaneously approves her acceptance of her responsibilities and limitations, loves her despite her folly, reminds us that she foolishly throws away her young life, and suggests that frigidity may be one of her hidden motivations. James refuses to oversimplify Isabel's complex act and the mixture of laudable and suspect motives behind it. Rather, he demands that readers retrospectively appreciate Isabel's development and use the knowledge thus derived to understand Henrietta's ambiguous final words properly. He refuses both to make the ending saccharine and to make interpretation an easy, automatic process for his reader.


IV


In the notebooks kept during the writing of *The Portrait of a Lady*, James anticipated that the ending—with its lack of an after-history of Isabel to satisfy reader expectations—would arouse criticism.

He seems to have felt that contemporary readers were not ready for endings that seemed unresolved and confusing:

> The obvious criticism of course will be that it is not finished— that I have not seen the heroine to the end of her situation— that I have left her *en l'air*.—This is both true and false. The *whole* of anything is never told; you can only take what groups together.[9]

"What groups together" is Isabel's definition of her character and decision to live out her mistake, whether or not the reader approves of that definition and decision. As an older James noted in his preface to the New York edition, *The Portrait of a Lady* is essentially a novel in which character supersedes plot; his point supports mine that the ending, in the 1881 edition, is confrontational in its relationship with the reader. It seeks to compel the reader's appreciation of character (both Isabel's and Henrietta's), by forcing the reader to become the ideal, attentive reader James desired or else to misread the novel completely.

The notebook entries confirm that James intended the reader to undergo the evaluative process I have indicated; he tells us that Caspar, at novel's end, is to see "Henrietta who has the last word— utters the last line of the story: a characteristic characterization of Isabel" (p. 18). Oddly, however, James gives support to an alternative reading in his revision of *The Portrait of a Lady* for the New York edition. In the revised version, Henrietta's final words are her "characteristic characterization" of *Caspar*, not Isabel:

> Henrietta had come out, closing the door behind her, and now she put out her hand and grasped his arm. "Look here, Mr. Goodwood," she said; "just you wait!"
> On which he looked up at her—but only to guess, from her face, with a revulsion, that she simply meant he was young. She stood shining at him with that cheap comfort, and it added, on the spot, thirty years to his life. She walked him

away with her, however, as if she had given him now the key to patience.

Less ambiguous than the original, and less demanding of the reader, the revision also seems flatter. We can only guess why James made the change. Most probably, the revision was a concession to mis-readings of the original ending, misreadings more common and less willful in James's day than in ours.

Since the publication of James's notebooks and F. O. Matthies-sen's *Henry James: The Major Phase* (New York: Oxford Univ. Press, 1944), the accepted interpretation of the ending to *The Portrait of a Lady* rejects the possibility that Henrietta's final words indicate Caspar's ultimate success and sees Isabel's dismissal of Caspar as final. Earlier reviewers and critics, however, often wildly misread the ending; the misreadings, in fact, go far toward ex-plaining James's characteristic complaints about the rarity of the ideal, attentive reader. All James's important contemporary re-viewers recognized that the ending to *Portrait*, like many of James's endings, deviates from the expectations established by endings to most nineteenth-century novels. Many condemned him for his ambiguity or "perversity." Not unrepresentative are the com-ments of the reviewer for *Spectator*:

> That he always likes to end his tales with a failure of anything like the old poetic justice, we all know. That perplexing re-lations should ravel themselves, rather then [sic] unravel themselves . . . is one of Mr. Henry James's canons of art. . . . He ends his *Portrait of a Lady*, if we do not wholly misinterpret the rather covert, not to say almost cowardly, hints of his last page, by calmly indicating that this ideal lady of his, whose belief in purity has done so much to alienate her from her husband . . . saw a "straight path" to a liaison with her rejected lover.[10]

Except for the reviewers for the *Atlantic Monthly* (which published *Portrait* in serial form) and *Galaxy*, most of the popular reviewers similarly misread the novel and its ending.

In mid-career, as demonstrated by the scornful rhetoric of "The Art of Fiction," James no doubt enjoyed tweaking the noses of unperceptive critics. He realized that the scenic ending—unpopular though it was—emphasized his role as fictional innovator. Moreover, he saw his endings as justified by his conception of character, which, in early reviews, is often condemned along with his way of ending a novel. Later in his career, as "the Master" composing his New York edition, James may have mellowed and softened toward wayward readers: he may have decided to set the record straight on Isabel's decision at the end of *Portrait*. It is also possible that, by the end of his career, he had so refined (or reduced) his audience that affronts to the reader who loved "happy endings" were no longer in order, and the flamboyant emphasis given by the original ending to the theory that character determines incident (and after-history) no longer necessary. At any rate, the revision brings into sharper focus the similarity I noted earlier between Morris Townsend's and Aunt Penniman's final scene in *Washington Square* and the end of *Portrait*, a similarity that, as I have said, shows James substituting his own private conventions for received popular conventions like the epilogue.

## V

In *The Ambassadors*, James beautifully achieves his "search for form" as the controlling principle of the ending, simultaneously building on his achievement thus far. The scenic ending, by now, and to the end of James's career, the characteristic form of Jamesian ending, could not possibly be dismissed (as James polemically dismissed epilogues) as "appended paragraphs." In fact, the last two parts of its twelve-part structure are the very heart of *The Ambassadors* and have appropriately received lavish attention from critics.

The final scene of the novel records Strether's last meeting with Maria Gostrey before returning to America and his rejection of a possible life with her as being too clearly a "gain" from his handling of Chad, which has broken off his Woolett engagement to Mrs. Newsome. The ending rests on one of the most basic of devices to give a sense that the work is ending—circularity (with some parallelism at work as well). In this scene, and in that which immediately precedes it (Strether's final talk with Chad before his departure), "it was as if his last day were oddly copying his first" (p. 362): as the text reminds us, encounters balance earlier encounters, and characters explicitly recall circumstances and situations from the initial meetings in Europe that began the novel.

The device is, however, a more complicated thematic device as well. In the first meeting between Strether and Maria, which opens the novel, Maria leads the way and gives Strether guidance. As Strether comes to realize in Paris: "He could toddle alone . . . it having been but the day before yesterday that he sat at her feet and held on by her garment and was fed by her hand" (pp. 207-08). In their final conversation, *Strether* sees most clearly, anticipates meanings, and verbally leads the way. Most significantly, he leads the way to a statement of the morality that prevents their marriage, a marriage which would have given *The Ambassadors* an entirely happy, conventional, and popular ending.

Strether begins by rejecting Maria's offer of her home as haven, a covert offer of herself in marriage. In doing so, he expands upon the ironic self-awareness that has (in the passage previously quoted) caused him to image himself as an infant. Candidly but with some embarrassment and sadness, Strether responds:

> "It [Maria's civilized, pleasant home] wouldn't give me—that would be the trouble—what it will, no doubt, still give you. I'm not," he explained, leaning back in his chair, but with his eyes on a small ripe, round melon—"in real harmony with what surrounds me. You *are*. I take it too hard. You don't. It makes—that's what it comes to in the end—a fool of me." (p. 371)

Attractive as his European experience has been, Strether recognizes that the European attitude is only a part of himself: he takes things "too hard," but he must accept himself as he is. Thus, although "It was awkward, it was almost stupid, not to seem to prize such things" as Maria's home and Maria herself, Strether finally meets her offer by renouncing it squarely and giving her his reason, a reason immediately clear to Maria though she pretends not to see it, stalling for time (p. 374).

Strether points out that he must go " 'To be right. . . . Not, out of the whole affair, to have got anything for myself' " (p. 375). He tells Maria: " 'you yourself would be the first to want me [to be right]' " (p. 375), recalling, no doubt, Maria's reason for leaving Paris for Mentone, thereby not interfering between Strether and Madame de Vionnet: "she had not interfered on any chance . . . that she might interfere to her profit" (p. 357). If, as Maria teases and many readers complain, Strether looks too hard for moral subtleties and acts rigidly, his actions, like Maria's stay in Mentone, are decided on "private, passionate lines, played strictly fair" (p. 358). In a world of moral relativities and ambiguities—such as Strether's has become with the wedding of his Parisian consciousness to his Woolett sense of things—the word "private" counts most. Maria, "Honest and fine . . . couldn't [greatly] pretend she didn't see it" (p. 375); she gently capitulates to the essence of what she loves in the man—the ability to make fine moral and aesthetic distinctions others would regard as unimportant, an ability broadened rather than compromised by his Parisian experience.

The novel fittingly ends with what David Lodge calls "the language of heightened cliché."[11] Strether concludes with the words, " 'Then there we are!' " an idiom used at many other points in the novel, when "where he was" was obscure to Strether even when, in his dealings with little Bilham and Miss Barrace, Chad and Marie de Vionnet, he most *thought* he knew. The rightness of his final pronouncement (and Maria's frank accession to it) contrasts vividly with the equivocating, misunderstood, or (on Strether's part) dogged uses of the expression earlier in the novel.

In a discussion with little Bilham, for example, Strether decides that the relationship between Chad and Madame de Vionnet is "virtuous"; therefore, "he knew, once more . . . where he was, and . . . he meant to stay there" (pp. 172-73). He accordingly begins to recite Madame de Vionnet's virtues "as if not for little Bilham's benefit alone," and concludes by summarizing her problematic relationship with Chad in this way:

> "I understand what a relation with such a woman—what such a high, fine friendship—may be. It can't be vulgar or coarse, anyway—and that's the point. . . . As to *how* it has so wonderfully worked [to improve Chad]—is not a thing I pretend to understand. I've to take it as I find it. There he is."
>
> (p. 173)

In bemused agreement, little Bilham echoes Strether's tag, " 'There he is!' " At times, Maria also teases Strether with the expression, which, as he often uses it, prissily aims at exactness and expresses his mental stolidity:

> "Dear old Paris," she seemed to explain. But there was more, and, with one of her turns, she risked it. . . . "You," she declared, "have been a good bit of it."
>
> He sat massive. "A good bit of what, ma'am?"
>
> "Why, of the wonderful consciousness of our friend here [Chad]. You've helped too, in your way, to float him to where he is."
>
> "And where the devil *is* he?"
>
> She passed it on with a laugh. "Where the devil, Strether, are you?"    (p. 84)

At the end of the novel, in his final conversation with Maria, Strether no longer mechanically takes stock of his experiences or blindly determines "where he meant to stay." He responds as he feels he must to the flow of events. Mentally lively and emotionally agile, he is Maria's equal in this conversation, *without* denying his innate moral seriousness. The contrast supports the reading of the novel that finds Strether, at novel's end, a more mature, sensitive, self-aware man than he had earlier been. "Where he is" at novel's end is obscure neither to Strether, nor, once the concordances between the ending and body of the novel have been perceived, to the reader, despite some readers' feelings that he ought to be somewhere else—for instance, preparing to stay in Paris and marry Maria.

James achieves closure in *The Ambassadors* and justifies Strether's decision to leave Paris not just in the final conversation between Strether and Maria, but also in the last talk that Strether has with Chad. Chad's actions and attitudes in this scene convince Strether that Chad sees him as aging, dependent, and rather fragile. Chad's actions confirm for Strether certain impressions of himself and of Chad's essential "restlessness," so dangerous for Madame de Vionnet. In repeatedly denying that he has "tired" of her, Chad indicates that he has entertained the possibility of tiring of her and will eventually do so. Several hundred pages into the after-history of the novel, Chad will become its villain; he will—as Strether senses—"take the cultural money and run."[12] Given this outcome to the affair between Chad and Madame de Vionnet, neither Strether nor James can afford to compromise Strether by having him remain in Paris; they would thereby seem partly to excuse Chad's later actions. Strether himself perceives the connections between Chad's future conduct and his need to leave Paris; on the way to visit Chad, he realizes: "He must do both things: he must see Chad, but he must go. The more he thought of the former of these duties, the more he felt himself making a subject of insistence of the latter" (p. 362).

In his final scene with Maria, Strether is alternately sad and proud, serious and charming. The dialogue of that scene, by which Strether convinces Maria that he is right, is perhaps also intended to convince the reader that a conventional "happy ending" could not be the right ending for *The Ambassadors*. There is affirmation in the ending to *The Ambassadors*, but not the glib affirmation of "marriages, babies, millions"; rather, James affirms the aesthetic form of his novel and his consistent, honest portrait of Strether, and Strether affirms his knowledge of himself, a self less urbane than he might have been, than he might even wish to be. As Strether realizes during his last conversation with Chad, and expresses in his favorite idiom, " 'No one in the world, I imagine, was ever so portentously solemn. There I am,' he added with another sigh, as if weary enough, on occasion, of this truth. 'I was made so.' " (p. 368). As in *The Portrait of a Lady*, a correct interpretation of the ending can be reached only by drawing the correct inferences about Strether's character through the perception of circularity and parallelism, and by retrospectively confirming these inferences at the end of the novel.

Early and influential critics of the novel, like F. R. Leavis, F. O. Matthiessen, and Yvor Winters, saw either weakness or perversity on Strether's or James's part in the ending to *The Ambassadors*.[13] Matthiessen and, even more strongly, Winters, note a resurgence of Strether's Puritanism at the end of the novel, a resurgence that negates all that Strether has supposedly gained while in Paris. More recent critics, like Frederick Crews, Charles Samuels, and David Lodge, have tended—as I do—to read the ending as affirmative, though they do so in different contexts and with some substantive differences in interpretation.[14] As in the case of *The Portrait of a Lady*, the turnabout in critical opinion is striking.

The contributions of Leavis, Matthiessen, and Winters to our understanding of James' writings has been immense. But in interpreting the ending of *The Ambassadors*, they stubbornly—and, I think, incorrectly—refuse to accept the ending as James wrote it. Newer interpretations are not always more nearly correct than older ones, but in this case I think they are. The new consensus about the ending to *The Ambassadors* indicates recent tolerance for unhappy endings, coupled with a willingness to assume that authors know what they are about during closure, unless definitive evidence to the contrary exists. Among other things, James bequeaths later novelists readers' confidence in the formal integrity of novels and in the appropriateness of the ending chosen by the author. This confidence is not always warranted, but, in the case of *The Ambassadors*, it is. In his final novel, *The Golden Bowl*, James puts his readers' good will to the test and—as many readers complain—he comes close to making the test too hard.

# SEVEN

## Gesture and the Ending of
## *The Golden Bowl*

### I

In his preface to "The Lesson of the Master," James defines his reader's ideal relationship to the text: "The reader is, on the evidence, left to conclude" (p. 229). James presents the reader of *The Golden Bowl*, however, with theories of interpretation hostile to the usual process of reaching firm conclusions. Consider, for example, an idea that enters Maggie's mind during the card game at Fawns, one never discredited in the novel:

> the full significance . . . [of a group of people interacting] could be no more after all than a matter of interpretation, differing always for a different interpreter.[1]

James's awareness of a principle so inimical to traditional critical procedures accounts in part for the astoundingly diverse interpretations critics have reached of *The Golden Bowl*.

James allows for "matter[s] of interpretation, differing always for a different interpreter," by providing an abundance (some say an over-abundance), of connections in the novel and by refusing to assume the interpretive authority that masters of nineteenth-century fiction like Hawthorne, Eliot, and Tolstoy exercise throughout their novels, and especially at their ends. James declines to gloss the final action of *The Golden Bowl* or to have Maggie gloss it for him. He declines even to designate clearly which of the motifs established in the novel should take priority in interpreting the final scene: "The reader is, on the evidence, left to conclude." The ending of *The Golden Bowl* is a good example of the scenic close-up ending, in its most extreme form.

A great deal of weight in the interpretation of *The Golden Bowl* must fall on its ending: it is not only the final scene in the novel, and thus the reader's final view of characters and action, but also the "end," or goal, of Maggie's efforts. Throughout the second half of the novel, she covertly strives to win back the Prince and to separate Amerigo and Charlotte without any disruption of her father's marriage or of her own. The Ververs' final visit marks the "success" of her actions. The next to last chapter of the novel adds additional importance to the final scene: both Maggie and Amerigo ask each other to "wait" to re-establish their relationship until the Ververs have departed. The future of this marriage—and of the two major characters in the novel—is thus to be decided in the final pages.

The characters' conduct during the visit is rigid, controlled, and, finally, evasive of the basic issues between them in just the way they intend it to be. When the Ververs have left, Maggie anxiously waits for the Prince to join her. His conduct in the final scene will inform her whether the "sacrifice" of her father and the elaborate performance she has given were worthwhile. In the monetary imagery typical of the novel, Maggie has paid a price for Amerigo, and his next actions will determine whether the price was too high. After depositing the Principino in his nursery, the Prince returns, and the final scene of the novel, which I will quote in full, unrolls:

> He opened the door however at last—he hadn't been away ten minutes; and then with her sight of him renewed to intensity she seemed to have a view of the number. His presence alone, as he paused to look at her, somehow made it the highest, and even before he had spoken she had begun to be paid in full. With that consciousness in fact an extraordinary thing occurred; the assurance of her safety so making her terror drop that already within the minute it had been changed to concern for his own anxiety, for everything that was deep in his being and everything that was fair in his face. So far as seeing that she was "paid" went he might have been holding out the money-bag for her to come and take it. But what instantly rose for her between the act and her acceptance was the sense that she must strike him as waiting for a confession. This in turn charged her with a new horror: if *that* was her proper payment she would go without money. His acknowl-

edgement hung there, too monstrously, at the expense of
Charlotte, before whose mastery of the greater style she had
just been standing dazzled. All she now knew accordingly was
that she should be ashamed to listen to the uttered word; all,
that is, but that she might dispose of it on the spot for ever.

"Isn't she too splendid?" she simply said, offering it to
explain and to finish.

"Oh splendid!" With which he came over to her.

"That's our help, you see," she added—to point further
her moral.

It kept him before her therefore, taking in—or trying to—
what she so wonderfully gave. He tried, too clearly, to please
her—to meet her in her own way; but with the result only
that, close to her, her face kept before him, his hands holding
her shoulders, his whole act enclosing her, he presently
echoed: " 'See'? I see nothing but *you*." And the truth of it
had with this force after a moment so strangely lighted his
eyes that as for pity and dread of them she buried her own
in his breast.     (XXIV, pp. 367-69)

Recognizing the importance of its ending, critics of the novel
have invariably offered readings of the final scene suitable to their
overall interpretations. Major critics like F. R. Leavis, F. O. Matthiessen, R. P. Blackmur, and Quentin Anderson emphasize Maggie's destructive role and her selfish manipulation of the other
characters. Matthiessen especially stresses the "obscene" way that
Adam Verver and his daughter view Charlotte and Amerigo as
"good things," as "concrete attestations of a rare power of pur-
chase" (*Bowl* XXIV, p. 360). Blackmur sees the final embrace
between Maggie and Amerigo as that of "a shade embracing a
shade," and Anderson finds the embrace an ominous one by which
"the genitally centered consciousness is banished."[2]

Dissenting from these major views in a short but influential
study, Frederick Crews praises Maggie's ability to use social mores
constructively to save her father's marriage and her own, and notes
Christian vocabulary associated with Maggie in the second half of

the novel. Despite his relatively favorable view of Maggie, however, Crews concludes that "*The Golden Bowl* ends, not on a note
of moral finality which James has carefully trained one of his
characters to strike, but rather on the same authentic dissonance,
the perpetual clash of interests, with which the novel began."[3]
Developing Crews' hints about Christian vocabulary into a more
inclusive theory, Dorothea Krook more strongly praises Maggie
and sees the ending as the consummation of Maggie's Christian
redemptive love, with the final action James's "supreme expression
of the moral beauty of his heroine."[4]

Recent critics overwhelmingly share Crews' emphasis on the
absence of "moral finality" in the novel. Some, continuing a long
tradition of disliking *The Golden Bowl* as the epitome of James's
later style, consider the novel seriously flawed by its ambiguities.[5]
Others, holding the majority view that it is an exciting and important novel, have interpreted its ambiguity of moral statement
as James's final epistemology. Thus, Sallie Sears in *The Negative
Imagination* maintains that James wishes the reader's sympathies
to be radically divided throughout the novel, and therefore builds
in dual reactions to all the action, including the morality of
Maggie's actions and the meaning of the final scene.[6] Thus, too,
Ruth B. Yeazell sees the world of *The Golden Bowl* as one of
epistemological uncertainty, with language that accommodates that
uncertainty through ambiguity (as, in Yeazell's view, Maggie's
does) being the most admirable, though not "purely" admirable
or morally transcendent as Krook would have it.[7]

These last two critics—Sears and Yeazell—define as fully as
possible the precise kind of ambiguity existing at the end of *The
Golden Bowl*: a controlled ambiguity of moral judgments on the
characters, despite the book's intense involvement with moral issues. They correctly and gracefully rescue James from charges that
the ending is hopelessly and pointlessly ambiguous and confirm
that James was self-aware during the closural process. Moreover,
they clear the ground for discussion of the novel and its ending
free from subjective and therefore conflicting moral judgments on

the characters. For although interpretations of the ending to *The Golden Bowl* have been numerous, they have been partial. In studies with broader focuses, critics have been unable to devote full attention to the ending and its links to the body of the novel. Moreover, in relying on the highly ambiguous dialogue of the final scene for interpretation, critics have reached radically different conclusions. The ending—largely because of its ambiguous dialogue—is indeed cryptic. But an interpretation that recognizes parallelism as the novel's closural pattern and explores concordances between the ending and the body of the novel—especially gestural patterns that convey to the reader feelings suppressed by the characters in conversation—can coherently interpret the ending of *The Golden Bowl* and illuminate the shape and meaning of the novel. James's characteristic comparison of his narrative techniques to those of the playwright or dramatist suggests the importance of gesture in the determination of meaning and the possibility of dramatic tension between what the characters say and what they feel.

## II

As a number of critics have recognized, relationships in *The Golden Bowl* may be viewed as a series of shifting balances among the four major characters. All of the action comes from shifting balances: Maggie's marriage determines the need for Verver's marriage, and the tight links between Maggie and Verver create the realignment of Charlotte and Amerigo. Moreover, Maggie's perception that Charlotte and Amerigo are acting in concert, are "treating" her identically, initiates the second half of the novel and leads to the Ververs' banishment to America. Similarly, Charlotte's recognition that the Prince has ceased to act in unison with her and is synchronizing his actions with Maggie's convinces her that she has lost him and should make a graceful exit. Balance controls the relationships among the four major characters, and the gestures in the final scene—Amerigo's grasping of Maggie's shoulders and Maggie's resting her head on his breast, burying her eyes—are important physical signals in the mental struggle between the two central characters.

Amerigo first perceives that something is wrong—that Maggie is troubled—when a projected trip abroad by Maggie and her father (which would leave Charlotte and Amerigo alone together) is canceled at a dinner party. As they return home, Amerigo decides to employ his considerable charm and physical appeal to smooth things over and avoid any possible trouble, much as he had earlier, and more successfully, done after his return from Gloucester (see XXIII, p. 378 and XXIV, pp. 28-29). Accordingly, he puts his arm around Maggie,

> and drew her close—indulged in the demonstration, the long firm embrace by his single arm, the infinite pressure of her whole person to his own, that such opportunities had so often suggested and prescribed.     (XXIV, pp. 55-56)

Aware of being "exquisitely solicited," Maggie nonetheless feels that "whatever he might do she mustn't be irresponsible." She then debates whether to accept Amerigo's physical overture or to postpone reconciliation:

> Yes, she was in his exerted grasp, and she knew what that was; but she was at the same time in the grasp of her conceived responsibility, and the extraordinary thing was that of the two intensities the second was presently to become the sharper. . . . She should have but to lay her head back on his shoulder with a certain movement to make it definite for him that she didn't resist.     (XXIV, pp. 56-57)

She refuses, however, to make the gesture and leaves incomplete the physical code they have developed for Amerigo's mastery and Maggie's submission. The incident signals the development of her will and marks an epoch in their relationship.

The remainder of the chapter in which this incident occurs underscores the importance of the gestural code. Instead of agreeing to go abroad with her father, Maggie proposes that Amerigo and

Verver go instead. The Prince agrees, but informs Maggie that he will ask Charlotte to propose the journey to Verver. In a section that recounts Maggie's thoughts, she perceives this as a slight defeat and feels that "It was almost as if—in the strangest way in the world—he were paying her back by the production of a small pang, that of a new uneasiness, for the way she had slipped from him during their drive" (XXIV, p. 67; see also p. 139, when Maggie again broods on the incident). The physical gestures that reappear in the final scene thus come to signify psychological warfare between husband and wife: Maggie's resting her head on the Prince's chest becomes a signal of nonresistance, her drawing apart a sign of independence and will. If we apply this code to the final scene, the result indicates a resurgence of the Prince's influence and Maggie's submission to his charm.

The completed physical action in the final scene needs, however, some further glossing. For although the Prince begins by resenting Maggie's resistance, he ends by falling more firmly in love with her because of it. Both Maggie and Charlotte realize what Fanny Assingham verbalizes: in revealing the hidden depths of her nature, Maggie enchants the Prince. As Fanny urges upon Maggie, one fact becomes increasingly clear: "The fact that your husband has never, never, never. . . been half so interested in you as now" (XXIV, p. 178). The Prince confirms this several times, and, in the final scene, utters in all sincerity, "I see nothing but *you*." Since this devotion from the Prince is, in fact, Maggie's goal, her troubled reaction in the last paragraph is problematic: we need to explain *why* Maggie is troubled, and what, besides herself, Maggie would like the Prince to "see."

### III

In lowering her head, Maggie makes the gesture of nonresistance she has restrained herself from making earlier. But in doing so, she risks lessening the interest she has recently aroused in the Prince. The princess-like conduct that has re-won Amerigo necessitates subsequent actions of which Maggie may not be capable.

She has, in earlier scenes, *forced* herself not to surrender, at least until she senses that the Prince truly desires her:

> She was keeping her head for a reason, for a cause. . . . A single touch from him—oh she should know it in case of its coming!—any brush of his hand, of his lips, of his voice, inspired by recognition of her probable interest as distinct from pity for her virtual gloom, would hand her over to him bound hand and foot. . . . She could keep it up with a change in sight, but she couldn't keep it up for ever. . . .
>
> (XXIV, pp. 141-42)

Maggie's image of being "handed over" "bound hand and foot" at a sign of authentic sexual interest shows her reluctance to assume mastery in their relationship. It indicates the difficulty of her position once she perceives that being of "interest" to the Prince grows directly from her assertion of power.

In the final scene, sensing Amerigo's now genuine involvement with her as woman and mate, Maggie stops "keeping it up," embraces Amerigo, and, in a sense, restores equal power in their relationship to him. He, has, however, misused power before. Unsure of whether he has changed—and no doubt hoping that he has—Maggie probes his feelings in the guarded dialogue about Charlotte, carefully gauging both what Amerigo says and how he looks while saying it. In this dialogue, Maggie shows compassion for her husband's guilt and for Charlotte's suffering, as well as an instinct for the preservation of her marriage, by continuing to avoid the explicit mention of adultery. Compassion for Charlotte is, not insignificantly, all on Maggie's part in this scene, suggesting that one of the things the Prince should "see," in addition to Maggie, is the effect of his conduct on others.

The "pity and dread" that prompt Maggie to bury her eyes are difficult to explain and, indeed, demand several explanations. At one level, Maggie responds to the Prince's "strangely lighted eyes" as Isabel Archer responds to Caspar Goodwood's kiss, which "was like a flash of lightning." The Jamesian heroine reacts ambivalently to sexuality, and the language and situation in this scene are sexually charged. Maggie recognizes and capitulates to the Prince's sexual charm but fears her loss of self, and experiences passion only with ambivalence. Hiding her eyes expresses gesturally her reluctance to acknowledge sexual desire for Amerigo.

The words "pity and dread" also echo, and I think deliberately echo, Aristotle's use in his *Poetics* of the words "pity and fear" when discussing audience reaction to Sophocles' *Oedipus Rex*. Both *Oedipus Rex* and *The Golden Bowl* play upon "seeing" as "knowing." The verbal echo is also appropriate given the somewhat incestuous relationship of Maggie and her father, and that of Charlotte and Amerigo. In Sophocles' tragedy, however, Oedipus acts self-destructively to bring everything to light and to have the truth fully stated; Maggie, on the other hand, acts consistently to avoid overt recognition and statement of the "incestuous" links between her husband and her father's wife. To pursue the revelation of incest (like Oedipus) is disastrous; to avoid positive knowledge (like Maggie) is morally ambiguous, but emotionally sound. Maggie thus acts less heroically, but more humanly, than Oedipus, and appropriately buries her eyes rather than blinding them.

In terms of the metaphoric structure of *The Golden Bowl*, Maggie ends as she began her investigation of Amerigo's conduct and nature, by choosing to proceed with "bandaged eyes"—eyes willing to forego the absolute truth about him in favor of a salvaged relationship with him. For the "pity and dread" in Maggie's eyes finally refer to the Prince himself: she pities and dreads the qualities she is forced to identify in him, to which, having sacrificed her father to regain Amerigo, she has attributed ultimate value. If we follow through the verbal analogy with Aristotle, Maggie's avoidance of clarifying explanations prevents the ending from being cathartic: the persistence of the Prince as amoral but eminently desirable necessitates the continuance, rather than the purgation, of pity and dread. The key lines in this connection are those that reveal Maggie's perception, immediately before her gesture of surrender, that "He tried, too clearly, to please her—to meet her in her own way." The lines refer to a crucial characteristic of the Prince: his absolute desire to please others—the chief source of his charm and polish, but simultaneously the source of his amorality and inability to develop an authentic moral sense.

The narrator of *The Golden Bowl* and every character in it (including Amerigo himself) recognize that his desire to please is an essential element in the Prince's nature. Their reactions to the quality become one method of moral characterization in the novel. Amerigo acknowledges his flaw to Fanny Assingham, and in so doing reveals that his amorality is eminently good natured:

> "I'm excellent, I really think, all round—except that I'm stupid. I can do pretty well anything I see. But I've got to see it first. . . . I don't in the least mind its having to be shown me—in fact I like that better." (XXIII, p. 30)

It is this yielding to the suggestions of others that prompts Amerigo to follow Charlotte's lead when she suggests that the logical outcome of their situation is adultery. Charlotte knows the Prince at least as well as he knows himself, but she places a favorable interpretation on his qualities. As Charlotte spins out verbal lures for greater intimacy on the grounds that they have done everything to avoid such intimacy, the Prince remains silent. Charlotte's gloss on his silence measures both her adoration of the Prince and her moral density in matters that concern him:

> She was to remember not a little meanwhile the particular prolonged silent look with which the Prince had met her allusion to these primary efforts at escape. She was inwardly to dwell on the element of the unuttered that her tone had caused to play up into his irresistible eyes. . . . He had been sufficiently off his guard to show some little wonder as to their having plotted so very hard against their destiny, and she knew well enough of course what in this connection was at the bottom of his thought, and what would have sounded out more or less if he hadn't happily saved himself from words. All men were brutes enough to catch when they might at such chances for dissent—for all the good it really did them; but the Prince's distinction was in being one of the few who

could check himself before acting on the impulse. This, obviously, was what counted in a man as delicacy.

(XXIII, pp. 289-90)

In a section which recounts Adam Verver's thoughts, the
American muses on the question of what makes his new son-in-
law so easy to live with and recalls his favorite solution. Contact
with Amerigo "was a contact with practically yielding lines and
curved surfaces. 'You're round, my boy,' he had said—'you're *all*,
you're variously and inexhaustibly round, when you might, by
all the chances, have been abominably square' " (XXIII, pp. 137-
38). The Prince's roundness and polished surface appeal to Verver's
high aesthetic sense as absolutely as the golden bowl itself would.
At the end of the same paragraph, the narrator, by interpreting
the same quality in an unflattering way, indicates the flaw both
in Amerigo and in Verver's aestheticism:

The young man, in other words, unconfusedly smiled—
though indeed as if assenting, from principle and habit, to
more than he understood. He liked all signs that things were
well, but he cared rather less *why* they were.

(XXIII, pp. 138-39)

Maggie's perception in the final paragraph of the novel that "He
tried, too clearly, to please her—to meet her in her own way," is
a more ambivalent perception than those of the other characters.
In the final scene, by evaluating his manner as well as his words,
she realizes that Amerigo's chief glory—his good nature and willingness to please—is the manifestation of his moral defects. Therefore, she feels "pity and dread" in not resisting Amerigo's charm.

## IV

Dorothea Krook interprets the ending of the novel as one in which
the Prince recognizes the higher worth of Maggie's moral standards
and surrenders his previously held aesthetic criteria to Maggie's
loftier moral ones. The final scene suggests, however, the opposite.

In the final meeting with her father and his wife, Maggie "had just been standing dazzled" before Charlotte's mastery of the "greater style," a style that preserves impeccable appearances, but belies both moral facts and the emotional torture felt by Charlotte in leaving Amerigo. Moreover, once Maggie is sure that the Prince is "worth" the sacrifice of her father—his worth depending upon his attraction to and attractiveness for her—she becomes concerned "for everything that was deep in his being and everything that was fair in his face." The conjunction of things "deep" in Amerigo's being and "fair" in his face is a peculiar one, things "deep" being moral or emotional, things "fair," superficially physical. Belonging to Maggie, as all perceptions in the final scene belong to her, it underscores weakness in her that should trouble any reader inclined (like Krook) to view her as a morally elevated, triumphant heroine.

Like the more obviously flawed Fanny and Charlotte, Maggie wants the Prince because he is "princely": self-assured, poised, well-mannered, charming, and yet (if we articulate what the women in the novel will not) pleasure-seeking, inadvertently pain-inflicting, and willing to take whatever moral line seems most expedient or comfortable. After all she has learned about Amerigo, Maggie should fully understand his nature and his inability to perceive moral issues. But she would probably *like* to believe that Amerigo has undergone a moral education, and she declines to face the truth about her husband until forced to by his conduct in the final scene. The Prince stands before Maggie "taking in— or trying to—" her message; he "tried, too clearly, to please her— to meet her in her own way." Maggie's interpolated perceptions emphasize that Amerigo is the same man he has always been: he meets Maggie in her own way, without any heightened moral consciousness, because he always meets people in their own way. In the final scene, his actions and words merely mimic those of his wife: as Maggie reluctantly realizes, they do not signal the transformation of the Prince or his insight into moral phenomena.

If, in fact, any character has authentically taken on the other's qualities, it is Maggie. She has re-won the Prince by adopting and by meeting his aesthetic standards—the maintenance of a polished, unruffled surface being, after all, the principle that controls Maggie's efforts in the second half of the novel. Now, her task accomplished, Maggie begins to measure the truth about the Prince and the "cost" of her victory to her own idealistic nature. Earlier in the novel, when speaking to Fanny, Maggie wants "The golden bowl—as it *was* to have been"—perfect and flawless (XXIV, p. 216). Here she learns (as Densher and Kate do at the end of *The Wings of the Dove*) that things "will never be as . . . [they] were." In the final scene, Maggie painfully realizes that a paradisal return to unconstrained intimacy with and untroubled adoration of the Prince is as impossible as her earlier impulses to escape into Edenic isolation with her father. At the end of *The Golden Bowl*, she chooses to accept the Prince despite his moral flaws, to accept a patched, imperfect relationship and to share that imperfection. But to one of Maggie's "serious" nature and "scant" "provision of irony," compromise is not without ambivalence.[8] Maggie buries her eyes as a means of avoiding the sight of the Prince, a sight that might force intolerable awareness of both Amerigo's nature and her own concession to it. She decides, at the end of the novel, to suppress both kinds of awareness to preserve her marriage. Neither demonically selfish nor divinely triumphant, Maggie acts out a painfully human compromise.

This interpretation of the ending to *The Golden Bowl* aims primarily to give a detailed explication of an important but controversial moment in literature. It also serves, however, to reemphasize something about *The Golden Bowl* (and, indeed, most great novels) that somehow gets forgotten in theoretical discussions, and that has been obscured by critical statements about the "epistemology" of *The Golden Bowl* or about the virtue or villainy of its heroine: great fictional characters confront emotionally charged and difficult situations. However elitist a novel may be— and *The Golden Bowl* is clearly elitist—novels present characters whose "lives" interest readers as representations of human emotions and of human dilemmas. A major work by a major novelist inevitably assumes interest for students and critics of the novel.

But in its basic story, *The Golden Bowl* is of considerably less esoteric interest, its plot being, in fact, the very stuff of soap operas. Transformed by James's treatment into a complex novel, the subject retains, and should retain, its common level of what is popularly called "human interest."

# EIGHT

## Story-Telling as Affirmation at the End of *Light in August*

### I

As is well known, Faulkner did almost no revising of his two early "tour de force" novels—*The Sound and the Fury* and *As I Lay Dying*. But he substantially revised *Light in August*, his third major novel, and his fifth novel.[1] Comparison of the finished text with two early manuscripts shows two key changes. First, Faulkner extensively revised so as to give the novel an optimistic ending through his use of circular form: *Light in August* begins and ends with Lena Grove, earth-mother figure, placidly journeying in search of a father for her child, rather than with Hightower—a less affirmative, more ambiguous character. Second, Faulkner changed the title of the novel from *Dark House* to *Light in August*. The original title evokes the two recluses, Joanna Burden and Hightower; the revised title alludes instead to Hightower after he has been partly redeemed, and especially to Lena Grove, since to be "light in August" is, in Southern idiom, "to give birth in the month of August."[2] The changes clearly indicate Faulkner's conscious shaping of the fiction to end his powerfully violent novel with gentle humor and peacefulness. For, as has been generally agreed, the final focus on Lena is intended by Faulkner as contrast and counterweight to the novel's central story—the devastatingly brutal tale of Joe Christmas.

Despite the general agreement on the intention behind the ending, and the ease with which readers have entered complementary relationships with Faulkner during closure, much of the criticism of *Light in August* has implicitly tried to justify its final chapter. Effectively taught by Henry James and other early Modernists, critics fully expected the ending of *Light in August* to round off its shape organically, although they had no specific expectations as to what form that ending had to take and no preference for a happy or unhappy ending. A number of critics have shown that the narrative opposition between Joe and Lena assumes power through parallelism, through contrasting motifs developed in the novel, especially motifs of movement as against stillness.[3] Some of these critics have viewed Lena as integrated with the community as Joe is not, with the community serving as "moral norm" and as the basis for affirmation at the end of the novel.[4] I find this view interesting but only partly responsive to the novel, since, in many instances, the community's notions are stale, racist *idées reçues* and, at the end of the novel, Lena and Byron are "on the road," out of a set social community, and this fact is one source of the ending's affirmation. Other critics have interpreted the novel mythically and designated the peacefulness of Lena as a mandala enclosing the scapegoat story of Joe Christmas.[5] Finally, some critics have bypassed Lena and the novel's final chapter in identifying affirmation at the end of the novel, turning instead to the next to last chapter and positing Hightower as the novel's moral center.[6]

The instinct to accept Faulkner's peaceful ending is a healthy one. But a more adequate basis for reading the ending as successful, if partial, affirmation is both needed and possible. The following discussion explores two new and, ultimately, related aspects of closure in *Light in August*. First, using the knowledge that Faulkner very consciously shaped the ending, it will show how the last three chapters ease the way for the peaceful ending both in their overall structure and in their establishment of key themes. In doing so, it will describe both parallel and circular patterns of closure. Next, it will explore the theme of story-telling in the novel, which becomes increasingly important in the final chapters and suggests that—as Faulkner said in his Nobel Prize speech—fiction-making "can be one of the props, the pillars to help [man] endure and prevail."[7]

## II

*Light in August* actually has three chapters that end the novel, each resolving one of its three organically linked plot centers. The most explosive of the plot lines, that concerning Joe Christmas, ends in a chapter with several marked shifts in point of view. It begins with Gavin Stevens' account of Christmas' escape, moves to a third-person history of Percy Grimm, and ends with one of the most gruesome events in all of fiction—Grimm's shooting and castration of Joe Christmas. The Hightower plot center ends with an apocalyptic meditation by Hightower at the window where, for thirty years, he has nightly evoked his grandfather's last cavalry charge and death in a chicken house. The quietest plot center, that concerning Lena Grove, ends with a furniture dealer's account of how Lena, now accompanied by Byron and her newborn child, journeys from Mississippi to Tennessee—ostensibly searching for Lucas Burch, but really (as the furniture dealer assures his wife) just traveling a bit before settling down with Byron.

The chapter that resolves the Christmas story (chapter nineteen) seems at first anticlimactic. At the end of the preceding chapter, Byron Bunch and the reader have been told that Christmas is dead; chapter nineteen tells how that happened—but only gradually, building very slowly to the frenzied intensity of the actual killing. Quietly, the opening of the chapter relays the townspeople's thoughts on the night of Joe Christmas' death:

> About the suppertables on that Monday night, what the town wondered was not so much how Christmas had escaped but why when free, he had taken refuge in the place which he did, where he must have known he would be certainly run to earth, and why when that occurred he neither surrendered nor resisted. It was as though he had set out and made his plans to passively commit suicide. (p. 419)

Faulkner then lists the townspeople's inadequate explanations for the novel's climactic events, in a passage strikingly similar to the opening of Hawthorne's "Conclusion" in *The Scarlet Letter*:

> There were many reasons, opinions, as to why he had fled to Hightower's house at the last. "Like to like," the easy, the immediate, ones said, remembering the old tales about the minister. Some believed it to have been sheer chance; others

said that the man had shown wisdom, since he would not have been suspected of being in the minister's house at all if someone had not seen him run across the back yard and run into the kitchen.    (p. 419)

For the next few pages, the novel develops one opinion at some length—the opinion of Gavin Stevens, "the District Attorney, a Harvard graduate, a Phi Beta Kappa" (p. 419). Because the novel's climactic events are reported without explanation at the end of chapter eighteen, the reader wants some analysis of what has happened and therefore is attentive to what Stevens has to say. He hopes, in fact, that the Phi Beta Kappa will hold the "key" to the novel's climactic events. But a sensitive reader can be only partly satisfied with what he finds in Stevens' section. Stevens believes that Mrs. Hines—having told her story to Hightower and only then understood it—attributed magical powers of relief and comfort to the minister. He speculates that she told her grandson about Hightower during a visit to the jail and that, intuitively impressed, after Christmas escaped he instinctively ran to the minister's house. Thus far, Stevens' account is fully conjectural, but possible and tantalizing; the reader must accept it or have no explanation at all for these events in the novel.

Quickly, however, his narration discredits itself. Its explanation of events in Hightower's house as related alternately to Christmas' "black blood" and "white blood" seems both racist and overdone. Faulkner apparently intended Stevens' narration to be suspect, despite (or, knowing Faulkner, because of) his Harvard Phi Beta Kappa. When critics confidently assumed that Stevens was Faulkner's spokesman in the novel, the author declared that Stevens' account "is an assumption, a rationalization."[8] And although Faulkner has certainly been known to lie about his intentions and methods, this time he seems to be telling the truth. For internal evidence in the novel suggests that Stevens' narration tries to do more than any narrative can or should. The omniscient narrator of *Light in August* reveals, for example, a great deal of crucial information about characters, motivations, incidents. But he deliberately refrains from providing any authorized view of events surrounding Christmas' escape and death. No rational cause or explanation can adequately account for the actions of characters like Mrs. Hines and Joe Christmas; they are not rational creatures and their motivations cannot be systematically analyzed and logically explained.

Stevens' explanation of Christmas' good actions as produced by his "white blood" and violent acts as produced by his "black blood" relies absolutely, moreover, on both the doubtful notion that Joe Christmas is in fact of mixed racial origins, and on the *idées reçues* of his community. And like the fixed and unfeeling notions of *The Scarlet Letter*'s Puritan community, the "accepted ideas" of Jefferson are unable to fathom what Hawthorne calls "the mysteries of the human heart." Several major examples exist in the novel, but one of the best concerns Joe Christmas' slaying of Joanna Burden. Once Lucas Burch provides a "cast of characters" for that event which includes Joe Christmas as "nigger," the community readily supplies a plot that casts Joanna Burden as pure, innocent victim. In rich detail, however, the novel has supplied a more complex scenario—one in which Joanna Burden arranges and provokes her own murder, one that might even partly exculpate Joe.

Reluctant to trust Stevens' account any further, Faulkner switches in mid-chapter back to the novel's typical narrative mode—third-person (occasionally becoming third-person subjective)—to give the history of Percy Grimm and to record Christmas' escape, the chase, and the butchery that follow swiftly, inexorably, and ritualistically. At the end of chapter nineteen, the climax of the novel—reported but not enacted earlier—finally occurs in the novel's narrative time: Christmas is shot and castrated by Grimm as the instrument of a force Faulkner calls "the Player." In the very last paragraph of the chapter, having pushed horror as far as it will go, the narrative gradually transfers attention from Christmas' death and mutilation to the reactions of Grimm's companions:

> For a long moment he looked up at them with peaceful and unfathomable and unbearable eyes. Then his face, body, all, seemed to collapse, to fall in upon itself, and from out the slashed garments about his hips and loins the pent black blood

seemed to rush like a released breath. It seemed to rush out of his pale body like the rush of sparks from a rising rocket; upon that black blast the man seemed to rise soaring into their memories forever and ever. They are not to lose it, in whatever peaceful valleys, beside whatever placid and reassuring streams of old age, in the mirroring faces of whatever children they will contemplate old disasters and newer hopes. It will be there, musing, quiet, steadfast, not fading and not particularly threatful, but of itself alone serene, of itself alone triumphant. Again from the town, deadened a little by the walls, the scream of the siren mounted toward its unbelievable crescendo, passing out of the realm of hearing.   (pp. 439-440)

Many of the terms in this passage aptly describe the relationship of the two last chapters in the novel to the horrors of Christmas' slaying. The destructive energies in the book are discharged in this cathartic moment. The image of Christmas hovers through the remainder of the novel as it does in the memories of Grimm's companions—"not particularly threatful," and not overtly remembered, but real and present and "not to be lost." Having built to its "unbelievable crescendo," the novel now builds away from it. The account of the bystanders' reactions both freezes the horror of the moment and begins to distance it. The last two chapters of the novel continue to brake the intensity of the Christmas chapter by deliberately focusing on different characters and more humane events.

## III

Like chapter nineteen, the final Hightower chapter begins slowly, gradually moving to its own climax—powerful, but distinctly less intense than the murder of Christmas. Its tone is elegiac; its subject, Hightower's family history and life as relived in his own consciousness. As the chapter begins, Hightower sits awaiting the phantom re-enactment of his grandfather's death, which has preoccupied him for a lifetime. But instead of the familiar ritual, he undergoes a more authentic experience. In *agon* with himself, he probes the springs of his actions and finds them selfish and self-interested. Apocalyptically, the chapter builds to Hightower's vision of a wheel of faces, "mirrors in which he watches himself" and "can read his doings" (p. 462). Once he acknowledges responsibility in the ruin of his own life and those of others, "The wheel, released, seems to rush on with a long sighing sound." The faces in the wheel (among them those of Mrs. Hightower, Christmas, and Grimm) "are not shaped with suffering, not shaped with anything: not horror, pain, not even reproach. They are peaceful, as though they have escaped into an apotheosis; his own is among them. In fact, they all look a little alike" (p. 465). Here, as in the final description of Christmas, a peaceful serenity is achieved in apotheosis even by the novel's doomed characters. The chapter then ends with the delayed appearance of his grandfather's phantom charge.

Hightower's fate at the end of the chapter has been a vexed critical issue. Many critics assumed that Hightower dies; but we have Faulkner's word for it that "Hightower didn't die."[9] Other critics have responded with the idea that he goes mad or that he becomes the apotheosis of human compassion. Such questions may finally be academic. In chapter twenty, it is clear that Hightower has the first (and very painful) moral self-insight of his life. It is equally clear that living man or dead, he has experienced vision too late for that vision to be effectual in the day-to-day world of living men. He has entered an "apotheosis": a state outside of ordinary experience. His face, like the faces of those he sees in vision, is void of any emotion recognizable as human, of any expression with which to face the living world. Moreover, after a self-effacing and self-accusatory reverie, Hightower's last words in the chapter reassert and excuse the self: " 'With all air, all heaven, filled with the lost and unheeded crying of all the living who ever lived, wailing still like lost children among the cold and terrible stars. . . . I wanted so little. I asked so little. It would seem. . . .' " (p. 466, Faulkner's ellipses). And at chapter's end, the habitual thundering hooves of his grandfather's horses limit Hightower's transcendence of his past. Though the men and horses "rush past, are gone . . . it seems to him that he still hears them: the wild bugles and the clashing sabres and the dying thunder of hooves" (p. 467). The image of the wheel, or circle, suggestive of vision through long artistic tradition, also suggests the circular street of Christmas' life—the insurmountable barrier of the past that dooms so many characters in this novel and forms a barrier Hightower can only partly cross.

Faulkner ends the chapter with deliberate ambiguity. Hightower is redeemed, but only partly and only too late. He experiences true compassion, but is himself a being in need of the reader's compassion. In chapter twenty, the weight of his total experience in life is appropriately allowed to stand beside the power of his final vision. Because it comes too late, that vision is ineffectual outside the mind of Hightower and can have no further bearing on the novel. Fittingly, the novel leaves him here, in an ambiguous state between life and death, between new insight and the vivid phantoms of the past.[10] With the Hightower chapter, the novel has moved beyond the horror of Christmas' death, but has still not achieved any vital affirmation. To do so, Faulkner must leave both Christmas and Hightower and turn to characters still able to participate in life.

IV

The last chapter in the novel, which resolves the Lena Grove and Byron Bunch plot center, is the most fully anticlimactic of the three concluding chapters. But as in Hawthorne's *The Scarlet Letter*, the anticlimax is deliberately contrived by a self-aware author. In formal terms, the ending is an epilogue, although very dissimilar to other epilogues I have examined. Its time is very close to the conclusion of the novel's major action (perhaps two to three weeks after Christmas' death and Hightower's reverie), and it is only minimally useful in providing after-histories of Lena and Byron, since any astute reader has long assumed that they will eventually marry. Like the epilogue to *War and Peace*, it combines overview and scenic techniques. Dominated by the furniture dealer's narration, the ending rechannels the powerful, violent energies of the novel, deliberately ending it on the simple, peaceful notes with which it began.

The furniture dealer's narration is comic, almost *fabliau*, in tone. To the salesman, Byron is "the kind of fellow you wouldn't see the first glance if he was alone by himself in the bottom of a empty concrete swimming pool" (p. 469). And his awkwardness and vacillation as would-be lover to Lena are a fully conventional source of humor. Similarly, Lena is a motherly, serene, and honest, but stupid and even rather "bovine," young country girl as she is presented in the final chapter.[11] The comic "after you Alphonse" scene when the furniture dealer and Byron Bunch "negotiate" over who will sleep in the comfortably equipped truck marvelously underscores both the funniness of Byron and Lena and their parasitic dependence on the good will of others:

> It was like those two fellows that used to be in the funny papers, those two Frenchmen that were always bowing and scraping at the other one to go first, making out like we had all come away from home just for the privilege of sleeping on the ground. . . . I reckon you might say that I won. Or that me and him won. Because it wound up by him fixing their blanket in the truck, like we all might have known all the time it would be, and me and him spreading mine out before the fire. I reckon he knew that would be the way of it, anyhow. If they had come all the way from south Alabama like she claimed.    (pp. 473-74)

But if the furniture dealer's reactions to the couple are humorous and simple, the reader's are more complex. The reader knows more, after all, than the furniture dealer can of Lena's and Byron's past and of the significance they have acquired as characters in the body of the novel. From the first pages of *Light in August*, Lena has assumed mythic, symbolic, earth-mother roles. And Byron's basic decency has similarly won him the reader's sympathy. Though they are not epic figures, of the major characters only Lena and Byron survive and endure. In the final chapter, they are for the reader life-affirming characters as compared to others in the novel—Christmas, Hightower, Joanna Burden, Percy Grimm. On the road, with no significant crimes or past to burden them, they escape the destructive forces that envelop the other characters.

The balance between comic and affirmative views of Lena and Byron at the end of *Light in August* enables Faulkner to perform a favorite trick in ending his novel: the investment of the banal, comic, or grotesque with positive significance. For like Anse with his new teeth and Cash with his gramophone at the end of *As I Lay Dying*, or Luster with his wagon at the end of *The Sound and the Fury*, Lena and Byron may be clownish, but they are alive and well. They muddle through life, but they get by—in Faulkner's universe, no mean achievement. At the end of *Light in August*, Faulkner gets his readers to accept Byron and Lena (appropriately nameless in the furniture dealer's narration) as symbols of continuing life: a little weak and foolish, a bit inept and dependent, but living, loving, acting, and surviving.

The basic function of the furniture dealer's narration is thus to prevent the ending of *Light in August* from seeming too grandly or artificially affirmative by providing a comical account of Lena and Byron. But his narration has several other purposes as well. The furniture dealer (also unnamed in the novel) has been on the road for more than a week. Upon his return home, he naturally enough winds up in bed with his wife, and in post-coital conversation relates the story of two hitch-hikers picked up in Mississippi, whom the reader recognizes as Byron Bunch and Lena Grove. One immediate point to note about the furniture dealer's narration relates to the "natural enough" quality of its setting. The furniture dealer and his wife are a "normal" couple and, in their good-natured bantering and sexual contentment, a clear contrast to other couples in the novel.

At the end of this text, the humor and warmth with which the furniture dealer regards human sexuality are genuinely refreshing. When the furniture dealer explains the genesis of Byron's plan to claim Lena by becoming her lover, for example, the following dialogue ensues:

". . . I begun to notice how there was something funny and kind of strained about him. Like when a man is determined to work himself up to where he will do something he wants to do and that he is scared to do. I dont mean it was like he was scared of what might happen to him, but like it was something that he would die before he would even think about doing it if he hadn't just tried everything else until he was desperate. That was before I knew. I just couldn't understand what in the world it could be then. . . ."

*What was it he aimed to do?* the wife says.

*You wait till I come to that part. Maybe I'll show you, too.*

. . .

*What was it?* the wife says

*I just showed you once. You ain't ready to be showed again, are you?*

*I reckon I dont mind if you dont. But I still dont see anything funny in that. How come it took him all that time and trouble, anyway?*

*It was because they were not married* the husband says. *It wasn't even his child. I didn't know it then, though.*

(pp. 471-72, Faulkner's emphasis)

In such passages, the furniture dealer's easygoing sexual attitudes and his wife's good-humored responses contrast sharply and effectively with images of sexuality presented earlier in the novel: the casual abandonment of Lena Grove by Lucas Burch, the rigid anti-sexuality of Hines and McEachern, the hurried coupling of the dietician and the doctor, Joe's tortured initiations into the mysteries of menstruation and intercourse, Joanna's repressed sexuality, Hightower's inability to meet his wife's needs, her shabby death in a Memphis hotel, the sexual fears of a community that finds Grimm as an instrument for castrating Christmas. The novel's presentation of sexuality up to the last chapter is uncompromisingly strong and unrelievedly violent. The healthy sexuality in the furniture dealer's chapter cannot and does not obliterate what has come before, nor does Faulkner wish it to. But the final chapter reminds the reader that matters charged with death and suffering can also be humorous and life-enriching.

## V

The most important aspect of the final chapter seems to me, however, to be its anecdotal quality. The furniture dealer takes a recent experience, orders it into narrative form, and places humane and humorous interpretations on his story. He communicates his tale to his wife, using it to enhance their relationship. The very act of story-telling, as exemplified by the furniture dealer, is healthful and restorative: it allows the individual to absorb his experiences and, as a reflective act, prevents consciousness from merely being carried along by the flux of events. In fact, the furniture dealer's narration crystallizes connections between themes in the novel: story-telling, its relationship to self-comprehension, and its ability to give human beings some control over the flow of experience.

Once again, the ending can be appreciated only by discerning parallelism and recognizing contrasts to the body of the novel. Only two characters tell stories before the last chapters of the novel—Lena and Byron. Lena, the least sophisticated story-teller in the book, has a secure grasp on her story and tells it "with that patient and transparent recapitulation of a lying child" (p. 22). She repeats her story gravely and mechanically to anyone she meets. She doesn't think about her audience, but she moves those who hear her and travels safely, even comfortably—her passport both the child she carries and the utter simplicity of her tale. As the link among the three plot centers, Byron suitably tells stories about other characters (Lena, Mrs. Hines, Joe Christmas), usually to Hightower as audience. Byron's interest in others and his compassion motivate his story-telling and make him a highly sympathetic character. But, like Lena, he is an unsophisticated teller of tales: he detaches his narratives from himself, declining to see their full relevance. Thus, Hightower perceives from Byron's stories that Byron is in love with Lena before Byron himself does. Bunch also rather passively looks to Hightower—his audience—

to make the moral and value judgments so integral a part of narration.

In contrast to Lena and Byron, the novel's doomed characters show no ability at all to analyze the self or order experience and are consequently unable to communicate with themselves or with others. Joe Christmas simply runs for thirty-three years "inside a circle," without ever telling his story to others or to himself. The one piece of information he regularly communicates is the idea that he has black blood in him, and this piece of story-telling is life-destroying rather than life-enriching: Joe uses it to avoid paying whores; others use it to beat and punish him. The story of Joe's black blood is of doubtful status in the novel: it is, after all, never proven, but always based on "hearsay" evidence, some of it (like Doc Hines') "planted." More crucially, this information is not something Joe concludes and announces in a genuine search for self-understanding. Rather, it is an idea others hand to him that Joe uncritically accepts.

By letting others tell his story and passively adopting that story as his own, Joe becomes the "pawn" of "the Player," a man inauthentic and doomed. In the hands of Faulkner as story-teller, Joe's life falls into clearly recognizable patterns: psychically linked difficulties with women, food, and the black race; an antipathy (sprung from his childhood with McEachern) to people praying over him; periodic eruptions of violence fatal to others and ultimately destructive to himself. If Joe were able to tell his story, a perception of destructive patterns and a partial break with them might have followed for him, as it does for Hightower in chapter twenty. But throughout his life, Joe refuses to put facts together, to follow a tale through to its conclusion. He murmurs brief cautionary remarks to himself: "I better move. I better get away from here." "I am going to do something." "Something is going to happen to me." But he never follows through on his promptings, never breaks through to an understanding of himself, to a "telling" of his story to himself or to others.

A similar failure informs the life of Joanna Burden. On the eve of the "second phase" of her relationship with Joe (the period of intense sexuality), she breaks her pattern of silence and (as Joe perceives it) surrenders "in words." She tells, in fact, the complete history of her family. But the novel does not present her narrative anecdotally or even in dialogue. It is rendered in indirect discourse, in a chillingly encyclopedic third person:

> Calvin Burden was the son of a minister named Nathaniel Burrington. The youngest of ten children, he ran away from home at the age of twelve, before he could write his name. . . .   (p. 228)

Her narrative is, moreover, curiously impersonal. Little of it pertains directly to Joanna; she gives few facts about herself except for the mere fact of her birth and the strong impression left on her by her father's theory that the black race is eternally cursed and a shadow under which all white men live. Like Hightower, she has no proper history uncontaminated by the history of her ancestors. She could make that tale her own only by reliving it in her consciousness and judging its effects on her life, much as Hightower does with his own life and family history in his final meditation. Killed by Christmas when she attempts to murder him and destroy herself with an ancestral pistol, she never gives herself the chance to tell her own story and thereby understand it.

At novel's end, the pressure toward story-telling, toward the power of narrative to cope with experience, becomes intense. After Christmas' death, as we have seen, the townspeople try to create a plot for his slaying, a story to make sense of the day's events. Like Christmas' account of his black blood and parts of Stevens', their narratives are, however, inauthentic because based upon the received ideas of the community. Gavin Stevens also attempts to shape the unshapeable, to attribute cause and effect, motive and will, where causes and motives may in fact be absent. Yet Stevens' idea that telling makes the teller see things "whole and real" as never before is fruitful in understanding the novel. His theory about the power of narrative to fix and clarify experience occurs as an explanation of Hightower's effect on Mrs. Hines:

". . . [Mrs. Hines] had been like an effigy with a mechanical voice being hauled about on a cart by that fellow Bunch and made to speak when he gave the signal, as when he took her last night to tell her story to Doctor Hightower.

"And she was still groping, you see. She was still trying to find something which that mind which had apparently not run very much in thirty years, could believe in, admit to be actual, real. And I think that she found it there, at Hightower's, for the first time: someone to whom she could tell it, who would listen to her. Very likely that was the first time she had ever told it. And very likely she learned it herself then for the first time, actually saw it whole and real at the same time with Hightower."    (p. 422)

To tell one's story—to oneself or another—is to "learn it for the first time," to "see it whole and real."

In his final chapter, Hightower, whose real story has yet to be told in the novel, tells himself of his family, his childhood, his fascination with the tale of his grandfather's death—and in the telling comes to some understanding and judgment of himself, some small measure of grace. In the case of Percy Grimm the same pattern holds. Grimm is unable to tell his own story and remains the tool of "the Player." The novel, on the other hand, halts the main line of action to give a complete history of Grimm, since simply to name or describe a character will not aid comprehension of his acts; only the orderly history of the man can do that.

In itself, the furniture dealer's narration is a humble thing: it deals with no cosmic issues, and chronicles no epic events. But it shows the imagination of a healthy individual in action. The furniture dealer shows interest in others and uses anecdote and story to enrich his personal experience. He perceives himself as a character, implicitly recognizes the roles played in life, and analyzes his own motivations. A man who tells someone else "he got me right nervous. . . . I was a little mad. . . . So I reckon I was short and grumpy maybe" (p. 473), has begun to place his actions in an objective context and has made the first step towards controlling his impulses. And a man who speculates about the motivations of others—as the furniture dealer speculates on those of Byron and Lena—may not always hit upon the truth, but has at least broken out of the self-absorption that cuts Hightower off from life until it is too late.

## VI

Faulkner's claims for the power of story-telling and narrative should be seen as modest and humble. Stories can cope with experience and thus are a basic human need, but they cannot always fully explain people and events. Some matters—those Hawthorne calls the "mysteries of the human heart"—remain inaccessible to verbalization and plot-making. Thus, all individual explanations (including Gavin Stevens') of why Joe Christmas flees to Hightower's house and submits to his death fail. The cumulative narrative of *Light in August* reveals much about Christmas, but it refuses finally to reveal all. For story-telling pushed too far or valued too absolutely can be as distorting and unhealthy as storytelling totally suppressed.

Several kinds of story-telling are allowed to discredit themselves in Faulkner's fictions. Stories that raise moral issues for the reader without seeming at all aware of the issues involved form one class of suspect narrative. "Was," in which the narrator comically treats the story of Tomey's Turl from a child's-eye-view is one example; in the same volume, in "The Bear," related events are revealed as both serious and tragic. Self-interested or biased narratives are more strongly discredited. Such narratives may be rhetorically effective and even immensely entertaining—like Jason's soliloquy in *The Sound and the Fury*. But they neither increase the teller's self-awareness nor (given their biased perspective) effectively uplift mankind. The classic examples of unhealthy story-telling in Faulkner's canon are, however, the narratives of Quentin Compson. His fiction of incest in *The Sound and the Fury* distorts reality and springs from his deep-seated neuroses. His narration of *Absalom, Absalom!*—although skillful and engrossing to the reader—is, for the narrator, perverse and unsound. Quentin constructs a plot for the destruction of the Sutpen family that "doubles" his own personal history. But he is unable to bear what Shreve so easily perceives—the narrative's reference to Quentin himself—and hence derives no benefits from it.[12]

To create a healthy narration, the story-teller must be self-conscious both about himself and about the narrative act. He must be sensitive to the complexities of reality and aware of fiction's limitations, but must also be doggedly willing to try to understand himself and to order the world in a way that tallies with felt experience. Fictions cannot be true in any absolute sense. But, as Faulkner said in his "Address Upon Receiving the Nobel Prize," "the poet's voice" and the stories it tells "can be one of the props, the pillars to help [man] endure and prevail."[13] The juxtaposition of "props" and "pillars" reveals much about Faulkner's sense of both the limitations and the powers of story-telling, and indicates Faulkner's self-awareness during closure in *Light in August*. The word "pillars" glorifies the poet's voice, evoking both our classical heritage and the institutions and buildings that symbolize our coherence into social communities. The word "prop" acknowledges the feebleness of the poet's voice, and indicates the precarious basis on which mankind sometimes "endures and prevails." As a poet aware of story-telling as both prop and pillar, Faulkner conscientiously strove to end major novels, like *Light in August*, on a note of at least partial affirmation. Such affirmation is the poet's "duty" to mankind, his way of helping man "endure and prevail."

An incident toward the end of *Light in August* beautifully captures both the inadequacy of words to human experience and their saving banality. The incident occurs when Gavin Stevens goes to meet a visiting friend, a college professor, at the local train station. Their meeting is told through the friend's eyes, effectively "making strange" the characters and their dialogue:

> When he [the professor] descended from the train he saw his friend [Stevens] at once. He believed that Stevens had come down to meet him until he saw that Stevens was engaged

with a queerlooking old couple whom he was putting on the
train. Looking at them, the professor saw a little, dirty old
man with a short goat's beard who seemed to be in a state
like catalepsy, and an old woman who must have been his
wife—a dumpy creature with a face like dough beneath a
nodding and soiled white plume, shapeless in a silk dress of
an outmoded shape and in color regal and moribund. . . . Still
unseen by his friend, he overheard Stevens' final words as the
flagman helped the old people into the vestibule: "Yes, yes,"
Stevens was saying, in a tone soothing and recapitulant; "he'll
be on the train tomorrow morning. I'll see to it. All you'll
have to do is to arrange for the funeral, the cemetery. You
take Granddad on home and put him to bed. I'll see that the
boy is on the train in the morning."   (pp. 420-21)

With a start, one realizes that "the boy" is Joe Christmas, and
"Granddad" Doc Hines. Stevens' words transpose all that is aberrant in these characters into a recognizable, humane pattern: the
concern of grandparents for the decent burial of their "boy." His
fiction is chillingly inadequate to the realities of the situation:
Hines has, after all, hardly played the part of a normal "Granddad,"
nor Christmas that of a beloved "boy." But it is not contemptible.
Stevens' words allow the Hineses to get on that train and go home.
They allow Stevens to do all that a decent man can under circumstances bizarre and inhumane.

In the best-known section of *As I Lay Dying*, Addie Bundren
insists that words falsify human experience:

"I learned that words are no good; that words don't ever fit
even what they are trying to say at.

"I would think how words go straight up in a thin line, quick
and harmless, and how terribly doing goes along the earth,
clinging to it, so that after a while the two lines are too far
apart for the same person to straddle from one to the other;
and that sin and love and fear are just sounds that people who

never sinned nor loved nor feared have for what they never had and cannot have until they forget the words.[14]

Faulkner's endorsement of anecdotes and stories at the end of *Light In August* does not totally deny what Addie says. Faulkner simply claims, and reminds us of the claim, that some aspects of human experience can and should be made anecdotal. In individual lives, a healthy coping with experience, communication with others, and understanding of self result. In fact, for individuals, anecdotes and stories perform on a smaller scale precisely the same functions that art performs for its audience and its society. When things "go by too fast" for us—as they do for Christmas, Hightower, Grimm, the community in the manhunt—we are the tools of "the Player," the pawns of events. When we slow things down in narrative— when we tell ourselves and others what is happening to ourselves and our world—we regain a measure of control.

# NINE

## Virginia Woolf, the Vision of *The Waves*, and the Novel's Double Ending

I

VIRGINIA Woolf left a rich record of the genesis and composition of *The Waves*, both in her personal diary and in the notebooks and drafts of the novel. This material provides provocative and indispensable points of departure for any discussion of its ending. Her comments begin as she nears the completion of *To the Lighthouse*, in 1926. While at her house in Rodmell, she confides to her diary:

> I wished to add some remarks to this, on the mystical side of this solitude; how it is not oneself but something in the universe that one's left with. It is this that is frightening & exciting in the midst of my profound gloom, depression, boredom, whatever it is: One sees a fin passing far out. What image can I reach to convey what I mean? Really there is none, I think. The interesting thing is that in all my feeling & thinking I have never come up against this before. Life is, soberly & accurately, the oddest affair; has in it the essence of reality. I used to feel this as a child—couldn't step across a puddle once I remember, for thinking, how strange—what am I? & etc. . . . All I mean to make is a note of a curious state of mind. I hazard the guess that it may be the impulse behind another book. . . . I want to trace my own process.[1]

Several important elements in the completed novel already exist in this journal entry, prior to its conscious inception. First, there is the remembrance of being a child afraid to cross a puddle—a personal remembrance from which the character Rhoda springs,[2] and one of many indications that *The Waves* is, for Woolf, an intensely personal novel. Second, weighty themes in the novel are already present here—"Life," "reality," "Being" ("what am I? & etc.")—with a distinction made between "life" and the "essence of reality." Third, the idea that no image will finally prove adequate to convey her vision is suggested by Woolf and later confirmed in the diaries during the writing of *The Waves*. Fourth, and most important, the image that comes closest to capturing the essence of her vision, that of "a fin passing far out" is recorded in her diary as a remarkable and intensely felt part of her experience and later given to Bernard in the novel, recurring with some frequency and shifting significance in the last section of the novel.

The new book begins to assume more definite shape in an entry that announces a new stage in Woolf's life: the stage that came with writing *To the Lighthouse* and freeing herself from being "unhealthily obsessed" with her parents (p. 208). At this early date in its composition (November, 1928), Woolf calls the book *The Moths* and conceives of it as "saturated" like poetry, and stripped of the social details usually found in novels (p. 209). The notion that *The Moths* would not be a conventional novel is one that she reiterates several times; she finally calls it a "play-poem" in deference to the "series of dramatic soliloquies" of which it is composed (p. 312). In its first draft version, *The Moths* was subtitled "the life of anyone" and "life in general." It was also given the alternative titles *Moments of Being* and *The Waves*, with the second chosen as the novel's title by the beginning of the second draft.[3]

Woolf's diary repeatedly testifies to her difficulties in writing the novel. She describes herself as "blundering" at the book (p. 275), and as not knowing "how to pull it together" (p. 285). As she herself records, it was the most difficult to write and the most complex of her novels. Part of the difficulty arose from the mystical vision which was the germ of the novel and the inadequacy of words and fiction to accurately convey that vision. And for Woolf, the question of how to end was a large part of the question of form and a considerable part of the book's difficulty. She speculates several times on the appropriate ending, usually alluding to "a gigantic conversation" or "a mosaic" of voices (pp. 285, 298), but always concluding, "I do not know." Ultimately, in the first and second drafts, and in the published novel, the "mosaic" of voices is abandoned in favor of a protracted soliloquy by Bernard. In his section, Bernard first reviews his life and those of his friends in an ambiguous, shadowy dinner setting with a chance acquaintance as auditor, and then confronts death in the condition of Woolf's own vision at Rodmell—solitude.

Woolf's diary records the completion of both the first draft (on April 29, 1930), and the second draft (on February 7, 1931), each time referring to her "mystical" vision at Rodmell and to her sense of relief and satisfaction that the hard work of writing the novel has completed another stage. At the completion of the first draft, she writes:

> And I have just finished, with this very nib-full of ink, the last sentence of The Waves. I think I should record this for my own information. Yes, it was the greatest stretch of mind I ever knew; certainly the last pages; I don't think they flop as much as usual. And I think I have kept starkly & ascetically to the plan. So much I will say in self-congratulation. But I have never written a book so full of holes & patches; that will need re-building, yes, not only re-modelling. I suspect the structure is wrong. Never mind. I might have done something easy & fluent; & this is a reach after that vision I had, the unhappy summer—or three weeks—at Rodmell, after finishing the Lighthouse.   (p. 302)

The entire novel was, in fact, extensively revised and rewritten; the ending of the first draft is only a bare outline of the ending of the finished novel.

At the completion of the second draft, the diary reveals another way that *The Waves* and its ending were intensely important, intensely emotional to Woolf—as a tribute to her dead brother Thoby:

> Here in the few minutes that remain, I must record, heaven be praised, the end of *The Waves*. I wrote the words O Death

fifteen minutes ago, having reeled across the last ten pages with some moments of such intensity and intoxication that I seemed only to stumble after my own voice, or almost, after some sort of speaker (as when I was mad) I was almost afraid, remembering the voices that used to fly ahead. Anyhow, it is done; and I have been sitting here these 15 minutes in a state of glory, and calm, and some tears, thinking of Thoby and if I could write Julian Thoby Stephen 1881-1906 on the first page. I suppose not. How physical the sense of triumph and relief is! Whether good or bad, it's done; and, as I certainly felt at the end, not merely finished, but rounded off, completed, the thing stated—how hastily, how fragmentarily I know; but I mean that I have netted that fin in the waste of water which appeared to me over the marshes at Rodmell when I was coming to an end of *To the Lighthouse*.

(*A Writer's Diary*, p. 165)

In the same diary entry, she also notes that in the novel's "last stages" she abandoned the search for coherent, worked-out images, fulfilling her prediction, at the time of her first diary entry on *The Waves*, that no one image or group of words would definitively communicate the mystical import of the vision from which the book had sprung:

What interests me in the last stage was the freedom and boldness with which my imagination picked up, used and tossed aside all the images, symbols which I had prepared. I am sure that this is the right way of using them—not in set pieces, as I had tried at first, coherently, but simply as images, never making them work out; only suggest.

(*A Writer's Diary*, p. 165)

The publication of the holograph drafts of *The Waves* in 1976 revealed, however, that she had not finally "netted" the meaning of that fin in the waste of waters at the conclusion of the second draft. The notebook outline of the novel and the second draft both end with Bernard's challenge to death as the enemy and the words

"O Death."[4] But the diary entries, despite their basic tone of triumph, hint at Woolf's slight dissatisfaction with the novel's end. And somewhere between the second draft and the final typescript, she added one line to the novel: "The waves broke on the shore."[5] The line, it is generally agreed, signifies the death of Bernard and (with its plural, "waves") probably the death of other characters or death in general. It looses the "chained beast stamping by the shore" perceived as threatening by Louis, but welcomed by Rhoda as "a tremendous shower, dissolving me."

Parallelism controls the ending, but parallelism of a kind different from that we have seen so far. The one-line epilogue is, in fact, anomalous in the structure of the novel. Each of the novel's nine sections has a poetic prologue, which describes a beach scene at a point from near sunrise to slightly after dark; each prologue includes some mention of waves forming or thudding, or massing, or falling, or (as in the final line) breaking. But no section except the last has an epilogue. The earlier sections—which cover the lives of Neville, Susan, Louis, Rhoda, Bernard, and Jinny from early childhood to old age in a progression which parallels that of the day in the prologues—simply taper off as the last of the characters in each section completes his dramatic soliloquy. In all but sections five and nine (the final section), all six characters speak. The final line clearly recalls the prologues (often called interludes), and in some sense "sums them up." But in its brevity, it cannot fully balance them. The final line thus parallels the prologues, but breaks the normal pattern of the sections and ends the novel with an asymmetrical difference and a surprising full stop. This final asymmetry emphasizes the asymmetry of the entire last section, which is the only section to have just one character speak.

The addition or omission of a single six-word line would seem to be a matter of colossal insignificance. But in *The Waves*, it just simply is not. For depending upon how Bernard's final section is interpreted and how the epilogue is related to Bernard's section, the meaning of this extraordinarily difficult novel shifts and changes. Woolf's confession (in the last diary entry quoted above)

that unresolved images abound at the end of the novel confirms
what any reader or critic of the novel knows: the book is at times
ambiguous and baffling, at times overcharged with images and
cross-references dazzlingly rich but intensely difficult to compre-
hend and order. The final section of the novel is among the most
difficult in the novel. Heeding Woolf's remarks, the discussion
which follows will not attempt to resolve all the patterns and cross-
patterns in Bernard's narration nor to discuss every image. But
it will attempt several things: to define the pressure Woolf's vision
exerts in the novel as a whole, and especially in the novel's final
section; to explain the appropriateness and meaning of Bernard's
final soliloquy; and, finally, to examine the relationship between
Bernard's final words and the novel's one-line, six-word epilogue.

## II

While preparing the holograph edition of *The Waves*, J. W. Graham published an interesting essay based on a comparison of the
two drafts, called "Point of View in *The Waves*: Some Services
of the Style."[6] As one of his observations, Graham notes that
Woolf began the novel with a clearly conceived omniscient narrator
and was oddly reluctant to abandon omniscient narration even
though it proved awkward and cumbersome in the developing
novel, and clashed with the book's "series of dramatic soliloquies."
He suggests that Woolf tried so hard for so long to retain the
omniscient narrator because she had outgrown the "cult of personality" that her subjective renderings of consciousness tended
to affirm and wanted to convey a sense of things *beyond* what any
of her characters perceive. In other words—and this is a comparison
Graham makes in passing but leaves undeveloped—she wished to
regain something of the role George Eliot had in *Middlemarch*:
the narrator as possessor of an Olympian point of view far superior
to the limited views of her characters, the narrator as seer. But
regaining the Olympian point of view possible in omniscient narration meant for Woolf a break with one of the constituent tech-

niques of modern fiction, a technique she had helped to develop and refine—the rejection of omniscient narration in favor of narration confined to the consciousness of characters.

Having set up a fascinating argument, Graham illogically abandons it, by seeing the omniscient narrator's role as usurped in the revised novel by Bernard's narration in the final section. Graham bases his position on stylistic affinities between the omniscient narrator's sections in the first draft and Bernard's final monologue. Whether intentionally or inadvertently, he implies that Bernard's vision in the last section is Olympian and privileged—equivalent to an omniscient narrator's. This is, indeed, a view implicitly shared by many critics of the novel,[7] who attribute the same affirmative, unifying value to Bernard's vision that Lily Briscoe's vision assumes at the end of To the Lighthouse. Yet there is really no reason to assume that the omniscient narrator's original place in the novel entirely disappears by the final draft: the interludes that precede each section are omnisciently narrated, as is the one-line epilogue. And if Bernard's vision equaled the omniscient narrator's, then the novel's final line (added to the second draft) would be simply redundant.

To appreciate the special pressures of closure in The Waves, the issues casually raised by Graham but left undeveloped must be explored—an exploration in which the comparison between Eliot's situation in Middlemarch and Woolf's in The Waves is instructive. Eliot can and must emphatically end Middlemarch with a philosophical discourse in which the omniscient authorial narrator makes clear what the characters and their story reveal about man, society, and the cosmos. She adopts the role of "Victorian sage" and is ready with the answers to questions raised in the novel. Indeed, she has carefully and artistically prepared for her Positivist philosophical conclusions by the development of verbal patterns that gradually reconcile the initially hostile epic and domestic levels of life. As the diaries reveal, Woolf in The Waves is also self-aware: she has a message to communicate, a vision she wants to impart to the reader. As her journal makes clear, she measures the success of the novel by its ability to suggest the contours of her vision.[8] But her vision and message are of a much vaguer, more private kind than Eliot's. And as has been widely noted about Woolf, she believes in the impossibility of any firm, clear, definite statement of the truth. "For nothing was simply one thing," thinks James in *To the Lighthouse* at a moment of maturity and growth. Says Bernard in *The Waves* in a statement with which Woolf agrees: "for ourselves, we resent teachers. Let a man get up and say, 'Behold, this is the truth,' and instantly I perceive a sandy cat filching a piece of fish in the background. Look, you have forgotten the cat, I say" (p. 187).

George Eliot would scoff at such a refusal of commitment. It is part of her strength as a novelist to say, in effect, "Behold the truth," without overlooking anything. Woolf's strength was, however, quite different. Her meaning must be "netted" at the end of the novel, but gently, unobtrusively. She does this by having the meaning emerge not solely from the omniscient epilogue, but from the epilogue as played against Bernard's soliloquy. The meaning of the ending depends on the blend of overview and close-up perspectives. To see Woolf's vision as equivalent to Bernard's or to the omniscient voice's is to misread the novel and to miss the fruitful tension at its end that allows Woolf to net her meaning without "forgetting the cat."

## III

The inclination to trust Bernard's insights at the end of *The Waves* is understandably great. On a first reading, *The Waves* flows by the reader, its meaning vague and difficult to paraphrase. The beginning of Bernard's final section lures the confused reader and promises enlightenment: " 'Now to sum up,' said Bernard. 'Now to explain to you the meaning of my life' " (p. 238). As a writer, Bernard seems a likely spokesman for the novelist, a fact that has perhaps led critics and readers to rely too much on him. Moreover, Bernard prefaces his "summing up" with a disclaimer that—in a Modernist novel by Virginia Woolf—augments rather than reduces his believability. Bernard explains that, "in order to make you understand, to give you my life, I must tell you a story—and there are so many, and so many—stories of childhood, stories of school, love, marriage, death, and so on; and none of them are true" (p. 238). Like James in *To the Lighthouse*, Bernard knows that any truth does not exclude alternative truths. Like Woolf herself in her essay "Modern Fiction," Bernard recognizes life as a "semi-transparent envelope," as a series of perceptions and sensations rather than as a clearly definable, single reality.[9]

In fact, to some extent, the reader must rely on Bernard's statements. For *of the six characters*, he is the *most nearly able* to communicate the author's vision. In a sense, Bernard truly does "sum up" the other characters. Like Neville and Louis, he writes and is successful in his chosen career; like Susan, he has a family and finds—for a time—joy in its rhythms. Like Jinny, he relishes society and conversation; like Rhoda, he is at times withdrawn and aware of a "world immune from change," which transcends career, family, and society (p. 107). Moreover, whereas each of the other characters remains relatively fixed in the novel, Bernard freely oscillates between differing approaches to life. As the most complex character, he also answers differently at various times in his life what may be called the novel's central questions: what is the proper relationship between the individual and the cosmos? Is "the essence of reality" the selves we cultivate or the universe which surrounds us? Can any line finally be drawn between the self and others, the self and the outer world, the self and the cosmos?

In his meditations on these questions, Bernard is once again the mean of the characters' extremes. Characters like Jinny and Neville emphasize the individual and the primacy of sexual love. Only superficially different from them, Susan values the extension of the individual through biological continuity. Traumatically made aware of the self when Jinny kissed him in the garden, Louis represses his awareness of the cosmos and concentrates on maintaining his precarious identity.[10] And at the opposite extreme from the others, Rhoda totally surrenders to her sense of oneness with the universe. None of these characters could narrate the final section as well as Bernard, because none could convey the two halves of Woolf's vision at Rodmell. Jinny, Neville, Susan, and Louis would ignore the cosmic, undifferentiated waste of waters that is one half of Woolf's vision. Rhoda would omit the other half of Woolf's vision—the fin suggestive of selfhood, of temporal, transient markers against the eternal waters. Attracted to both the undifferentiated cosmos and to the social world of the individual, Bernard is the character who can *best* "sum up" the novel and *begin* to articulate the balance Woolf envisions between the individual and the universe. To approach Woolf's vision we must, in fact, work through Bernard's final section, as will the remainder of this chapter. In my discussion, I will borrow a term from psychology—one fully consistent with the novel's own imagery—to describe the acute awareness of the universe and effacement of the individual self experienced to different degrees by the characters; I will call such cosmic feelings the "oceanic" sense.[11]

## IV

The characteristic movement of many of Bernard's sections is a rising and falling engagement with the "oceanic." In the novel's fourth section, the section of full maturity for the characters, Bernard's soliloquy occurs in one of the novel's favorite settings—a railroad station, a place where the individual merges into larger, mass configurations of people. Bernard's thoughts on this effacement of the individual are typical of him: he begins by thinking of himself, slips into a cosmic sense of reality, withdraws from his feelings of union with external things, and, finally, reflects on both his engagement with and removal from the "oceanic":

> "I am become part of this speed, this missile, hurled at the city. I am numbed to tolerance and acquiescence. . . . Over us all broods a splendid unanimity. We are enlarged and solemnised and brushed into uniformity as with the grey wing of some enormous goose. . . . I do not wish to be the first through the gate, to assume the burden of individual life. . . .

"Having dropped off satisfied like a child from the breast, I am at liberty now to sink down, deep, into what passes, this omnipresent, general life. . . . The surface of my mind slips along like a pale-grey stream reflecting what passes. . . .

"Yet behold, it returns. One cannot extinguish that persistent smell. It steals in through some crack in the structure— one's identity. I am not part of the street—no, I observe the street. One splits off, therefore.    (pp. 111-115)

The same rising and falling engagement with the "oceanic" is evident in the two crucial dinner scenes—the first a farewell dinner the young characters have for Percival, the second a commemorative dinner for the six characters, now grown middle-aged. When for a moment—a moment that, for Bernard, "was all . . . was enough"—the characters experience a sense of union with each other, Bernard articulates that union and coins the expressive image of the many-sided flower to convey its essence:

We have come together . . . to make one thing, not enduring— for what endures?—but seen by many eyes simultaneously. There is a red carnation in that vase. A single flower as we sat here waiting, but now a seven-sided flower, many-petalled, red, puce, purple-shaded, stiff with silver-tinted leaves—a whole flower to which every eye brings its own contribution.
(p. 127)

And, at the second dinner party:

"The flower," said Bernard, "the red carnation that stood in the vase on the table of the restaurant when we dined together with Percival is become a six-sided flower; made of six lives . . . a many-faceted flower. Let us stop for a moment; let us behold what we have made. Let it blaze against the yew trees. One life. There. It is over. Gone out."    (p. 229)

Yet in a falling motion away from the "oceanic," Bernard is also the character who recognizes that unifying moments pass, and that in the next moments each self resumes its individuality. Bernard characteristically both recognizes the "oceanic" and releases it as soon as he salutes it.

Bernard's narration in the last section of the novel condenses and emphasizes this rising and falling engagement with the oceanic and expands its applicability. In the first section of his "summing-up" chapter—his long monologue to a shadowy dinner companion—Bernard summarizes his own life and those of his friends and suggests that the pattern of rising and falling engagement with the "oceanic" is the overall pattern of every man's life. The novel's last section thus fulfills its original subtitle, "the life of anyone." Like Freud,[12] Bernard posits "in the beginning" a period of undifferentiated selfhood void of sensation. Shortly after birth, with the beginning of external stimuli, this "oceanic" sense is lost, a loss Bernard wishes could be spared others:

> "In the beginning, there was the nursery, with windows opening on to a garden, and beyond that the sea. . . . Then Mrs. Constable raised the sponge above her head, squeezed it, and out shot, right, left, all down the spine, arrows of sensation. And so, as long as we draw breath, for the rest of time, if we knock against a chair, a table, or a woman, we are pierced with arrows of sensation—if we walk in a garden, if we drink this wine. Sometimes indeed, when I pass a cottage with a light in the window where a child has been born, I could implore them not to squeeze the sponge over that new body.
> (p. 239)

In his own life, however, Bernard accepts the loss of the "oceanic" and the differentiation from others that comes as children react to external stimuli: "[when Susan cried] I felt my indifference melt. Neville did not melt. 'Therefore,' I said, 'I am myself, not Neville,' a wonderful discovery" (p. 240). But soon, the sense of differentiation from others becomes painful, not wonderful: "Louis was disgusted by the nature of human flesh; Rhoda by our cruelty; Susan could not share; Neville wanted order; Jinny love; and so on. We suffered terribly as we became separate bodies" (p. 241).

Caught up in the business of life—work, parties, writing, love affairs, marriage, children—the individual scarcely notices that time passes. For the most part, life proceeds smoothly and regularly:

> "Life is pleasant. Life is good. The mere process of life is satisfactory. . . . Something always has to be done next. Tuesday follows Monday; Wednesday Tuesday. Each spreads the same ripple of well-being, repeats the same curve of rhythm; covers fresh sand with a chill or ebbs a little slackly without. So the being grows rings; identity becomes robust.
>
> (pp. 261-62)

Yet for Bernard and for most men, "some doubt remained, some note of interrogation" about whether day-to-day life is a "covering over" of the true essence of things. On occasion, some chance event reveals the "oceanic" nature of reality, lifts "the corner of a curtain concealing the populous undifferentiated chaos of life which surged behind the outlines of my friends and the willow tree" (p. 249). In his life and those of his friends, the two dinner parties are chief among those events which capture the essence of things:

> half-way through dinner, we felt enlarge itself round us the huge blackness of what is outside us, of what we are not. The wind, the rush of wheels became the roar of time, and we rushed—where? And who were we? We were extinguished for a moment, went out like sparks in burnt paper and the blackness roared. Past time, past history we went. . . . I could not recover myself from the endless throwing away, dissipation, flooding forth without our willing it and rushing soundlessly away out there under the arches of the bridge, round some clump of trees or an island, out where seabirds sit on stakes, over the roughened water to become waves in the sea—I could not recover myself from that dissipation.
>
> (pp. 277-79)

Implicit in Bernard's narration of "the life of anyone" is the sense that although pressure toward the cosmic feeling is intense in sensitive beings, the "oceanic" interferes with life in the every-day world. Rhoda's marked inability to survive because of her intense attraction to the cosmic underscores Bernard's point: too strong an attachment to the "oceanic" impedes mature life. Yet the distinction made in Woolf's diary between "life" and "the essence of reality" should be remembered: ordinary routines and the responsibilities of work, society, and family constitute what is commonly called "life"; but "the essence of reality" is the "oceanic" sense of oneness with the universe which is only in-termittent in normal existence.[13]

Woolf's distinction is similar to that made by Mrs. Ramsay in *To the Lighthouse*, when she experiences "triumph over life" as a "core of darkness."[14] The Mrs. Ramsay the characters see and remember is a social being—a wife, a mother, a hostess, a soother of social tensions, an artistic creator of splendid, resonant, har-monic moments. But when alone, "Losing personality," she "could be herself, by herself," and becomes a "wedge-shaped core of darkness" (pp. 96, 95). Mrs. Ramsay's inner harmony and strength derive from her meditative moments of oneness with inanimate things (p. 97). Yet she regularly withdraws from her mystic states, perhaps to care for her husband (as at the end of chapter eleven), perhaps to perform another of her social roles. Moreover, she depends upon her husband to "save" her from her mystic ab-sorptions; she feels "his mind like a raised hand shadowing her mind" (p. 184). Thus, in *To the Lighthouse*, as more emphatically in *The Waves*, "oceanic" experience allows freer participation in "the essence of reality." But, for Mrs. Ramsay, it is necessarily, and even beneficially, hindered by the normal business of daily life.

In *The Waves*, however, the social reality within which char-acters live is far vaguer and more peripheral than in *To the Light-house*. Characters have social roles—as spouses, parents, hosts, guests—but the novel never directly portrays them functioning in these roles. As Woolf herself notes, *The Waves* is the most mystical of all her books.[15] Consequently, in *The Waves*, the "oceanic" becomes more persistent and more radical than in *To the Lighthouse*. As "the essence of reality," an essence almost untempered by scenes of domestic or social life, the "oceanic" necessarily exerts a powerful influence on all aspects of *The Waves* and persists with great force at its ending.

With its juxtaposition of interludes set on a beach and sections that record stages in the characters' lives, the very form of the novel suggests an "oceanic" identity between the processes of nature during a day and the psychological and social growth of the individual. Elements of style similarly mirror the "oceanic." The uniform style, vocabulary, and images used by Woolf to register the conscious and unconscious thoughts of her characters in soliloquy is a constant verbal equivalent of the "oceanic" sense that there is an underlying unity to reality that transcends the diversity of individual lives.[16] The construction of each section further mirrors the "oceanic." For most of the novel, the characters' soliloquies interlace, creating a web of recorded statements rather than a series of discrete utterances. Examples exist everywhere in the text:

> [end of Neville's soliloquy] But nature is too vegetable, too vapid. She has only sublimities and vastitudes and water and leaves. I begin to wish for firelight, privacy, and the limbs of one person."
>
> "I begin to wish," said Louis, "for night to come. . . .
>
> (p. 52)

At the dinner parties, this interlacing occurs most strikingly: the characters' intertwined utterances evoke a Greek chorus and have the effect of a choral poem. Boundaries between characters' minds seemingly dissolve, and their thoughts form a smooth and seamless web:

> "The leaf danced in the hedge without any one to blow it," said Jinny.
>
> "In the sun-baked corner," said Louis, "the petals swam on depths of green."
>
> "At Elvedon the gardeners swept and swept with their great brooms, and the woman sat at a table writing," said Bernard.

"From these close-furled balls of string we draw now every filament," said Louis, "remembering, when we meet."

"And then," said Bernard, "the cab came to the door . . . we were going to school. . . . A second severance from the body of our mother."

"And Miss Lambert, Miss Cutting, and Miss Bard," said Jinny, "monumental ladies, white-ruffed, stone-coloured, enigmatic, with amethyst rings moving like virginal tapers. . . ."

"Bells rang punctually," said Susan, "maids scuffled and giggled. . . . But from one attic there was a blue view, a distant view of a field unstained by the corruption of this regimented, unreal existence."

"Down from our heads veils fell," said Rhoda. "We clasped the flowers with their green leaves rustling in garlands."

"We changed, we became unrecognisable," said Louis. "Exposed to all these different lights, what we had in us (for we are all so different) came intermittently, in violent patches, spaced by blank voids, to the surface as if some acid had dropped unequally on the plate. I was this, Neville that, Rhoda different again, and Bernard too."     (pp. 124-26)

At these moments of intense union, another pressure the "oceanic" exerts in the novel comes to the surface: significantly, all the characters—even those normally indifferent or hostile to the "oceanic"—tell the story of a splitting-off, one from the other, "A second severance from the body of our mother." All the characters—and especially Louis, Rhoda, and Bernard—at moments feel with intensity and express by images a sense of themselves as having split off from some greater reality, as having lost an original state free from distinctions between inner and outer.

Finally, throughout the novel and especially in the last section, the images used for the development of individual selves (a development that, in itself, diminishes the cosmic feeling) nevertheless show the pervasive role that the "oceanic" plays in the novel. Bernard's favorite image for human development—"the being grows rings"—asserts, for example, an identity between human and nonhuman life, between men and trees. If we recall the germ of the novel in Woolf's vision at Rodmell, this pressure toward the "oceanic" in the novel is hardly surprising. The fin turns amid a waste of waters; the individual, however cherished, is only a transient "fin" against the relentless cosmic flux.

Understood in this way, the cosmic feeling and the "oceanic" sense are warnings of man's mortality, reminders and precursors of death itself. Bernard himself tellingly speculates that moments of "oceanic" unity are a foretaste of death. His speculation comes as, in the last section, he recalls his feelings immediately after the moment of unity at the second dinner party:

> "Was this then, this streaming away mixed with Susan, Jinny, Neville, Rhoda, Louis, a sort of death? A new assembly of elements? Some hint of what was to come? . . . Later, walking down Fleet Street at the rush hour, I recalled that moment; I continued it. 'Must I for ever,' I said, 'beat my spoon on the tablecloth? Shall I not, too, consent?' " (p. 279)

The question of whether Bernard will "consent" to the "oceanic" and to the death it resembles is a crucial one at the end of the novel. For Bernard's instinctive recoil from the "oceanic" as a precursor of death finally prevents Bernard from being fully able to articulate Woolf's vision and necessitates the addition of the one-line epilogue to prevent distortion.

## V

As Bernard recalls in his final soliloquy, when he was a child and first became aware of "what is unescapable in our lot; death,"

> the presence of an enemy had asserted itself; the need for opposition had stung me. I had jumped up and cried, 'Let's explore.' The horror of the situation was ended. (p. 269)

As a man, he continues to repeat the same strategy—the coining of phrases to deny death's reality—whenever confronted by the "oceanic" dissolution of self which is a foretaste of death. When, in his final section, Bernard recalls the second dinner party and its moment when "blackness roared," he also notes his own in-stinctive reaction to that moment:

> Past time, past history we went. For me this lasts but one second. It is ended by my own pugnacity. I strike the table with a spoon. If I could measure things with compasses I would, but since my only measure is a phrase, I make phrases—I forget what, on this occasion.    (p. 277)

Other examples recur throughout the novel, and, in the last section, are couched in terms of "fighting the enemy" that anticipate Bernard's last words in defiance of death.

Bernard's strategy survives even what has mistakenly been taken as a transforming experience for him—a moment of vision com-pared metaphorically to seeing an eclipse of the sun. He recounts this experience (again to his shadowy listener) in the second major portion of his final soliloquy, near the end of the novel; contrary to what some critics have assumed, the vision has occurred in the past, and is not occurring at the moment that Bernard speaks.[17] In his visionary moment, "A space was cleared in [his] mind," and he saw "the world . . . without a self" (pp. 283, 287). In this extreme moment of his life, his phrases failed him:

> "I spoke to that self who has been with me in many tre-mendous adventures . . . the man who has collected himself in moments of emergency and banged his spoon on the table, saying, 'I will not consent.'
> "This self now as I leant over the gate looking down over fields rolling in waves of colour beneath me made no answer. He threw up no opposition. He attempted no phrase. His fist did not form. I waited. I listened. Nothing came, nothing. I cried then with a sudden conviction of complete desertion, Now there is nothing. No fin breaks the waste of this im-measurable sea. Life has destroyed me. No echo comes when I speak, no varied words. This is more truly death than the death of friends, than the death of youth.    (pp. 283-84)

But typically, for Bernard, the moment passed as an eclipse passes, and a sense of self returned:

> it fades . . . it undergoes a gradual transformation, becomes, even in the course of one short walk, habitual—this [vision-ary] scene also. . . . One breathes in and out substantial breath; down in the valley the train draws across the fields lop-eared with smoke.
> "But for a moment. . . . the pages of the picture-book had stopped and had said, 'Look. This is the truth.' (p. 287)

Under the pressure of remembering this moment and recounting it to his shadowy dinner companion, Bernard moves once again into an "oceanic" sense of union with others, which is often (mistakenly) cited as the essential and final statement in Bernard's section:

> And now I ask, "Who am I?" I have been talking of Bernard, Neville, Jinny, Susan, Rhoda and Louis. Am I all of them? Am I one and distinct? I do not know. We sat here together. But now Percival is dead, and Rhoda is dead; we are divided; we are not here. Yet I cannot find any obstacle separating us. There is no division between me and them. As I talked I felt, "I am you." This difference we make so much of, this identity we so feverishly cherish, was overcome. (pp. 288-89)

But Bernard's dissolution of the self does not stop at this first stage of the oceanic (a sense of union with persons known); he welcomes all of his potential selves, "shadows of people one might have been; unborn selves" (p. 289). Descending ever deeper into the "oceanic," Bernard feels his body rise "tier upon tier like some cool temple" and becomes "Immeasurably receptive, holding everything, trembling with fullness" (p. 291). He takes upon him "the mystery of things" (p. 291).

At the end of this very vague and ambiguous section (Woolf had as much difficulty as anyone in communicating mystic states of mind), Bernard unwillingly returns to the reality of being an elderly man at a table in a restaurant, returns to the "I, I, I" (p. 296). Under pressure of his companion's eye,

Once more, I who had thought myself immune, who had said,
'Now I am rid of all that,' find that the wave has tumbled
me over, head over heels, scattering my possessions, leaving
me to collect, to assemble, to heap together, summon my
forces, rise and confront the enemy.    (p. 293)

I regain the sense of the complexity and the reality and the
struggle, for which I thank you.    (p. 294)

At this point, very near the end of the novel, Bernard's soliloquy
enters its final stage: he leaves his vague dinner companion and
walks in solitude to get the train home. He prays, "Let me cast
and throw away this veil of being" (p. 294), and vows "I have
done with phrases" (p. 295). Although he obeys his routine, he
resents being forced into the old habits, into the limited "I, I, I"
(p. 296).

But despite his vow not to make phrases, the habits of a lifetime
do not instantly break for Bernard. At the very end of the novel,
he is confronted with death itself as he walks to the train station.
Faced with death—the final and greatest "oceanic" experience—
Bernard falls back on his familiar phrases, uttered in images and
in a context which belie their efficacy. Although he definitively
recognizes the "oceanic," and spurs himself toward it as "the
eternal renewal, the incessant rise and fall and fall and rise again"
(p. 297), his old pugnacity returns and he paradoxically greets
death as an enemy, with words of defiance:

"And in me too the wave rises. It swells; it arches its back.
I am aware once more of a new desire, something rising
beneath me like the proud horse whose rider first spurs and
then pulls him back. What enemy do we now perceive advancing against us, you whom I ride now, as we stand pawing
this stretch of pavement? It is death. Death is the enemy. It
is death against whom I ride with my spear couched and my
hair flying back like a young man's, like Percival's, when he
galloped in India. I strike spurs into my horse. Against you
I will fling myself, unvanquished and unyielding, O Death!

The novel ends with the omniscient epilogue:

*The waves broke on the shore.*    (p. 297)

What occurs, then, at the end of *The Waves*, is a gesture of resistance by Bernard to what he knows is irresistible and to what has been the pervasive and dominant direction of the novel—the dissolution of the self, the triumph of the "oceanic" sense over the sense of selfhood, the inevitability of death. Woolf allows him to make his gesture of resistance because it fulfills his character and serves as a tribute to selfhood and—if we return to the hint in her diaries—to Thoby Stephen. But she adds the one-line epilogue lest the novel seem to suggest that the "oceanic" can finally be challenged by the will of the individual. In accordance with her credo in *To the Lighthouse*, Woolf declares that "nothing was simply one thing," and sees both the inevitable and the futile in Bernard's phrases, his will to fight death and order undifferentiated nature around himself.

Woolf's vision at Rodmell had two components: *a fin* turning in *a waste of waters*. The vision of the omniscient voice in the interludes and in the final line is too relentlessly objective a view of the cosmos, too hostile to the illusion of man's importance which sustains human life, to be fully Woolf's; it could not see that fin turning. But Bernard's last words are too dedicated to the significance of an individual's gestures and phrases. Both the epilogue and Bernard's last words are necessary at the end of the novel to express Woolf's vision. Bernard's gesture of resistance expresses the natural refusal of the biological self to dissolve and to cease existence in its accustomed form—the fin turning and making itself noted against a grey background. Every self—unless unformed and ill-equipped for life like Rhoda's—owes life this gesture of integrity, this greeting of death as enemy. Woolf's periods of madness and disorientation—which contribute to the character of Rhoda—had surely taught her this. But the underlying "oceanic" sense toward which the characters, the events, and the very form of the novel tend demands the final one-line, six-word epilogue, which echoes Bernard's "six-sided flower" and ends the novel with an affirmation of the essential unity and continuity of things, a unity and continuity that transcend the specific and the individual.

From an individual's viewpoint, when the wave of individual life breaks, the individual self is tragically lost. But from a cosmic point of view, at the very moment of dissolution, the wave rejoins the undifferentiated life force and awaits regrouping into another of its embodiments. The novel's highly stylized double ending effectively communicates the essential meaning of Woolf's vision. Feeling its success, she greets the novel's favorable reviews with an expression of triumph: "so it wasn't all wasted then. I mean this vision I had here has some force upon other minds."[18]

IN THE introduction, I noted that identification of endings as formal kinds like "epilogue" or "scene," though a helpful first step, tells us much less than we need to know about endings and closures. Identification of closural strategies using terms like circularity and parallelism, overview and close-up, complementary and incongruent, self-aware and self-deceiving takes us much further toward understanding how closure works in novels. But like any theoretical system, mine has its limitations and must ultimately be used as a way of entering into the complexities of individual texts rather than as a way of explaining away those complexities.

Compare, for example, the first and last novels I discuss—Eliot's *Middlemarch* and Woolf's *The Waves*. Eliot's ending is an epilogue, circular in pattern, overview in technique, which assumes a complementary relationship between author and reader during closure. *The Waves* ends with an epilogue, parallel in pattern, overview in technique, which also assumes a complementary relationship beween author and reader during closure. Both authors are self-aware. My terminology allows us to see unexpected and previously unperceived similarities between strategies of closure in Eliot's Victorian novel and in Woolf's Modernist one, while simultaneously pressing us to explore their differences. If any of my readers is tempted to rattle off terms rather than to use those terms to analyze attentively closures, my book will have failed in its attempt to provide a vocabulary for the description of closure that *initiates* rather than precludes further discussion.

I may prevent misuses of my approach if I point out the limitations of some of my terms and reiterate a basic but crucial point: any form, pattern, technique, or overall strategy of closure may have a variety of contents and effects. A theoretical framework for the discussion of closure can help us define particular contents and effects, but cannot, in itself, substitute for practical critical analyses, and for the kinds of fine distinctions called for by a given text. To create a taxonomy that would cover every possible variation in closural pattern, technique, or strategy would require a system more cumbersome and more elaborate than the Ptolemaic view of the universe in its last days. Instead, I have chosen to retain a workable, coherent, straightforward system responsive to the texts it describes. My position bears comparison to Wayne Booth's in *A Rhetoric of Irony* (Chicago: Univ. of Chicago Press, 1974), when he points out that although two works may employ the same kinds of irony and hence fit into the same descriptive "box," they will not be similar to each other in all, or even in most, ways.

The frequency with which the novels I have examined end in a circular return to the beginning of the work provides a convenient example. Of texts discussed here, *Middlemarch, Bleak House, The Scarlet Letter, Vanity Fair, L'Education sentimentale, The Ambassadors,* and *Light in August* end in this way.[1] Yet in most of these novels, completion of the circular pattern would seem mechanical, and even rather suspect as a method of resolution, were it not for the thematic contrasts or concordances established by the novel between beginning, middle, and end. The conclusion of *Middlemarch,* for example, is important not because it balances the St. Theresa beginning, but because it completes verbal patterns in the novel and provides Eliot with an opportunity to explain the importance of marriages reported in the text. Similarly, Faulkner's beginning and ending with Lena Grove would be glib and too simple were it not for the thematic contrasts Faulkner establishes between Joe Christmas' story and Lena's, and for the theme of story-telling as affirmation. The precise way circularity works in a novel cannot be summarized by the simple label.

The meaning implied by circularity, moreover, varies radically from novel to novel. A circular ending may suggest growth and change in a character by showing him behaving differently in a situation similar to that which began a novel, as in *The Ambassadors;* or it may show stagnation or stasis in a character, as in *L'Education sentimentale.* It may return to the novel's initial themes in order to resolve them (as in *Middlemarch*), to repeat them (as in *Vanity Fair*), or to reaffirm an ambivalence developed throughout the novel (as in *The Scarlet Letter*). Alternatively, a

circular ending may be largely a formal element, with little thematic significance. A circular ending can be used to give a novel
a consolatory, relatively happy ending, a bitterly ironic and unhappy one, or something in between; the endings of *Light in
August*, *L'Education sentimentale*, and *Middlemarch* respectively
illustrate these possibilities.

Despite its limitations, however, the approach I propose has a
number of practical advantages over existing analyses of closure
in novels. First, as I have already maintained, it provides a flexible
vocabulary to describe endings and closures—aspects of literature
that have aroused widespread and enduring interest. Second, it
provides a way out of the polemical approaches to closure of critics
like Girard and Friedman (discussed in the introduction), with their
insistence that the "novelistic" endings of nineteenth-century texts
are better than endings in twentieth-century texts, or that the
"open" endings of twentieth-century novels are "truer" than the
"closed" endings in nineteenth-century ones. Third, my approach
to closure indicates connections between literature and life established by endings, connections often overlooked in recent studies
of closure. I shall reserve discussion of this third advantage of my
approach to closure, since more needs to be said about the second.

## II

Certain generalizations about the historical development of closural
strategies can be drawn from the progression of my chapters. Some
of these generalizations confirm observations that have been made
about the broader history of the novel; others qualify or revise
such observations. Following writers like Roland Barthes, for example, critics have been accustomed to see a radical discontinuity
in both society and the novel, beginning about 1850, a discontinuity
demonstrated in the writings of Flaubert. Thus, according to
Barthes:

> Between the third person as used by Balzac and that used by
> Flaubert, there is a world of difference (that of 1848): in the
> former we have a view of History which is harsh, but coherent

and certain of its principles, the triumph of an order; in the latter, an art which in order to escape its pangs of conscience either exaggerates conventions or frantically attempts to destroy them.[2]

The process of "exaggerating conventions" or "frantically seeking to destroy them" often underlies confrontational endings, as we have seen them in novels by Thackeray, Flaubert, and James. Such endings began to appear in the late 1840's and are very different in tone and intent from earlier endings (most not really worthy of detailed attention), which poked fun at existing conventions for ending *without* entering a confrontational relationship with the reader during closure. I am thinking here of endings like that to Scott's *Old Mortality*, and those to most of Austen's novels, endings of a kind mentioned earlier in this study.[3]

Within twenty years after the turn of the present century, as experimentation with endings and the rise of the "art novel" revised reader expectations, confrontational endings began to fade. Early Modernists, like James, opened up reader expectations for, and acceptance of, new kinds of endings. Thus, authors like Faulkner and Woolf, writing after the early Modernists, simply *assumed* readers would accept their endings. In the novels I have examined, Faulkner and Woolf felt little need to anticipate an incongruent relationship during closure, to work for a congruent one, or to write a confrontational ending. Indeed, they wrote with full confidence that their reader would be the ideal reader, even though this has not always proven to be the case. Their sense of their audience was radically different from that shown by James (who lamented the absence of the ideal reader), or even from those shown by writers like Eliot, Hawthorne, and Tolstoy (who educated their readers).

Thus far, my system confirms the idea of *discontinuities* in the history of the novel, discontinuities naturally reflected in two important aspects of novelistic shape—endings and closures. My approach simultaneously, however, reveals *continuities* in the novelistic tradition. It is, for example, striking that for their endings novels of both the nineteenth and twentieth centuries use overview techniques, close-up techniques, or some combination of the two, and that novels of both centuries follow circular, parallel, incomplete, tangential, and linking patterns. We can justifiably maintain that Faulkner's ending has as much in common with Hawthorne's, or Woolf's with Eliot's, as either has with the endings of Henry James, even though James, Faulkner, and Woolf are Modernists, and the others are not. Indeed, if we take a broader approach to the history of fiction, the terms I propose to describe closure would work for earlier narrative forms, just as many of the terms Robert Scholes and Robert Kellogg apply to character, plot, and point of view in *The Nature of Narrative* work for narratives of all periods.[4] Most critics of how novels end—like Girard, Friedman, Kermode— did not lead us to expect such similarities to exist.

## III

In a recent study, *Making Sense of Literature*, John Reichert considers the nature of evaluating literature and the question of what makes a given work of literature "good." He replies with the simple yet sophisticated question: "Good for what?"[5] We may ask the same question and give the same answer in evaluating closures. The endings of *Bleak House* and *War and Peace* are "good" for allaying Dickens' and Tolstoy's anxieties about the value of family life and for pleasing readers inclined to sentimentalize domesticity. They are not, however, "good" as programs to reform society or as prescriptions for how individuals should live. The ending of *Middlemarch* is "good" for providing a consolatory view of the individual's role in bettering a sometimes hostile world; Flaubert's ending in *L'Education sentimentale* is "good" for discomforting the reader and for showing the folly of many common human aspirations. By avoiding implicit value judgments linked to its descriptive terms, my approach to closure acknowledges many ways that an ending can be "good," and allows each novel to be examined in its own terms.

Some of my observations—like that of the ease with which post-Jamesian authors assume complementary relationships with read-

ers during closure—and the generally chronological sequence of
my chapters may inadvertently, however, suggest an evaluative
generalization frequently made: the generalization that endings
and closures in recent novels are somehow "better" and more
complex than those in older novels. In reality, I mean to challenge
that generalization, and would like now to do so. When Alan
Friedman asserts in *The Turn of the Novel* that twentieth-century
endings are "truer" and more interesting than those in nineteenth-
century novels, he provides the best-known and most highly developed statement of the position in favor of recent fiction.[6] But
although he is the most vulnerable critic holding this view, Friedman is not alone. Smith and Kermode occasionally seem to suggest
that Modernist "open" endings deserve fuller discussion than older
endings do, if only because they are both in the process of defining
the "open" ending. Lightly made comments by otherwise percep-
tive critics reinforce the same misconception. I select two examples
among many: the dismissal of nineteenth-century endings as
"lacking sophistication" in a recent book on the novel; the statement that most nineteenth-century endings are an epistemological
"form of deception, veiling the abyss" in an article in the *New
York Review of Books*.[7] The very vocabulary of the last statement
betrays a Modernist bias. All these critics implicitly invoke a deceptive standard for discussing and evaluating endings—the criterion of newness.

Sensibly applied, a criterion calling for novelty of effect works
against modern novels as often as it does against older ones. Endings in which hero marries heroine and lives happily ever after
will, for example, hardly startle most readers familiar with fairy
tales, dramatic comedy, or popular fiction. In the nineteenth-century, an ending of this kind was, indeed, often "merely conventional." And by reaching a purely mechanical conclusion, authors
like Dickens in fact weakened their works. But in contemporary
novels, an old-fashioned happy ending can be downright refreshing, as for example, in Fowles' *Daniel Martin*, a novel only intermittently distinguished.

Even endings that self-consciously strove for newness against the model of the marital happy ending—as I have maintained that Henry James's did—are effective not primarily because they are "new," but because they arose as the appropriate endings to novels constructed along particular patterns of plot and character. Jamesian endings are "good" not because they differ from nineteenth-century endings, but because they suit Jamesian fictions. We might argue, indeed, that the effectiveness of Jamesian endings depends in part on their recognizable deviation from older patterns. James basically complicates and inverts, after all, the expected elements of the conventional marital happy ending. Instead of a joyous marriage, group or community focus, chastisement of vice and rewarding of virtue, James gives us the rejection of ordinary married happiness and love, a focus on two characters, and ambiguity surrounding questions of vice and virtue. And knowledge of the older, "conventional" format increases the impact of the newer, "unconventional" one.

Admirers of the "new" in novelistic closure should also consider the effect of "open" endings, once a "new" and dynamic form, in recent novels like Fowles' *The French Lieutenant's Woman*, Jong's *Fear of Flying*, and Malamud's *The Tenants*.[8] In *The French Lieutenant's Woman*, a novel that takes a backward look at the Victorian period, the ending suitably toys with the popular nineteenth-century after-history convention. It twists the technique by providing two alternative epilogues, either (or neither) of which may be believed by the reader: the first a "happy ending" in which Sarah and Charles are reunited by their child; the second an ending in which Charles angrily leaves a feminist, independent Sarah in the Rossettis' house, without ever discovering the existence of his child. Fowles builds freedom into the ending because "there is no intervening god [in human affairs] beyond *the actions of men* (and of women) *in pursuit* of their ends."[9] Like the impresario who turns back the clock fifteen minutes to make the second ending possible, the novelist provides possibilities of closure consistent with character, but refuses to present definitive, conclusive facts.

*Fear of Flying* and *The Tenants* undercut the possibility of ending a novel and, like Fowles' work, are self-consciously "open." The simpler of the two, *Fear of Flying*, ends with the heroine, Isadora Wing, awaiting the return of her husband, whom she has flagrantly deserted earlier in the novel. Wing arrives, the door begins to open, the novel ends. Its climax and potential reunion are clipped off the text. As in Fowles' novel, the effect is striking, but somehow "gimmicky," and is curiously paraphrasable, as the endings of most of the novels I have studied are not. A contemporary reader immediately gets the point and nods in recognition of a model "open" ending. A form of conclusion that would once have been shocking and new has become thoroughly expected and conventional.

Of the three, Malamud's *The Tenants* is the most complexly concerned with closure and its difficulty, which is to find a "sufficient ending, the one that must be if the book is to be as good as it must."[10] The novel itself ends four times, the first time after a mere twenty-three pages. To emphasize closure as a theme even more heavily, the plot features a writer named Lesser who is having great difficulty finishing his novel, and an unfinished painting upon which he broods. The novel's self-conscious involvement with closure is further announced on its book jacket and in its first sentence: "Lesser catching sight of himself in his lonely glass wakes to finish his book" (p. 3). At the actual end of the novel, Lesser and Willie— a black writer with whom Lesser has entered artistic and sexual rivalries—destroy each other in an ambiguously dreamlike scene: Lesser plunges an axe through Willie's brain as the black man castrates Lesser with a razor. This action is followed by the words "The End," and by the book's fourth and final ending, a plea for mercy uttered by the landlord, Levenspiel, with the word "mercy" printed for a solid fourteen lines of the text.

*The Tenants* is a carefully written novel, and a detailed analysis of the endings would certainly be possible. It would be possible, for example, to explore the structural resemblance between Levenspiel's plea and Willie's poem "Manifested Destiny," and other elements of parallelism. Or the gradual takeover of racist stereotypes in the men's relationship might be considered. Or the question of whether the third and most violent ending is (like the first and second), fantasy rather than fact might be answered and further questions asked: does the novel maintain that endings are illusory and never achieved in life? If so, is the inability to conclude a sign of weakness or of strength? But the text does not really inspire such questions. Ironically, or prophetically, it is the weakest part of an often interesting novel.

More clearly than the other two recent novels mentioned here, Malamud's indicates why none of these "open" endings is especially effective: the idea of the "open"ending seems to precede the creation of the novel; it does not emerge from the work as inevitable and right. Indeed, there is a mechanical, *idées reçues*, quality to these endings, similar to that at the end of Dickens' novels and at the end of purely conventional fiction in any period. By the nineteen-sixties and nineteen-seventies, the "open" ending had become too trite and expected to have great imaginative force. "Open"endings can be as "merely conventional" as the older techniques for ending they replaced. Far from being absolute, then, the criterion of newness must always be applied with a nervous glance around to see what novelists are writing and how audiences are reacting. The "new" becomes the familiar and tired relatively soon in the novel genre.[11]

One further complication may be added at this point to the too simple idea that innovative endings are good endings: in the hands of an imaginative artist, even a stale form of ending can become vital and new. Consider, for example, Nabokov's use of the after-history convention in *Lolita*. Playfully, Nabokov gives after-histories of his characters not at the end of his novel, but at its beginning, in the bogus "Foreword" supposedly written by "John Ray, Jr., Ph.D." Ray snickeringly condescends to give "a few details" about the later lives of figures in the story,

> For the benefit of old-fashioned readers who wish to follow the destinies of "real" people beyond the "true" story.[12]

Among the details, some are significant and some are not. Important details include the death of Humbert Humbert "in captivity," and the death of Lolita, several months later, "giving birth to a stillborn girl, on Christmas Day 1952, in Gray Star, a settlement in the remotest Northwest" (p. 6).

The effect of giving after-histories at the beginning of the book is peculiar, and differs on first and subsequent readings of the novel. When encountering the novel for the first time, the reader is essentially indifferent to the fates of all the characters, except possibly to that of the text's supposed author, Humbert Humbert. Indeed, the reader *should* be indifferent, since he as yet knows nothing of the characters he is mockingly expected to care for as "old-fashioned readers" cared for Little Nell and Jane Eyre; even the title character, Lolita, appears in her after-history disguised by the name Dolly Schiller. On a second or subsequent reading, however, we realize that Nabokov has played several tricks on his reader beyond that of writing a fake introduction. For example, although "Ray" implies that any reader who cares about characters as "real people" is hopelessly naive, Nabokov provides dates, names, and details that would convince the truly naive reader that the characters *are* real people. Moreover, the circumstances of Lolita's death are curiously moving, despite their heavy-handed symbolism. Certainly, a reader who finishes the novel without remembering what happens to Lolita has missed something important to the novel. And the reader's view of Humbert Humbert becomes, I think, more marked by pathos if he reads Humbert's remarks (particularly his closing remarks, in which Humbert wrongly assumes that Lolita survives him by many years) with an awareness of the after-histories. In his use of after-histories, Nabokov both parodies an old-fashioned convention for ending and reminds us of the convention's roots and continuing source of potential power—the natural empathy that even sophisticated readers can be made to feel for characters as representations of human beings.

After being praised for many years, the "open" ending has recently come under critical attack and, insofar as it has become "merely conventional," rightly so.[13] In a sense, from the beginning of its use, the term "open" ending was an unfortunate one. Every novel, including an "open" one, establishes by its ending a "closed" network of internal relationships. And even endings that produce a feeling of finality, as most endings involving a shift in time scale do, may be relatively "open" or relatively "closed" when compared to similar endings. The distant historical perspective of the endings to *Middlemarch* and *The Scarlet Letter* may serve as examples of relatively "closed" endings that use the time-shift technique; the short span elapsed between epilogue and novel and the ending on a dash in *Bleak House* and *War and Peace* may serve as examples of relatively "open" endings using this technique. Moreover, application of the terms "open" and "closed" can sometimes be very much a matter of interpretation, as it is in *War and Peace*. As I have interpreted them, novels like *Light in August* and *The Waves* should be considered "closed," although a critic like Friedman would probably wish to call them "open."

## IV

I return now to the third practical advantage of my approach to closure: by taking account of the author's preoccupations and the reader's experience during closure, the approach I suggest reasserts the relevance of closure to the people who participate in it—author and reader. In the introduction, I have already indicated a number of ways in which closure pertains to human experience.[14] I should like to conclude by exploring one more connection between closure, the shape of fictions, and the shape of life that my terminology (particularly the last two sets of terms) helps to indicate.

As I noted in the introduction, a great deal has been made of the idea that endings in fictions falsify life by distorting the subjective, non-retrospective experience of man "in the middest." As I have maintained, we can avoid the partiality of this view by recognizing the analogies as well as the differences between living and reading. But we should also note that this idea denies some basic conventions of the reading experience. Anyone who reads a novel knows, after all, that he is dealing with a representation of experience that can be expected to include elements of *harmonia* (arrangement), as well as of *mimesis* (imitation). That he reads poems or novels at all indicates the value of the shaping and ordering of experience that constitutes literary art.

By acknowledging frankly the shaping, ordering qualities of literature—its "faking" as Sartre sees it—we can speak of endings not as "true" or "false," but speak instead of the direction in which "faking" takes place. Most of the novels I have examined are intensely concerned not just with language or form, but also with complex characterization and with propositions about human experience. Accordingly, their endings "fake" by using the novel's form to compel the reader's understanding of character or theme. Some of the novels I have examined "fake" to suggest optimistic or consolatory views of human experience. With equal validity, others "fake" to imitate or stress experiences of discontent, uncertainty, futility, absurdity, or banality. Some novels succeed in capturing more than one view of human experience by providing more than one ending—as, for example, *The Waves* does. In fictions less concerned with characterization and with propositions about human experience than most of the novels I have examined, however, an ending may properly "fake" to achieve a more purely formal or language-based, less strongly thematic or character-based, sense that a novel has reached an appropriate conclusion.

In a famous essay, the Russian Formalist Victor Shklovsky discusses defamiliarization as a function of literature: by "making things strange," literature reveals the "stoniness" of a stone; it makes us feel the essence of things.[15] I have already argued that endings invite the retrospective analysis of a text and create the illusion of life halted and poised for analysis. If we expand Shklovsky's idea slightly and apply it to endings and closures, we can then say that, in major fictions, effective endings command a novel to "stand still here" in a way that defamiliarizes and makes us feel anew the artfulness of a fictional structure, the essence of some human experience, or both.[16]

At the end of *The Golden Bowl*, James compels us to understand Maggie's motivations, to feel the ambivalences and tensions that accompany human compromises, and the need of the compromiser to will them away. In *Middlemarch* and *The Scarlet Letter*, Eliot and Hawthorne make us aware (as if we never were) of the limitations imposed by social orders and the sense of frustration men and women have always experienced. In *Light in August*, Faulkner makes us feel the aberrant forces behind Christmas, Hightower, and Joanna Burden, and also makes us acknowledge the ability of men to forget and move on, and the power of anecdote to order and cheer, if not to improve, the world. At the end of *War and Peace*, Tolstoy makes us feel, as if for the first time, the happiness found in rhythms of family life, and the precariousness of that happiness. In *L'Education sentimentale*, Flaubert makes us feel the banality of experience and the distances and gaps between desire and fufillment, man and man. No paraphrase can, however, finally convey the richness of what each text makes us feel about even the most common of human experiences. For each of these endings makes us feel anew the power of literary form to challenge the intellect and engage the emotions by its particular shaping of fiction in closure.

## Introduction

[1] *Aspects of the Novel* (1927; New York: Harcourt, Brace and World, rpt. 1954), pp. 26-27.

[2] Preface to *Roderick Hudson*, rpt. in *The Art of the Novel*, ed. R. P. Blackmur (1907; New York: Scribner's, 1962), p. 6.

[3] J. Hillis Miller takes this position in several recent essays. See, for example, "Ariadne's Thread," *Critical Inquiry*, 3 (Autumn, 1976) 56-77 and "The Problematic Ending in Narrative," *Nineteenth-Century Fiction*, 33: 1 (June, 1978), 3-7.

[4] James, p. 6.

[5] Forster, pp. 149-69.

[6] James, p. 5.

[7] The term "retrospective patterning" is used throughout Barbara Herrnstein Smith's *Poetic Closure* (Chicago: Univ. of Chicago Press, 1968).

[8] *Poetics*, trans. S. H. Butcher (New York: Hill and Wang, 1961), p. 65.

[9] (Chicago: Univ. of Chicago Press, 1978).

[10] *Strains of Discord: Studies in Literary Openness* (Ithaca: Cornell Univ. Press, 1968).

[11] (New York: Oxford Univ. Press, 1966).

[12] Herodotus shows awareness of this principle in the history of King Croesus when, after the fall of his empire and his capture by the Persians, Croesus understands the truth of Solon's words that "no man could be considered happy until he was dead." See *The Histories*, trans. Aubrey de Selincourt (Baltimore: Penguin, 1965), p. 48.

A biography of King Oedipus or of another tragic hero would be a very different document from Greek dramas, in part because events and words misunderstood in the play by characters like Oedipus would become portentous and receive emphasis in a retrospective narration.

[13] (Paris: Gallimard, 1938), pp. 62-63; trans. Lloyd Alexander (New York: New Directions, 1974), p. 39.

[14] Sartre, p. 63; p. 40.

[15] Kermode, p. 148.

[16] "Narrative Fictions and Reality," *Novel*, 11 (Fall, 1977), 40-50.

[17] In the experience of literature, such tentative guessing has been called establishing the "intrinsic genre" of an utterance, the "intrinsic genre" being "that sense of the whole by means of which an interpreter can correctly understand any part in its determinacy." See E. D. Hirsch, Jr., *Validity in Interpretation* (New Haven: Yale Univ. Press, 1967), p. 86.

[18] Trans. Yvonne Freccero (1961; Baltimore: Johns Hopkins Univ. Press, 1965),

p. 296. The original French title was *Mensonge romantique et vérité romanesque.*

[19] (New York: Oxford Univ. Press, 1966), p. 188.

[20] 33: 1 (June, 1978); (Berkeley: Univ. of California Press, 1979).

[21] Boris Eikhenbaum, "O'Henry and the Theory of the Short Story," rpt. *Readings in Russian Poetics*, ed. Ladislav Matejka and Krystyna Pomorska (Cambridge, Mass.: M.I.T. Press, 1971), p. 232. The essay originally appeared in the nineteen-twenties.

[22] "The Art of Fiction," rpt. in *The American Tradition in Literature*, vol. 2, eds. Sculley Bradley, Richard Croom Beatty and E. Hudson Long (1884; New York: Norton, 1967), p. 833.

[23] Gide provides explicit comments on the motivations behind his ending to *Les Faux Monnayeurs*. See (in English) *Journal of the Counterfeiters*, trans. Justin O'Brien, in *The Counterfeiters* (1927; New York: Modern Library, 1955), pp. 447, 449, and 450. For the French original, see *Journal des Faux Monnayeurs*, *Œuvres Complètes d'André Gide*, vol. XIII (Brussels: NRF, 1937), pp. 57-58, 60, 61-62.

[24] I translate from the French Houssiaux edition (1837-43; Paris: Houssiaux, 1955).

[25] Trans., Constance Garnett (1866; New York: Bantam, 1958), p. 472.

[26] See Lubbock's *The Craft of Fiction* (1921; New York: Viking, 1957).

[27] The phrase, used extensively by Kermode, is Sir Philip Sidney's.

[28] *The Rhetoric of Fiction* (Chicago: Univ. of Chicago Press, 1961), p. 74.

[29] See the end of this introduction for a discussion of the intentional fallacy and how it applies to my work. For support of my position, see the statement by Paul Ricoeur in *Interpretation Theory: Discourse and the Surplus of Meaning* (Fort Worth: Texas Christian Univ. Press, 1976), p. 30.

[30] The two best-known proponents of reader-response approaches are Stanley Fish and Wolfgang Iser. See especially Iser's book, *The Act of Reading: a Theory of Aesthetic Response* (Baltimore: Johns Hopkins Univ. Press, 1978). Also useful is a debate recently printed in *Novel*: Edward Bloom, ed., "In Defense of Authors and Readers," 11: 1 (Fall, 1977), 5-25.

[31] Especially useful sources include Richard Stang, *The Theory of the Novel in England 1850-1870* (New York: Columbia Univ. Press, 1959); Richard Altick, *The English Common Reader* (Chicago: Univ. of Chicago Press, 1957); and the volumes in the Critical Heritage Series published by Barnes and Noble.

[32] See Karl Kroeber, *Styles in Fictional Structure: the Art of Jane Austen, Charlotte Brontë, George Eliot* (Princeton: Princeton Univ. Press, 1971).

## Chapter One

[1] I borrow the term "after-history," which he uses to define the epilogue, from Boris Eikhenbaum; see introduction, p. 11 and note 21.

[2] (1816; New York: Everyman, 1968), p. 429.

[3] See the ending to Dickens' *Pickwick Papers* (1837; New York: New American

Library, 1964), p. 861, and that to Trollope's *The Warden* (1855; New York: New American Library, 1964), p. 198, respectively.

[4] George Eliot, *Middlemarch* Cabinet edition (Edinburgh and London: William Blackwood and Sons, 1877-1880), III, p. 455. As for all texts used repeatedly for quotations, subsequent page references will be incorporated into the text.

[5] Several critics have commented on "web" metaphors in *Middlemarch*. See, for example, Quentin Anderson, "George Eliot in *Middlemarch*," rpt. in *The Pelican Guide to English Literature: From Dickens to Hardy*, vol. VI, ed. Boris Ford (London: Penguin, 1958), pp. 274-93.

[6] *The George Eliot Letters*, ed. Gordon S. Haight, vol. V (New Haven: Yale Univ. Press, 1954), p. 168.

[7] *Letters*, II, p. 324.

[8] See *Letters*, II, pp. 324-26, 328, 334.

[9] *Letters*, II, pp. 325-26.

[10] As is well known, *Middlemarch* incorporates an earlier, shorter narrative called "Miss Brooke" with the story of Lydgate. The two plotlines were not conceived together but were brought together by Eliot as clearly parallel. See Jerome Beaty, *Middlemarch From Notebook to Novel: A Study of George Eliot's Creative Method* (Urbana: Univ. of Illinois Press, 1960).

[11] *Letters*, V, p. 58.

[12] *Letters*, V, p. 261.

[13] In a revision of the ending, Eliot wisely omitted a section from this passage (after "imperfect social state"), which too narrowly and stridently blamed the community for Dorothea's marriage to Casaubon. See the footnote in the Riverside edition for the original version.

[14] For detailed studies of Positivist influences on Eliot, see the following: Thakur Guru Prasad, *Comtism in the Novels of George Eliot* (Lucknow, India: 1968); Bernard J. Paris, *Experiments in Life: George Eliot's Quest for Values* (Detroit: Wayne State Univ. Press, 1965); U. C. Knoeflmacher, *Religious Humanism in the Victorian Novel* (Princeton: Princeton Univ. Press, 1965).

[15] See *The Compact Edition of the Oxford English Dictionary*, vol. I (Oxford: Oxford Univ. Press, 1971), p. 1764.

## Chapter Two

[1] See Introduction, note 22.

[2] Unsigned review, *Bentley's Miscellany*, xxxiv, October, 1853, rpt. in *Dickens: The Critical Heritage*, ed. Philip Collins (New York: Barnes and Noble, 1971), p. 287.

[3] *The Moral Art of Dickens* (New York: Oxford, 1970), p. 13.

[4] Richard J. Dunn, "Far, Far Better Things," *Dickens Studies Annual*, vol. 7, ed. Robert B. Partlow, Jr. (London: Feffer and Simons, 1978), pp. 221-38. Alexander Welsh, *The City of Dickens* (Oxford: Clarendon Press, 1971), pp. 220-27. Garrett

Stewart, "The New Mortality of *Bleak House,*" *ELH,* vol. 45 (1978), 443-487.
Edward Said, *Beginnings: Intention and Method* (New York: Basic Books, 1975).

[5] *PMLA.* 88 (1973), pp. 429-39.

[6] P. 438.

[7] *Bleak House,* Norton Critical edition, eds. George Ford and Sylvère Monod
(New York: Norton, 1977), p. 5. Although it is a paperback edition, the Norton
is becoming the standard edition of *Bleak House.* See the editors' comments on
existing hardcover editions of the novel on pp. 807-11.

[8] See especially Steven Marcus, *Dickens: From Pickwick to Dombey* (New York:
Basic Books, 1965), pp. 46, 60, and 255; see also T.A. Jackson, *Charles Dickens:
The Progress of a Radical* (New York: Haskell, 1971); and Mario Praz, *The Hero
in Eclipse in Victorian Fiction* (New York: Oxford, 1956). Steven Marcus, like
George Ford in *Dickens and his Readers* (Princeton: Princeton Univ. Press, 1955),
sees Dickens' political message as mild enough to win him an audience both from
those desiring reform and those in favor of the status quo. See Marcus, pp. 46 and
60 and Ford, p. 80.

Among those who defend Dickens from charges that his social message was
expedient, not effective, are his early biographer, John Forster, and G. K. Chesterton
in *Charles Dickens* (1906; New York: Dodd, Mead & Co., 1920). Perhaps the most
elegant word on the subject is that of George Orwell in his essay, "Charles
Dickens": "His radicalism is of the vaguest kind, and yet one always knows that
it is there. That is the difference between being a moralist and a politician." See
*Inside the Whale* (1940; London: Penguin, 1962), p. 81.

[9] Rpt. in *Bleak House: A Casebook,* ed. A. E. Dyson (London: Macmillan, 1969),
p. 93.

[10] Earlier in the novel, Krook notes that should Flite ever release her birds they
would be an easy prey to birds not used to captivity. This unsentimental view of
the matter occurs, typically, near the beginning, not near the end of the novel.

[11] *The Form of Victorian Fiction* (Notre Dame: Univ. of Indiana Press, 1970),
pp. 110-12.

[12] Viewed symbolically, the last moments of the novel—in which Allan suggests
that Esther is more beautiful than ever—reinforce the novel's drive at the end
to excel past happiness and contentment.

[13] Most of my readers will be familiar with this aspect of Dickens' life. Despite
having a large family and a strong public image as a happy family man, Dickens
always felt ambivalent toward his wife and idealized and admired her sisters, who
shared the Dickens' home. The marriage ended scandalously in 1858 (after twenty-
five years), with Dickens' separation and estrangement from his wife and children
and his increasing involvement with a younger mistress, Ellen Ternan, who is the
model for Estella in *Great Expectations.*

[14] "Dickens and Social Ideas," *Dickens 1970,* ed. Michael Slater (New York: Stein
and Day, 1970), p. 87.

[15] Issue no. 1 (March 30, 1850), p. 1. Quotations below from same source.

## Chapter Three

¹ *War and Peace*, trans. Aylmer Maude (1869; New York: Norton, 1966), pp. 4 and 10. I follow Maude in transliterating all Russian names in this chapter, except when convention dictates a variant spelling, e.g., Tolstoy. The Norton text follows that of the Oxford Centenary Edition of Tolstoy's Works, published in 1928. This translation has become standard, but is often quite difficult to obtain. The Norton text has, therefore, assumed the role of standard translation. The same is true for the edition of *Anna Karenina* used later in this chapter. Since I do not read Russian, I have had to rely on translations of Russian critics and criticism written in English or French in this dicussion of Tolstoy.

² In the original Russian edition, Tolstoy wrote a single epilogue, which may be divided into two parts—the familial or narrative epilogue and the philosophical epilogue. I follow Maude's translation in referring to the familial ending to the narrative sections of *War and Peace* as the first epilogue, the philosophical ending as the second epilogue.

³ Boris Eikhenbaum explores *War and Peace*'s relationship to English novels and their treatment of families in the untranslated *Lev Tolstoy*, II (Leningrad, 1931), parts 3 and 4. Another untranslated source, G. Volkov, "*Voina i mir*. Neizdannyye teksty" (Lit, nas., 33-36, pp. 286, 350, 380), examines the original ending. I found references to both in an unpublished dissertation written in English by Michael H. Futrell called "Dickens and Three Russian Novelists: Gogol, Dostoyevsky, Tolstoy," submitted to the University of London in 1965, pp. 271-72. In *What is Art?* Tolstoy includes Dickens and Eliot among writers of the highest form of art. The idealization of the family we have seen at different levels in Dickens and Eliot may have been one basis for Tolstoy's attraction to these English writers. See also Nicholas Apostolov, "Tolstoy & Dickens," *Family Views of Tolstoy*, trans. and ed. Louise and Aylmer Maude (London: Allen & Unwin, 1926).

⁴ Michael Katz, Professor of Russian at Williams College, is preparing a book on dreams in Russian literature and called this to my attention.

⁵ By contemporary standards, Tolstoy's views on male and female differences are certainly sexist. My interest is, however, in how Tolstoy's beliefs affect closure and not in debating Tolstoy's views.

⁶ (New York: Dutton, 1971), and (New York: Simon and Schuster, 1966).

⁷ This is Lukács' own summary of his views in *Studies in European Realism* (1938; New York: Grosset and Dunlap, 1965), p. 3.

⁸ P. 3.

⁹ Leo Tolstoy, *My Confession* (New York: Walter Scott Publishing Company, n.d.), p. 23.

¹⁰ Tolstoy identifies in himself a syndrome many have identified in Dickens, who also idealized family life but had a notoriously stormy and unsuccessful marriage. See chapter two, note 13.

¹¹ Leo Tolstoy, *Anna Karenina*, trans. Louise and Aylmer Maude (1878; New

York: Norton, 1970), p. 1. As for *War and Peace*, the Norton edition has become the standard text of the novel in translation.

[12] See chapters VIII, IX, X for Tolstoy's account of this process in his own life, which duplicates almost word by word this section of *Resurrection*.

[13] Leo Tolstoy, *Resurrection*, trans. Vera Traill (1903; New York: New American Library, 1961), p. 427. No really satisfactory translation of *Resurrection* exists. Faced with a choice between the difficult to obtain translation by Louise Maude in the Oxford Centenary edition and the widely available translation by Vera Traill in the Signet paperback, I have chosen the latter.

[14] As with Dickens' life, the basic facts of Tolstoy's are probably familiar to most readers. After a series of feuds between Tolstoy's family and his disciples, Tolstoy, at eighty-two, felt compelled to leave his home and renounce his family. Traveling alone, he died ten days later at a railroad hotel.

## Chapter Four

[1] "Editor's Introduction," *The Portable Hawthorne*, rev. ed. (New York: Viking, 1971), p. 18.

[2] *The Power of Blackness* (New York: Knopf, 1958), p. 74.

[3] The prologue also contains, of course, Hawthorne's account of finding the scarlet A and the genesis of the novel.

[4] *The Scarlet Letter, The Centenary Edition of the Works of Nathaniel Hawthorne*, vol. I, (1850; United States: Ohio State Univ. Press, 1962), p. 38.

[5] The factual information above is taken from Edith Roelker Curtis, *A Season in Utopia: The Story of Brook Farm* (New York: Nelson, 1961). Quotations from Hawthorne's letters are from Nathaniel Hawthorne, *Passages from the American Notebooks* (Boston: Houghton Mifflin, 1883), pp. 227, 229, 234.

[6] Mark Van Doren, *Nathaniel Hawthorne*, The American Men of Letters Series (U.S.A.: William Sloane Associates, 1949), p. 109.

[7] Rpt. in Katherine Burton, *Paradise Planters: The Story of Brook Farm* (London: Longmans, Green & Co., 1939), p. 149.

[8] *Notebooks*, p. 229.

[9] *Notebooks*, pp. 241, 236.

[10] *Notebooks*, p. 232.

[11] *Notebooks*, p. 237.

[12] *Notebooks*, p. 237.

[13] Curtis, pp. 261-63, 279-80.

[14] Hawthorne's sense of society as mechanized is comparable to Dickens'. Their common focus on prisons, cemeteries, and bureaucratic governmental offices as the primary symbols of the social order reveals an affinity of artistic temperament. In Hawthorne's novel, however, the ideal of community exists as an abstract, almost spiritual concept, whereas in Dickens' novels it is given mundane, concrete form in the idealized, miniature society of family and friends.

[15] The distinction here is similar to that between the ethical codes of Middlemarch the town and *Middlemarch* the novel in George Eliot's work. See Quentin Anderson, "George Eliot in *Middlemarch*," previously cited in chapter one, note 5.

[16] Here once again, Hawthorne is similar to the European realists George Eliot and Leo Tolstoy, both of whom emphasize the integrity and interiority of unverbalized emotional experience.

[17] When D. H. Lawrence applies his famous dictum, "Never trust the teller, trust the tale" to *The Scarlet Letter* in *Studies in Classic American Literature*, he surely refers to this lack of emotional congruence. But his advice is difficult to follow: like Eliot in *Middlemarch* and Tolstoy in *War and Peace*, Hawthorne is so integral a part of *The Scarlet Letter* that if the reader were to ignore authorial commentary, there would be very little left of the novel. Yet Lawrence correctly senses that Hawthorne manipulates his tale and his reader, suppressing their most romantic elements.

[18] The relevant letter (to Horatio Bridge, written in February, 1850) is not available for direct quotation. It is, however, quoted by Randall Stewart in *Nathaniel Hawthorne: A Biography* (New Haven: Yale Univ. Press, 1948), p. 95.

## Chapter Five

[1] William Makepeace Thackeray, *Vanity Fair*, Riverside paperback edition (Boston: Houghton Mifflin, 1963), p. 6. The best hardcover edition of the novel is that published by Oxford University Press in 1908, edited by George Saintsbury. Because of some textual errors and a lack of wide availability, however, it is not really a standard edition. I have chosen to use instead the excellent and popular edition edited by the Tillotsons.

[2] See Kathleen Tillotson, *Novels of the Eighteen-Forties* (Oxford: Oxford Univ. Press, 1954), p. 256.

[3] See Stuart Tave, *The Amiable Humorist: A Study in the Comic Theory and Criticism of the Eighteenth and Early Nineteenth Centuries* (Chicago: Univ. of Chicago Press, 1962), pp. 226-31.

[4] *The Letters and Private Papers of William Makepeace Thackeray*, ed. Gordon N. Ray, vol. II (Cambridge: Harvard Univ. Press, 1945-46), p. 423.

[5] *The Exposure of Luxury: Radical Themes in Thackeray* (London: Peter Owen, 1972), p. 168.

[6] P. 256.

[7] See Mario Praz, *The Hero in Eclipse in Victorian Fiction* (see chapter two, note eight), and Gordon N. Ray, *The Buried Life: A Study of the Relationship between Thackeray's Fiction and his Personal History* (Cambridge: Harvard Univ. Press, 1952).

[8] The French text is taken from the standard Conard edition (Paris: Conard,

1930), p. 600. English translations are from the best available translation, that by Robert Baldrick (London: Penguin, 1970), p. 411.

⁹ Not all critics share my view of the first concluding chapter, but views that emphasize ideal love in the scene require awkward qualification and critical maneuvering. Even an interpretation that calls the scene one of "transcending love" and finds it "deeply touching" must admit that elements in the text support the view that the scene is "a conscious and cruelly ironic subversion of whatever idealism was present in the relationship." See Victor Brombert, *The Novels of Flaubert: A Study of Themes and Techniques* (Princeton: Princeton Univ. Press, 1966), p. 150. Brombert's study includes the most thorough discussion of the ending of which I am aware, and it overlaps with mine at several points, as does Jonathan Culler's in *Flaubert: The Uses of Uncertainty* (Ithaca: Cornell Univ. Press, 1974). See also Enid Starkie, *Flaubert: the Master* (New York: Atheneum, 1971), p. 173, who speculates that Flaubert's reunion with Elisa Schlésinger (the model for Mme. Arnoux), softened Flaubert's satire in the scene and accounts for its occasional moving moments.

¹⁰ In a general discussion of Flaubert, Harry Levin notes that the Ideal and the Spleen are closely allied in his nature, with the Spleen ultimately triumphant. See *The Gates of Horn* (New York: Oxford, 1963), p. 301. Ideal love enters this scene, but is defeated by the Spleen: it may surface briefly and is implicit in the characters' romantic language, but it is submerged by a well-chosen word or phrase belonging to the author.

¹¹ Balzac's novel was published in 1835-36.

¹² Without applying the idea specifically to the ending, Benjamin Bart notes the inverted picaresque elements in the novel. See *Flaubert* (Syracuse: Syracuse Univ. Press, 1967), pp. 478-79.

¹³ Brombert emphasizes this point, for which I am indebted to him. The allusion occurs on pp. 52-53 of the French text. Most critics of the novel consider it an ironic *Bildungsroman*, a view suggested by the book's title and confirmed by its ending.

¹⁴ My discussion of this aspect of the ending coincides with Brombert's on several issues.

¹⁵ The repetition of a key emblematic event is also characteristic of the *récit*; sometimes the narrator is unaware of the event's significance, sometimes he is aware.

¹⁶ The endings to Flaubert's novels set in the nineteenth century differ from those of his non-novelistic works, especially those set outside of modern France dealing symbolically with artistic experience. At the end of "La Legende de saint Julien, l'hopitalier" (1876), and *La Tentation de saint Antoine* (1874), for example, the endings as most critics read them celebrate artistic union with the absolute. See Jules de Gaultier, *Le Bovarysme* (Paris: Mercure de France, 1902). The difference between these endings and that of *L'Education* supports my point that

Flaubert's negative views on the nineteenth century and his suppression of personal ideals in his novel contribute to the work's splenetic parody.

[17] The best evidence of Flaubert's artistic and personal sensibility is to be found in his letters, especially those to Louise Colet. Also useful are the studies by Bart and Starkie, cited above. The letters are most widely available in English in an edition translated and edited by Francis Steegmuller, *Selected Letters of Flaubert* (New York: Farrar, Straus, 1953). For the complete original letters, see Gustave Flaubert, *Correspondence* (Paris: Conard, 1954), vol. 4, supplement to *Œuvres Complètes de Gustave Flaubert* (Paris: Conard, 1910). Of special interest is a letter to Turgenev in which Flaubert praises Tolstoy's *War and Peace* but dislikes the final sections, in which Tolstoy remolds the generalized marital after-history to express his personal ideology; see *Lettres inédites à Tourgueneff* (Monaco: Rocher, 1946), p. 218.

[18] See Jack P. Rawlins, *Thackeray's Novels: A Fiction that is True* (Berkeley: Univ. of California Press, 1974), p. 63.

## Chapter Six

[1] See introduction, note 22.

[2] This and all subsequent references to James's prefaces refer to the edition collected by R. P. Blackmur under the title, *The Art of the Novel*, p. 114. See introduction, note 2.

[3] See Northrop Frye's discussion in *Anatomy of Criticism* (Princeton: Princeton Univ. Press, 1957), p. 44.

[4] See introduction, p. 11 and note 21.

[5] I paraphrase James's famous remarks in the preface to *Roderick Hudson*, pp. 5-6.

[6] *The Complete Tales of Henry James*, vol. 2, ed. Leon Edel (Philadelphia: Lippincott, 1962), p. 60. Edel uses not the New York edition, but the first book version of each story, since these versions benefited from James's corrections and revisions but preserve the development of his style. In rejecting the use of the New York edition in this chapter dealing with James's development, I have followed the same principle. I have chosen texts that print the first British editions of the novels (often the Methuen editions). The Signet paperback editions, to which all parenthetical page references for the novels refer, have the additional virtue of being widely available and easily accessible.

[7] "Afterword" to the Signet edition (New York: New American Library, 1964), p. 189.

[8] I am indebted to William Veeder for pointing out the metaphoric nature of the concluding sentence; see his interesting study, *Henry James—The Lessons of the Master: Popular Fiction and Personal Style in the Nineteenth Century* (Chicago: Univ. of Chicago Press, 1975), pp. 203-04.

⁹ *The Notebooks of Henry James*, ed. F. O. Matthiessen and Kenneth B. Murdock (1947; New York: Oxford Univ. Press, 1971), p. 18.

¹⁰ Unsigned review, rpt. in *Henry James: The Critical Heritage*, ed. Roger Gard (London: Routledge and Kegan Paul, 1968), pp. 95-96. I have relied on Mr. Gard's collection of reviews, since my purpose here was not to do an exhaustive study of contemporary commentary on James's novels.

¹¹ *The Language of Fiction* (New York: Columbia Univ. Press, 1966), p. 196.

¹² I borrow the phrase from my colleague, Don Gifford.

¹³ *The Great Tradition* (1937; New York: New York Univ. Press, 1967); *Henry James: The Major Phase* (New York: Oxford Univ. Press, 1944); and *Maule's Curse* (Norfolk, Conn.: New Directions, 1938), respectively.

¹⁴ *The Tragedy of Manners: Moral Drama in the Later Novels of Henry James* (New Haven: Yale Univ. Press, 1971); *The Ambiguity of Henry James* (Urbana, Ill.: Univ. of Illinois Press, 1971); and *The Language of Fiction* (see note 11) respectively.

## Chapter Seven

¹ *The Golden Bowl, The Novels and Tales of Henry James*, the New York edition, 26 vols. (1905; New York: Scribner's, 1907-09), XXIV, pp. 243-44.

² F. R. Leavis' comments occur in *The Great Tradition*, pp. 159-60, F. O. Matthiessen's in *Henry James: The Major Phase*, p. 100 (see chapter six, note 13), R. P. Blackmur's in "Introduction to *The Golden Bowl*," *The Golden Bowl* (New York: Grove Press, 1952), pp. xx-xxi, and Quentin Anderson's in *The Imperial Self* (New York: Knopf, 1971), p. 184.

³ Crews, p. 114 (see chapter six, note 14).

⁴ *The Ordeal of Consciousness in Henry James* (Cambridge: Oxford Univ. Press, 1962), p. 319.

⁵ Among critics who fault *The Golden Bowl* are John Middleton Murry, Andre Gide, H. G. Wells, F. R. Leavis, Yvor Winters, and Wayne Booth. A study which expands this position and raises further questions about Maggie is Charles Samuels' *The Ambiguity of Henry James*, p. 173 (see chapter six, note 14).

⁶ (Ithaca: Cornell Univ. Press, 1968), p. 173.

⁷ "Talking in James," *PMLA*, 91: 1 (January, 1976), pp. 74-76. In a book-length study that appeared after the first draft of this chapter was completed—*Language and Knowledge in the Late Novels of Henry James* (Chicago: Univ. of Chicago Press, 1976)—Yeazell expands her position: the two-part structure of the novel, which presents Maggie's views as the last and most comprehensive, forces the reader to identify with her, simultaneously suggesting that Maggie's views are both too "confining" and a willful creation of a fiction of harmony that masks the real tensions still present between Maggie and Amerigo (p. 124). This last point clearly has connections with my own argument, although I differ from Yeazell on

the issue of Maggie's triumph, and see the tensions in the novel as clearly conveyed by gesture, as distinct from dialogue (Yeazell's focus), in the final scene.

[8] James repeatedly makes comments—which critics usually ignore—about Maggie's serious, intense, naively unironic nature. See, for example, XXIV, pp. 35, 284 (from which my quotation comes), 332, 337.

## Chapter Eight

[1] The University of Texas at Austin has a few pages of an early manuscript. The Alderman Library at the University of Virginia has a slightly later, but complete, 188-page manuscript. Information about revisions and manuscripts is taken from François Pitavy, *Faulkner's Light in August* (Bloomington, Ind.: Univ. of Indiana Press, 1971), pp. 8-11.

[2] When asked about the title, Faulkner also spoke of "a day or two" in August when "there's a lambence, a luminous quality to the light, as though it came not just from today but from back in the old classic times . . . and that's all the title meant, it was just to me a pleasant, evocative title." See Frederick L. Gwynn and Joseph L. Blotner, eds., *Faulkner in the University: Class Conferences at the University of Virginia* (Charlottesville, Va.: Univ. of Virginia Press, 1959), p. 375. Hightower's meditation begins in the "final copper light of afternoon" and ends in "the lambent suspension of August" (pp. 441, 465). The title thus also refers to Hightower's meditation and partial redemption. All page references for *Light in August* refer to the original hardcover edition (New York: Random House, 1932).

[3] See, for example, Alfred Kazin, "The Stillness of *Light in August*," *Partisan Review* 24 (Autumn, 1957), pp. 519-38; Richard P. Adams, *Faulkner: Myth and Motion* (Princeton: Princeton Univ. Press, 1968), pp. 84-95; and Darrel Abel, "Frozen Movement in *Light in August*," rpt. *Twentieth-Century Interpretations of Light in August* (Englewood Cliffs, N.J.: Prentice-Hall, 1969), pp. 42-55.

[4] The original statement of this view is in Cleanth Brooks, *William Faulkner: the Yoknapatawpha Country* (New Haven: Yale Univ. Press, 1963).

[5] See, for example, Robert M. Slabey, "Myth and Ritual in *Light in August*," *Texas Studies in Language and Literature*, 2 (Autumn, 1960), pp. 328-49, and Walter Brylowski, *Faulkner's Olympian Laugh: Myth in the Novels* (Detroit: Wayne State Univ. Press, 1968).

[6] See Carl Benson, "Thematic Design in *Light in August*," *South Atlantic Quarterly* (October, 1954), pp. 540-55. Benson's essay (like Kazin's and Brooks') has been reprinted many times.

[7] "Address Upon Receiving the Nobel Prize for Literature," *Essays, Speeches, and Public Letters*, ed. James B. Meriwether (New York: Random House, 1965), p. 120.

[8] Gwynn and Blotner, p. 72.

⁹ Gwynn and Blotner, p. 75.

¹⁰ In a remarkably pithy and comprehensive study of the novel, François Pitavy suggests that Hightower's seeing the charge may be a cathartic liberation from the past, which now recedes into memory, p. 33. Pitavy believes, as I do, that Hightower remains a highly ambiguous figure in the novel.

¹¹ The adjective "bovine" is Pitavy's, p. 118.

¹² This interpretation of *Absalom, Absalom!* is that of John T. Irwin in *Doubling and Incest/Repetition and Revenge: A Speculative Reading of Faulkner* (Baltimore: Johns Hopkins Univ. Press, 1975).

¹³ *Essays, Speeches, and Public Letters*, p. 120.

¹⁴ (New York: Random House, 1930), pp. 163 and 165-66.

## Chapter Nine

¹ Virginia Woolf, *The Diary of Virginia Woolf*, vol. III, ed. Anne Olivier Bell, assisted by Andrew McNeillie.(New York: Harcourt, Brace, Jovanovich, 1980), p. 113. For two of the diary entries (written in 1931, a year not yet covered in the Bell edition), it was necessary to quote from *A Writer's Diary* (New York: Harcourt, Brace and Co., 1954).

² See Virginia Woolf, *The Waves* (New York: Harcourt, Brace and Co., 1931), pp. 158-59. Earlier in this book, when quoting from a passage of dialogue, but not from the beginning or to the end of that dialogue, I have occasionally added quotation marks to indicate that, in the novel, a character speaks the quoted material. Given the complex punctuation of *The Waves*, however, this system has been changed for chapter nine. When quoting from *The Waves*, I have reproduced only those quotation marks actually in the portion of the text quoted even though, at times, this results in passages that look odd (as, for example, when a passage begins with quotation marks but does not end with quotation marks). It may help for the reader to remember that, except for the one-line epilogue, all material quoted in this chapter is "spoken" by the characters.

³ See J. W. Graham, transcriber and editor, *Virginia Woolf, The Waves: The Two Holograph Drafts* (London: Univ. of Toronto Press, 1976). The title page of the first draft lists the subtitles and alternative titles, the title page of the second draft, simply *The Waves*. Hereafter cited as *Holograph Drafts*.

⁴ *Holograph Drafts*, pp. 768 and 743.

⁵ Exactly when the line was added cannot be precisely determined. The typescripts of the novel between the second draft and the proofs were apparently destroyed, probably by Woolf herself. See Graham, "Introduction" to *Holograph Drafts*, p. 29.

⁶ In *Virginia Woolf: A Collection of Criticism*, ed. Thomas S. W. Lewis (New York: McGraw Hill, 1975), pp. 94-112. Hereafter cited as "Point of View."

⁷ See, for example, James Hafley, *The Glass Roof: Virginia Woolf as Novelist*

(Berkeley: Univ. of California Press, 1954); Alice Van Buren Kelley, *The Novels of Virginia Woolf* (Chicago: Univ. of Chicago Press, 1971); Jean O. Love, *Worlds in Consciousness: Mythopoetic Thought in the Novels of Virginia Woolf* (Berkeley: Univ. of California Press, 1970); James Naremore, *The World Without a Self: Virginia Woolf and the Novel* (New Haven: Yale Univ. Press, 1973). The tendency to emphasize Bernard's vision at the end of *The Waves* may be partly explained as an understandable but somewhat misguided attempt to see the ending as similar to that of *To the Lighthouse*, which ends with Lily Briscoe's triumphant unifying vision.

[8] Graham, "Introduction" to *Holograph Drafts*, p. 16.

[9] See Woolf's essay "Modern Fiction" in *Collected Essays*, II (1919; London: Hogarth, 1966), pp. 103-10.

[10] This incident, among the most resonant in the novel, occurs on pp. 182-83.

[11] The term "oceanic" was used by Freud to describe "a feeling of an indissoluble bond, of being one with the external world as a whole." See *Civilization and its Discontents, The Standard Edition of the Complete Psychological Works of Sigmund Freud*, vol. XXI (London: Hogarth, 1961), p. 65. Freud believed that the "oceanic sense" is a vestigial remnant of the infantile ego that survives to different degrees in different individuals, and is completely absent in most mature beings. Although no available evidence from her essays, diaries, letters, or library indicates that Woolf systematically absorbed Freudian concepts, she certainly knew of his theories. Leonard Woolf mentions the Bloomsbury group's fascination with Freud in his autobiography; see *Beginning Again: An Autobiography of the Years 1911-1918* (New York: Harbrace, 1964), pp. 37 and 167-68 and *Downhill All the Way: An Autobiography of the Years 1919-1939* (New York: Harbrace, 1967), pp. 95-96. The Hogarth Press was the first to publish Freud's complete works in English. Woolf's conception of ego development parallels Freud's to some extent and may have been indirectly influenced by him.

[12] See *Civilization and its Discontents*, pp. 66-68.

[13] On this point, Woolf's difference from Freud is clear. Freud considers the "oceanic" an infantile illusion; Woolf sees it as an authentic intuition about the cosmos that is diminished as the ego matures, but that will periodically reassert itself in sensitive beings.

[14] (New York: Harcourt, Brace and World, 1927), p. 96.

[15] *Diary of Virginia Woolf*, pp. 113, 117-18.

[16] Hafley, p. 108.

[17] That the incident Bernard recounts occurred in the past and was not literally an eclipse is not difficult to prove. Bernard introduces the incident in the past tense, not in the present tense used to describe incidents in the restaurant. And he clearly uses the eclipse as a metaphor for the experience: "*It was like the eclipse* when the sun went out. . . ." (p. 374, my emphasis).

[18] *A Writer's Diary*, p. 170.

## Conclusion

[1] I refer to Thackeray's preface, "Before the Curtain," rather than to the first chapter of the novel.

I primarily see circularity as the pattern controlling the ending to *The Ambassadors*. That circularity is, however, supported by a network of parallel patterns as well.

[2] *Writing Degree Zero*, trans. Annette Lavers and Colin Smith (1953; Boston: Beacon Press, 1975), p. 38.

[3] See the beginning of chapter one.

[4] (New York: Oxford, 1966).

[5] (Chicago: Univ. of Chicago Press, 1978), pp. 180-85.

[6] See introduction, pp. 9-10.

[7] The first quotation is from Douglas Hewitt, *The Approach to Fiction* (Great Britain: Longman, 1972), p. 180; the second is from Michael Wood, "Victims of Survival," *The New York Review of Books*, February 7, 1974, p. 12.

[8] (New York: Signet, 1969); (New York: Holt, Rinehart & Winston, 1973); and (New York: Farrar, Straus & Giroux, 1971), respectively.

[9] Fowles, p. 365.

[10] Malamud, p. 108.

[11] Several critics, including Victor Shklovsky and Harry Levin, make the constant renovation of conventions a definitive aspect of the novel.

[12] Vladimir Nabokov, *Lolita* (1955; New York: Berkley, 1966), p. 6.

[13] See John Gardner's *On Moral Fiction* (New York: Basic Books, 1978) for the best-known example. See also David Richter, *Fable's End* (Chicago: Univ. of Chicago Press, 1974), pp. 2-7 and Patrick Swinden, *Unofficial Selves: Character in the Novel from Dickens to the Present Day* (Bristol: Macmillan, 1973), pp. 5-26.

[14] See introduction, pp. 3-5 and 8.

[15] "Art as Technique," trans. Lee Lemon and Marion J. Reis, rpt. in *Russian Formalist Criticism: Four Essays* (1917; Lincoln, Nebraska: Univ. of Nebraska Press, 1965), p. 12.

[16] The phrase "stand still here" is from Virginia Woolf's *To the Lighthouse*. It occurs when Lily Briscoe reflects that the goals of art and the goals of Mrs. Ramsay's way of living are to make "Life stand still here" (p. 240).

The list below includes only works footnoted in the text.

Adams, Richard P. *William Faulkner: Myth and Motion.* Princeton: Princeton Univ. Press, 1968.

Adams, Robert M. *Strains of Discord: Studies in Literary Openness.* Ithaca: Cornell Univ. Press, 1958.

Anderson, Quentin. "George Eliot in *Middlemarch.*" Rpt. in *The Pelican Guide to English Literature: From Dickens to Hardy.* Ed. Boris Ford. London: Penguin, 1958. VI, pp. 274-93.

————. *The Imperial Self.* New York: Knopf, 1971.

Apostolov, Nicholas. "Tolstoy and Dickens." *Family Views of Tolstoy.* Trans. and ed. Louise and Aylmer Maude. London: Allen & Unwin, 1926.

Aristotle. *Poetics.* Trans. S. H. Butcher. New York: Hill and Wang, 1961.

Bart, Benjamin. *Flaubert.* Syracuse: Syracuse Univ. Press, 1967.

Barthes, Roland. *Writing Degree Zero.* Trans. Annette Lavers and Colin Smith. 1953; Boston: Beacon, 1967.

Beaty, Jerome. *Middlemarch From Notebook to Novel: A Study of George Eliot's Creative Method.* Urbana: Univ. of Illinois Press, 1960.

Berlin, Isaiah. *The Hedgehog and the Fox: An Essay on Tolstoy's View of History.* New York: Simon and Schuster, 1966.

Blackmur, R. P. "Introduction." *The Golden Bowl.* New York: Grove Press, 1952.

Booth, Wayne. *The Rhetoric of Fiction.* Chicago: Univ. of Chicago Press, 1961.

————. *A Rhetoric of Irony.* Chicago: Univ. of Chicago Press, 1974.

Brombert, Victor. *The Novels of Flaubert: A Study of Themes and Techniques.* Princeton: Princeton Univ. Press, 1966.

Brooks, Cleanth. *William Faulkner: the Yoknapatawpha Country.* New Haven: Yale Univ. Press, 1963.

Chesterton, G. K. *Charles Dickens.* 1906; New York: Dodd, Mead, and Co., 1920.

Cowley, Malcolm. "Introduction." *The Portable Hawthorne.* Rev. ed. 1928; New York: Viking, 1971.

Crews, Frederick. *The Tragedy of Manners: Moral Drama in the Later Novels of Henry James.* 1957; New Haven: Yale Univ. Press, 1971.

Culler, Jonathan. *Flaubert: the Uses of Uncertainty*. Ithaca: Cornell Univ. Press, 1974.

Curtis, Edith Roelker. *A Season in Utopia: the Story of Brook Farm*. New York: Nelson, 1961.

Dickens, Charles. *Bleak House*. 1853; New York: Norton, 1977.

———. *Household Words*. Issue 1, March 30, 1850.

———. *Pickwick Papers*. 1837; New York: New American Library, 1964.

Dunn, Richard J. "Far, Far Better Things," *Dickens Studies Annual*. Vol. 7. Editor, Robert B. Partlow, Jr. London: Feffer and Simons, 1978.

Eikhenbaum, Boris. *Lev Tolstoy*. Leningrad: 1931.

Eliot, George. *The George Eliot Letters*. Ed. Gordon S. Haight. Vols. II, V. New Haven: Yale Univ. Press, 1954.

———. *Middlemarch*. Cabinet edition. vol. III. 1867; Edinburgh and London: William Blackwood and Sons, 1877-1880.

Faulkner, William. "Address Upon Receiving the Noble Prize for Literature." *Essays, Speeches, and Public Letters*. Ed. James B. Meriwether. New York: Random House, 1965.

———. *As I Lay Dying*. New York: Random House, 1930.

———. *Light in August*. New York: Random House, 1932.

Flaubert, Gustave. *Correspondence*. Œuvres Complètes de Gustave Flaubert. 4 vol. supplement. Paris: Conard, 1910.

———. *L'Education sentimentale*. Œuvres Complètes de Gustave Flaubert. Vol. 7. 1869; Paris: Conard, 1930.

———. *Lettres inédites à Tourgueneff*. Monaco: Rocher, 1946.

———. *Madame Bovary*. Œuvres Complètes de Gustave Flaubert. Vol. 8. 1850; Paris: Conard, 1921.

———. *Sentimental Education*. Trans. Robert Baldrick. 1869; London: Penguin, 1970.

Ford, G. H. *Dickens and His Readers*. Princeton: Princeton Univ. Press, 1955.

Forster, E. M. *Aspects of the Novel*. 1927; New York: Harcourt, Brace and World, 1954.

Forster, John. *The Life of Charles Dickens*. 1874; London: Dent, 1966.

Fowles, John. *The French Lieutenant's Woman*. Signet edition. New York: New American Library, 1969.

Freud, Sigmund. *Civilization and its Discontents*. The Standard Edition of the Complete Psychological Works of Sigmund Freud. Vol. XXI. London: Hogarth, 1961.

Friedman, Alan. *The Turn of the Novel*. New York: Oxford, 1966.

BIBLIOGRAPHY

Frye, Northrop. *Anatomy of Criticism: Four Essays*. Princeton: Princeton Univ. Press. 1971.

Futrell, Michael. "Dickens and Three Russian Novelists: Gogol, Dostoyevsky, Tolstoy." Diss. Univ. of London, 1965.

Gard, Roger, ed. *Henry James: the Critical Heritage*. London: Routledge and Kegan Paul, 1968.

Gardner, John. *On Moral Fiction*. New York: Basic Books, 1978.

de Gaultier, Jules. *Le Bovarysme*. Paris: Mercure de France, 1902.

Girard, Réné. *Deceit, Desire, and the Novel*. Trans. Yvonne Freccero. 1961; Baltimore: Johns Hopkins Univ. Press, 1965.

Graham, J. W., ed. and transcriber. *Virginia Woolf, The Waves: The Two Holograph Drafts*. London: Univ. of Toronto Press, 1976.

Gwynn, Frederick L. and Joseph Blotner, eds. *Faulkner in the University: Class Conferences at the University of Virginia*. Charlottesville: Univ. of Virginia Press, 1959.

Hafley, James. *The Glass Roof: Virginia Woolf as Novelist*. Berkeley: Univ. of California Press, 1954.

Hardy, Barbara. *The Exposure of Luxury: Radical Themes in Thackeray*. London: Peter Owen, 1972.

————. *The Moral Art of Dickens*. New York: Oxford, 1970.

Hawthorne, Nathaniel. *Passages from the American Notebooks*. Boston: Houghton Mifflin. 1883.

————. *The Scarlet Letter*. The Centenary Edition of the Works of Nathaniel Hawthorne. Vol. I. 1850; United States: Ohio State Univ. Press, 1962.

Herodotus. *The Histories*. Trans. Aubrey de Selincourt. Baltimore: Penguin, 1965.

Hewitt, Douglas. *The Approach to Fiction*. Great Britain: Longman, 1972.

Hirsch, E. D. *Validity in Interpretation*. New Haven: Yale Univ. Press, 1967.

Irwin, John T. *Doubling and Incest/Repetition and Revenge: A Speculative Reading of Faulkner*. Baltimore: Johns Hopkins Univ. Press, 1975.

Jackson, T. A. *Charles Dickens: The Progress of a Radical*. New York: Haskell, 1971.

James, Henry. *The Ambassadors*. Signet edition. 1903; New York: New American Library, 1960.

————. *The American*. Signet edition. 1875; New York: New American Library, 1963.

James, Henry. "The Art of Fiction." Rpt. in *The American Tradition in Literature*. Ed. Sculley Bradley, Richard Croom Beatty and E. Hudson Long. Vol. 2. 1884; New York: Norton, 1967.

――――. *The Art of the Novel*. Ed. R. P. Blackmur. New York: Scribner's, 1962.

――――. *The Complete Tales of Henry James*. Ed. Leon Edel. Vol. 2. Philadelphia: Lippincott, 1962.

――――. *The Europeans*. Signet edition. 1878; New York: New American Library, 1964.

――――. *The Notebooks of Henry James*. Ed. F. O. Matthiessen and Kenneth B. Murdock. 1947; New York: Oxford Univ. Press, 1961.

――――. *The Golden Bowl*. *The Novels and Tales of Henry James*. Vols. XXIII and XXIV. The New York edition. 1905; New York: Scribner's, 1907-1909.

――――. *The Portrait of a Lady*. Signet edition. 1881; New York: New American Library, 1963.

Johnson, Edgar. *Charles Dickens, his tragedy and triumph*. Vol. II. New York: Simon and Schuster, 1952.

Jong, Erica. *Fear of Flying*. New York: Holt, Rinehart and Winston, 1973.

Kazin, Alfred. "The Stillness of *Light in August*." *Partisan Review*. 24 (Autumn, 1957), 519-38.

Kelley, Alice Van Buren. *The Novels of Virginia Woolf*. Chicago: Univ. of Chicago Press, 1971.

Kermode, Frank. *The Sense of an Ending*. New York: Oxford, 1966.

Knoeflmacher, U. C. *Religious Humanism in the Victorian Novel*. Princeton: Princeton Univ. Press, 1965.

Kroeber, Karl. *Styles in Fictional Structure: the Art of Jane Austen, Charlotte Brontë, George Eliot*. Princeton: Princeton Univ. Press, 1971.

Krook, Dorothea. *The Ordeal of Consciousness in Henry James*. Cambridge: Oxford Univ. Press, 1962.

Lawrence, D. H. *Studies in Classic American Literature*. London: M. Secker, 1933.

Leavis, F. R. *The Great Tradition*. 1937; New York: New York Univ. Press, 1967.

Levin, Harry. *The Gates of Horn*. New York: Oxford, 1963.

――――. *The Power of Blackness*. New York: Knopf, 1958.

Lewis, Thomas S. W., ed. *Virginia Woolf: A Collection of Criticism*. New York: McGraw Hill, 1975.

Lodge, David. *The Language of Fiction*. New York: Columbia Univ. Press, 1966.

BIBLIOGRAPHY

Love, Jean. *Worlds in Consciousness: Mythopoetic Thought in the Novels of Virginia Woolf*. Berkeley: Univ. of California Press, 1970.

Lukács, Georg. *Studies in European Realism*. 1938; New York: Grosset and Dunlap, 1964.

Malamud, Bernard. *The Tenants*. New York: Farrar, Straus and Giroux, 1971.

Marcus, Steven. *Dickens: From Pickwick to Dombey*. New York: Basic Books, 1965.

Matthiessen, F. O. *Henry James: The Major Phase*. New York: Oxford Univ. Press, 1944.

Miller, J. Hillis. "Ariadne's Thread." *Critical Inquiry*. 3 (Autumn, 1976), 56-77.

————. *The Form of Victorian Fiction*. Notre Dame: Univ. of Notre Dame Press, 1970.

————. "The Problematic Ending in Narrative." *Nineteenth-Century Fiction*. 33: 1 (June, 1978), 3-7.

Nabokov, Vladimir. *Lolita*. 1955; New York: Berkley, 1966.

Naremore, James. *The World Without a Self: Virginia Woolf and the Novel*. New Haven: Yale Univ. Press, 1973.

*Narrative Endings*. Berkeley: Univ. of California Press, 1979.

*Nineteenth-Century Fiction*. 33: 1 (June, 1978).

Orwell, George. "Charles Dickens." *Inside the Whale*. 1940; London: Penguin, 1962.

Paris, Bernard J. *Experiments in Life*. Detroit: Wayne State Univ. Press, 1965.

Pitavy, François. *Faulkner's Light in August*. Bloomington: Univ. of Indiana Press, 1971.

Prasad, Thakur Guru. *Comtism in the Novels of George Eliot*. Lucknow, India, 1968.

Praz, Mario. *The Hero in Eclipse in Victorian Fiction*. London: Oxford Univ. Press, 1956.

Rawlins, Jack P. *Thackeray's Novels: A Fiction that is True*. Berkeley: Univ. of California Press, 1974.

Ray, Gordon N. *The Buried Life: A Study of the Relationship between Thackeray's Fiction and his Personal History*. Cambridge: Harvard Univ. Press, 1952.

Reichert, John. *Making Sense of Literature*. Chicago: Univ. of Chicago Press, 1978.

Richter, David. *Fable's End: Completeness and Closure in Rhetorical Fiction*. Chicago: Univ. of Chicago Press, 1974.

Said, Edward. *Beginnings: Intention and Method*. New York: Basic Books, 1975.

Samuels, Charles. *The Ambiguity of Henry James*. Urbana: Univ. of Illinois Press, 1968.

Sartre, Jean-Paul. *La Nausée*. Paris: Gallimard, 1938.

————. *Nausea*. Trans. Lloyd Alexander. New York: New Directions, 1974.

Scholes, Robert and Robert Kellogg. *The Nature of Narrative*. London: Oxford, 1966.

Scott, Sir Walter. *Old Mortality*. 1816; New York: Everyman, 1968.

Shklovsky, Victor. "Art as Technique." Rpt. in *Russian Formalist Criticism: Four Essays*. Trans. Lee Lemon and Marion J. Reis. 1917; Lincoln: Univ. Of Nebraska Press, 1965, pp. 3-25.

Shroder, Maurice Z. "The Novel as a Genre." Rpt. in *The Theory of the Novel*. Ed. Philip Stevick. 1963; London: Macmillan, 1967, pp. 13-29.

Slabey, Robert M. "Myth and Ritual in *Light in August*." *Texas Studies in Language and Literature*, 2 (Autumn, 1960), 328-49.

Smith, Barbara Herrnstein. *Poetic Closure*. Chicago: Univ. of Chicago Press, 1968.

Starkie, Enid. *Flaubert: the Master*. New York: Atheneum, 1971.

Steiner, George. *Tolstoy or Dostoevsky: an Essay in the Old Criticism*. New York: Dutton, 1971.

Stewart, Garrett. "The New Mortality of *Bleak House*," *ELH*, Vol. 45, 443-87.

Stewart, Randall. *Nathaniel Hawthorne: A Biography*. New Haven: Yale Univ. Press, 1948.

Swinden, Patrick. *Unofficial Selves: Character in the Novel from Dickens to the Present Day*. Bristol: Macmillan, 1973.

Tave, Stuart M. *The Amiable Humorist: A Study in the Comic Theory and Criticism of the Eighteenth and Early Nineteenth Centuries*. Chicago: Univ. of Chicago Press, 1962.

Thackeray, William Makepeace. *The Letters and Private Papers of William Makepeace Thackeray*. Ed. Gordon N. Ray. Vol. II. Cambridge: Harvard Univ. Press, 1945-46.

————. *Vanity Fair*. Riverside edition. Boston: Houghton Mifflin, 1963.

Tillotson, Kathleen. *Novels of the Eighteen-Forties*. Oxford: Oxford Univ. Press, 1954.

Tolstoy, Leo. *Anna Karenina*. Trans. Louise and Aylmer Maude. 1878; New York: Norton, 1970.

———. *My Confession.* New York: Walter Scott Pub. Co., n.d.

———. *Resurrection.* Trans. Vera Traill. Signet edition. 1903; New York: New American Library, 1961.

———. *War and Peace.* The Maude translation. 1869; New York: Norton, 1966.

———. *What is Art?* Trans. Aylmer Maude. 1896; New York: Bobbs-Merrill, 1960.

Trollope, Anthony. *The Warden.* Signet edition. 1855; New York: New American Library, 1964.

Veeder, William. *Henry James—The Lessons of the Master: Popular Fiction and Personal Style in the Nineteenth Century.* Chicago: Univ. of Chicago Press, 1975.

Welsh, Alexander. *The City of Dickens.* Oxford: Clarendon Press, 1971.

Williams, Raymond. "Dickens and Social Ideas." *Dickens 1970.* Ed. Michael Slater. New York: Stern and Day, 1970.

Winters, Yvor. *Maule's Curse: Seven Studies in the History of American Obscurantism: Hawthorne, Cooper, Melville, Poe, Emerson, Jones Very, Emily Dickinson, Henry James.* Norfolk, Conn.: New Directions, 1938.

Wood, Michael. "Victims of Survival." *The New York Review of Books,* February 7, 1974.

Woolf, Leonard. *Beginning Again: An Autobiography of the Years 1911-1918.* New York: Harbrace, 1964.

———. *Downhill All the Way: An Autobiography of the Years 1919-1939.* New York: Harbrace, 1967.

Woolf, Virginia. "Modern Fiction." *The Common Reader.* 1925; New York: Harcourt, Brace and Co., 1948.

———. *To the Lighthouse.* New York: Harcourt, Brace and Co., 1927.

———. *The Waves.* New York: Harcourt, Brace and Co., 1931.

Yeazell, Ruth B. *Language and Knowledge in the Late Novels of Henry James.* Chicago: Univ. of Chicago Press, 1976.

———. "Talking in James." *PMLA.* 91: 1 (January, 1976), 66-77.

Zwerdling, Alex. "Esther Summerson Rehabilitated." *PMLA.* Vol. 88 (1973), 429-39.

Novels extensively discussed in the text have been indexed separately from the names of their authors; cross references have been made in these cases.

Library of Congress Cataloging in Publication Data

Torgovnick, Marianna, 1949-
Closure in the novel.

Bibliography: p.
Includes index.
1. Fiction—Technique.    2. Closure (Rhetoric)
3. Fiction—19th century—History and criticism.
4. Fiction—20th century—History and criticism.
I. Title.
PN3378.T6        808.3        80-8581
ISBN 0-691-06464-4